300 TEATIME TREATS
cakes, sweets & desserts

300 TEATIME TREATS
cakes, sweets & desserts

More than 300 scrumptious cakes, cookies, tarts, pies, pancakes, puddings and desserts – each recipe shown step by step in more than 900 tempting photographs

CONTRIBUTING EDITOR:
VALERIE FERGUSON

LORENZ BOOKS

This edition is published by Lorenz Books

Lorenz Books is an imprint of Anness Publishing Limited
Hermes House, 88–89 Blackfriars Road, London SE1 8HA
tel. 020 7401 2077; fax 020 7633 9499
www.lorenzbooks.com; www.annesspublishing.com

If you like the images in this book and would like to investigate using them for publishing,
promotions or advertising, please visit our website www.practicalpictures.com for more information.

© Anness Publishing Limited 2006

UK agent: The Manning Partnership Ltd
tel. 01225 478444; fax 01225 478440; sales@manning-partnership.co.uk

UK distributor: Grantham Book Services Ltd
tel. 01476 541080; fax 01476 541061; orders@gbs.tbs-ltd.co.uk

North American agent/distributor: National Book Network
tel. 301 459 3366; fax 301 429 5746; www.nbnbooks.com

Australian agent/distributor: Pan Macmillan Australia
tel. 1300 135 113; fax 1300 135 103; customer.service@macmillan.com.au

New Zealand agent/distributor: David Bateman Ltd, tel. (09) 415 7664; fax (09) 415 8892

A CIP catalogue record for this book is available from the British Library.

Publisher: Joanna Lorenz
Editorial Director: Helen Sudell
Editors: Joanne Rippon and Elizabeth Woodland
Series Designer: Bobbie Colgate Stone
Designers: Andrew Heath and Adelle Morris
Jacket Designer: Balley Design Associates
Production Controller: Lee Sargent

Recipes contributed by: Catherine Atkinson, Angela Boggiano, Janet Brinkworth, Kathy Brown,
Carla Capalbo, Frances Cleary, Carole Clements, Trisha Davies, Roz Denny, Nicola Diggins,
Joanna Farrow, Rafi Fernandez, Christine France, Sarah Gates, Shirley Gill, Rosamund Grant,
Carole Handslip, Janine Hosegood, Sarah Lewis, Gilly Love, Lesley Mackley, Norma MacMillan,
Maggie Mayhew, Norma Miller, Katherine Richmond, Anne Sheasby, Liz Trigg, Laura Washburn,
Steven Wheeler, Elizabeth Wolf-Cohen, Jeni Wright.

Photography: Karl Adamson, Edward Allwright, Steve Baxter, Louise Dare, James Duncan,
John Freeman, Ian Garlick, Michelle Garrett, Amanda Heywood, Janine Hosegood, David Jordan,
Don Last, William Lingwood, Patrick McLeavey, Michael Michaels, Thomas Odulate, Polly Wreford.

Previously published in two separate volumes, *Sweet Treats* and *Afternoon Teas, Homemade Bakes
and Party Cakes*

Notes

Bracketed terms are intended for American readers.

For all recipes, quantities are given in both metric and imperial measures and, where appropriate, in standard
cups and spoons. Follow one set, but not a mixture; they are not interchangeable.

Standard spoon and cup measures are level. 1 tsp = 5ml, 1 tbsp = 15ml, 1 cup = 250ml/8fl oz.

Australian standard tablespoons are 20ml. Australian readers should use 3 tsp in place of 1 tbsp for measuring
small quantities of gelatine, flour, salt, etc.

Medium (US large) eggs are used unless otherwise stated.

Contents

Introduction

Afternoon tea is a meal we don't often have time for these days, which makes it even more special when we do. In these pages both beginners and more experienced home bakers will find inspirational ideas for every teatime occasion. The book is divided into 16 chapters. The Basic Recipes and Techniques section gives recipes for

the cake bases that are used later in the book – quick-mix sponge cake, Madeira cake, and rich fruit cake – as well as the different types of icing, marzipan, apricot glaze and sugar flowers. The helpful techniques pages provide step-by-step instructions for such things as preparing cake tins (pans), making pastry and bottling preserves. The rest of the book offers a superb collection of teatime recipes including: fruity treats; pastries; pies and tarts; trifles and puddings; soufflés and meringues; cookies; bakes and breads; jams, jellies and preserves; cakes and gâteaux; and delectable iced desserts. Whatever the occasion, you will be sure to find the ideal teatime treat.

BASIC RECIPES
AND TECHNIQUES

MAKING AND DECORATING CAKES

To obtain the best results when making cakes, it is necessary to have a selection of good equipment.

Above: A selection of useful items for cake-making and decorating.

• Accurate weighing scales, measuring spoons and cups are available in both metric and imperial measurements. Always measure level when using spoons unless otherwise stated in the recipe.

• A set of mixing bowls in various sizes and a selection of wooden spoons are essential items. However, an electric hand-held beater will save time and make cake-making easier.

• Cake tins (pans); the most useful are round or square in sizes 15 cm/6 in, 20 cm/8 in and 25 cm/10 in.

• Cooling racks; at least two racks are useful for cake-making and decorating.

• A serrated knife for cutting the cooled cake without it crumbling.

• Pastry brush for glazing cakes.

• A heavy rolling pin for rolling out marzipan and sugarpaste icing.

• Pastry and small cookie cutters in various shapes and sizes for cutting sugarpaste icing shapes.

• A palette knife or metal spatula for spreading

• Piping (pastry) bags and a variety of nozzles of different sizes and shapes (or you can use baking parchment cones with the nozzles).

• A turntable is not essential but makes icing much easier.

• Sable paintbrushes for painting fine details on to cakes.

• Silver cake boards for presenting decorated cakes.

SUCCESSFUL CAKE-MAKING

There are a few simple guidelines which must be followed to achieve the best results when making any cake.

• Always use the correct shape and size of tin (pan) for the recipe you have chosen and make sure it is properly prepared and lined.
• Check that you have all the necessary ingredients measured correctly and that they are at the right temperature before you start mixing.
• Ensure soft margarine is kept chilled in the refrigerator to maintain the right consistency. Leave butter out to reach room temperature.

• Sift all dry ingredients to help aerate the mixture and to disperse lumps.
• Use the correct sugar. Caster (superfine) sugar creams more easily with fats than granulated sugar, and is used where a fine and soft texture is required. Soft brown sugar is used when making heavier cakes.
• Use good quality fruit and peel for fruit cakes. Sometimes sultanas (golden raisins) can become hard if they are stored for too long.
• When making cakes by hand, beat well with a wooden spoon until the mixture is light and glossy; scrape down the mixture from the sides of the bowl during beating with a plastic mixing spatula to ensure even mixing.
• If a cake is being made in a food processor or an electric mixer, be very careful not to overprocess or overbeat. Scrape down the batter with a plastic spatula during mixing.

• If ingredients have to be folded into a mixture, use a plastic spatula with a flexible blade.
• Level cake mixtures with a palette knife or metal spatula before baking.
• Check that your oven is preheated to the temperature that is stated in the recipe. Failure to do this will affect the rising of the cake and the cooking time.
• If the cake appears to be cooked before the given time, it may indicate that the oven is too hot; conversely, if it takes longer to cook, it may mean the oven is too cool.
• The temperature of the cake mixture can cause the cooking time to vary. If conditions are cold, the mixture will be cold and take longer to cook and if it is warm the cooking time will be slightly quicker.
• The surface of the cake should be evenly browned and level; if the cake is overcooked or risen to one side, then the heat in the oven is uneven or the oven shelf is not level.

PREPARING CAKE TINS

Lining a Shallow Cake Tin

Lining tins (pans) is important so that the cake comes out of the tin without breaking or sticking to the base of the tin. This method is simple, but essential.

1 Place the tin on a piece of baking parchment, draw around the base with a pencil and cut out the paper inside this line to fit tightly.

2 Grease the base and sides of the tin with melted lard or soft margarine. Grease the paper and then place it neatly into the tin. It is now ready for filling with the cake mixture.

3 To line the sides of a tin: Cut a strip of paper long enough to wrap around the outside of the tin and overlap by 4 cm/1½ in. It should be wider than the depth of the tin by 2.5 cm/1 in.

4 Fold the strip lengthways at the 2.5 cm/1 in point and crease. Snip at regular intervals from the edge to the crease along the fold. Line the side of the tin, with the snipped part of the strip on and overlapping the base. Press the bottom lining in (Steps 1 and 2).

5 For square and rectangular cake tins, fold the paper and crease it with your fingernail to fit snugly into the corners of the tin. Then press the bottom paper lining into place.

Lining a Deep Cake Tin

1 Place the tin (pan) on a double thickness of baking parchment. Draw around the base with a pencil. Cut out the marked shape with a pair of scissors.

2 Cut a strip of double-thickness baking parchment long enough to wrap around the outside of the tin, leaving a small overlap. It should stand 2.5 cm/1 in above the top of the tin.

3 Brush the base and sides of the tin with melted vegetable fat or oil. Place the double strip of paper inside the tin, pressing well against the sides and making sharp creases if it must fit into corners. Place the cut-out shape in the base of the tin and press it flat.

4 Brush the base and side papers well with melted vegetable fat or oil. Place a strip of double-thickness brown paper around the outside of the tin and tie securely with a string.

Line a baking sheet with three or four layers of brown paper and stand the tin on top.

Greasing and Flouring

For some cake recipes, the tin (pan) does not need to be lined with paper, but just greased, or sometimes greased and floured.

1 To grease a tin: If using butter or margarine, hold a small piece in kitchen paper (or use your fingers), and rub it all over the base and side of the tin to make a thin, even coating. If using oil, brush a small amount on with a pastry brush.

2 To flour a tin: Put a small scoop of flour in the centre of the greased tin. Tip and rotate the tin to coat the base and side. Shake out excess flour, tapping to dislodge any pockets.

Quick-mix Sponge Cake

Choose chocolate, lemon or orange flavouring for this light and versatile sponge cake, or leave it plain.

Makes 1 x 20 cm/8 in round or 18 cm/7 in square cake

INGREDIENTS
115 g/4 oz/1 cup self-raising (self-rising) flour
5 ml/1 tsp baking powder
115 g/4 oz/½ cup soft margarine
115 g/4 oz/½ cup caster (superfine) sugar
2 eggs

FOR THE FLAVOURINGS
Chocolate: 15 ml/1 tbsp unsweetened
    cocoa powder blended with 15 ml/1 tbsp
    boiling water
Lemon: 10 ml/2 tsp grated lemon rind
Orange: 15 ml/1 tbsp grated orange rind

1 Grease and line a 20 cm/8 in round tin (pan) or 18 cm/7 in square tin.

2 Preheat the oven to 160°C/325°F/ Gas 3. Sift the flour and baking powder into a bowl. Add the margarine, sugar and eggs with the chosen flavourings, if using.

3 Beat with a wooden spoon for 2–3 minutes. The mixture should be pale in colour and slightly glossy.

4 Spoon the mixture into the cake tin and smooth the surface. Bake in the centre of the oven for 30–40 minutes, or until a skewer inserted into the centre comes out clean.

5 Turn out on to a wire rack, remove the lining paper and leave to cool completely.

Madeira Cake

This is a richer basic cake which is ideal for decorating.

Makes 1 x 20 cm/8 in round or 18 cm/7 in square cake

INGREDIENTS
225 g/8 oz/2 cups plain (all-purpose) flour
5 ml/1 tsp baking powder
225 g/8 oz/1 cup butter or margarine,
    at room temperature
225 g/8 oz/generous 1 cup caster (superfine)
    sugar
grated rind of 1 lemon
5 ml/1 tsp vanilla extract
4 eggs

1 Preheat the oven to 160°C/325°F/ Gas 3. Grease and line a cake tin (pan). Sift the flour and baking powder into a bowl. Set the mixture aside.

2 Cream the butter or margarine, adding the caster sugar about 30 ml/ 2 tbsp at a time, until light and fluffy. Stir in the lemon rind and vanilla extract. Add the eggs, one at a time, beating for 1 minute after each addition. Add the flour mixture and stir until just combined.

3 Pour the cake mixture into the prepared tin and tap lightly to level. Bake for about 1¼ hours, or until a metal skewer inserted in the centre comes out clean.

4 Cool in the tin on a wire rack for 10 minutes, then turn the cake out and leave to cool completely.

Rich Fruit Cake

Make this cake a few weeks before icing, wrap well and store in an airtight container to mature.

Makes 1 x 20 cm/8 in round or 18 cm/7 in square cake

INGREDIENTS
375 g/13 oz/1¾ cups currants
250 g/9 oz/1½ cups sultanas (golden raisins)
150 g/5 oz/1 cup raisins
90 g/3½ oz/scant ½ cup glacé (candied) cherries, halved
90 g/3½ oz/scant 1 cup almonds, chopped
65 g/2½ oz/scant ½ cup mixed (candied) peel
grated rind of 1 lemon
40 ml/2½ tbsp brandy
250 g/9 oz/2¼ cups plain (all-purpose) flour
6.5 ml/1¼ tsp mixed (apple pie) spice
2.5 ml/½ tsp freshly grated nutmeg
65 g/2½ oz/generous ½ cup ground almonds
200 g/7 oz/scant 1 cup soft margarine or butter
225 g/8 oz/1 cup soft brown sugar
15 ml/1 tbsp black treacle (molasses)
5 eggs, beaten

1 Preheat the oven to 140°C/275°F/ Gas 1. Grease and line the base and sides of a 20 cm/8 in round or 18 cm/ 7 in square cake tin (pan) with a double thickness of baking parchment.

2 Sift the flour and combine with the other ingredients in a mixing bowl. Beat with a wooden spoon for 5 minutes. Spoon into the prepared tin. Make a slight depression in the centre.

3 Bake in the centre of the oven for 3–3½ hours. Test the cake after 3 hours. If it is ready it will feel firm, and a skewer inserted in the centre will come out clean. Cover the top loosely with foil if it starts to brown too quickly.

4 Leave to cool completely in the tin, then turn out. The lining paper can be left on to keep the cake moist.

Butter Icing

The creamy rich flavour and silky smoothness of butter icing is popular with both children and adults.

Makes 350 g/12 oz/1½ cups

INGREDIENTS
225 g/8 oz/2 cups icing (confectioners')
   sugar, sifted
75 g/3 oz/6 tbsp soft margarine or
   butter, softened
5 ml/1 tsp vanilla extract
10–15 ml/2–3 tsp milk

FOR THE FLAVOURINGS
Chocolate: Blend 15 ml/1 tbsp unsweetened
   cocoa powder with 15 ml/1 tbsp hot water.
   Cool before beating into the icing.
Coffee: Blend 10 ml/2 tsp coffee powder
   with 15 ml/1 tbsp boiling water. Omit the
   milk. Cool before beating the mixture into
   the icing.
Lemon, orange or lime: Replace the vanilla
   extract and milk with lemon, orange or
   lime juice and 10 ml/2 tsp finely grated
   citrus rind. Omit the rind if using the icing
   for piping. Lightly tint the icing with food
   colouring, if wished.

COOK'S TIP: Use Butter Icing for
fillings, toppings and as a thin
coating over a cake before adding
Sugarpaste Icing.
   The icing will keep for up to
3 days in an airtight container stored
in the refrigerator.

1 Put the icing sugar, margarine or butter, vanilla extract and 5 ml/1 tsp of the milk into a bowl.

2 Beat with a wooden spoon or an electric mixer until creamy. Add sufficient extra milk, a little at a time until the icing has a light, smooth and fluffy consistency.

3 To make flavoured butter icing, follow the instructions for chocolate, coffee or citrus flavourings given above for the flavour of your choice.

Marzipan

This can be used on its own, under an icing or for modelling.

Makes 450 g/1 lb/3 cups

INGREDIENTS
225 g/8 oz/2 cups ground almonds
115 g/4 oz/½ cup caster (superfine) sugar
115 g/4 oz/1 cup icing (confectioners') sugar, sifted
5 ml/1 tsp lemon juice
a few drops of almond extract
1 small (US medium) egg, or 1 medium (US large) egg white

1 Stir the ground almonds and caster and icing sugars together in a bowl until evenly mixed. Make a well in the centre and add the lemon juice, almond extract and enough egg or egg white to mix to a soft, but firm dough, using a wooden spoon.

2 Form the marzipan into a ball. Lightly dust a surface with icing sugar and knead the marzipan until smooth. Wrap in clear film (plastic wrap) or store in a polythene bag until needed.

Sugarpaste Icing

Sugarpaste (fondant) icing is wonderfully pliable and can be coloured, moulded and shaped.

Makes 350 g/12 oz/2¼ cups

INGREDIENTS
1 egg white
15 ml/1 tbsp liquid glucose, warmed
350 g/12 oz/3 cups icing (confectioners') sugar, sifted

1 Put the egg white and glucose in a mixing bowl. Stir them together to break up the egg white. Add the icing sugar and mix together with a palette knife, using a chopping action, until well blended and the icing begins to bind together. Knead the mixture with your fingers until it forms a ball.

2 Knead the sugarpaste on a work surface lightly dusted with icing sugar for several minutes until smooth, soft and pliable. If the icing is too soft, knead in some more sifted sugar until it reaches the right consistency.

BASIC RECIPES AND TECHNIQUES

Royal Icing

Use for a truly professional finish. This recipe makes enough icing to cover the top and sides of an 18 cm/7 in round cake.

Makes 675 g/1½ lb/4½ cups

INGREDIENTS
3 egg whites
about 675 g/1½ lb/6 cups icing
   (confectioners') sugar, sifted
7.5 ml/½ tsp glycerine
a few drops of lemon juice

1 Put the egg whites in a bowl and stir lightly with a fork or a wooden spoon to break them up.

2 Gradually add the icing sugar, beating well with a wooden spoon after each addition. Add enough icing sugar to make a smooth, shiny icing that has the consistency of very stiff meringue. Do not use an electric mixer as this will make the icing too fluffy.

COOK'S TIP: This recipe is for an icing consistency suitable for flat icing a marzipanned rich fruit cake. When the spoon is lifted, the icing should form a sharp point, with a slight curve at the end, known as "soft peak".

   For piping, the icing needs to be slightly stiffer. It should form a fine sharp peak when the spoon is lifted. Add more icing (confectioners') sugar to achieve this consistency.

3 Beat in the glycerine and lemon juice. Leave for 1 hour, or up to 24 hours before using, covered with damp clear film (plastic wrap), then stir to burst any air bubbles.

Fudge Frosting

This rich, darkly delicious frosting can transform a simple sponge into an excitingly decorated novelty cake.

Makes 350 g/12 oz/2¼ cups

INGREDIENTS
50 g/2 oz/2 squares plain (semisweet)
   chocolate, chopped into small pieces
225 g/8 oz/1½ cups icing (confectioners')
   sugar, sifted
50 g/2 oz/¼ cup butter or margarine
45 ml/3 tbsp milk or single (light) cream
5 ml/1 tsp vanilla extract

1 Put the chocolate, icing sugar, butter or margarine, milk or cream and vanilla extract in a heavy pan.

2 Stir over a very low heat until the chocolate and butter or margarine melt. Remove from the heat and stir until evenly blended.

3 Beat the icing frequently as it cools until it thickens sufficiently to use for spreading or piping.

4 Use immediately and work quickly once it has reached the right consistency, otherwise it will be difficult to spread.

Glacé Icing

This icing can be made in just a few minutes and can be varied by adding a little food colouring or a flavouring such as coffee.

Makes 225 g/8 oz/1 cup

INGREDIENTS
225 g/8 oz/2 cups icing (confectioners')
  sugar
30–45 ml/2–3 tbsp warm water or
  fruit juice
food colouring or flavouring
  (optional)

1 Sift the icing sugar into a bowl. Using a wooden spoon, gradually stir in enough liquid to make an icing that is the consistency of thick cream.

2 Beat well until the icing is completely smooth. It should be thick enough to coat the back of the spoon. If it is too runny, beat in a little more sifted icing sugar.

3 Beat in a few drops of food colouring or flavouring, if using.

4 Use the icing immediately for coating or piping.

Apricot Glaze

Use the glaze to brush cakes before applying marzipan, or use for glazing fruits on gâteaux and cakes.

Makes 450 g/1 lb/1½ cups

INGREDIENTS
450 g/1 lb/1½ cups apricot jam
45 ml/3 tbsp water

1 Place the jam and water in a pan. Heat gently, stirring occasionally until melted. Boil rapidly for 1 minute.

2 Remove from the heat and rub through a sieve (strainer), pressing the fruit against the sides of the sieve with the back of a wooden spoon. Discard the skins left in the sieve.

3 Use a pastry brush to cover the entire surface of the cake.

Sugar-frosted Flowers

These pretty edible flowers may be used when a dainty and elegant decoration is required for a cake.

To cover about 20 flowers.

INGREDIENTS
Edible flowers, such as pansies,
    primroses, violets, roses, freesias
    or nasturtiums
1 egg white
caster (superfine) sugar

1 Trim the stems from the flowers leaving approximately 2 cm/¾ in if possible. Wash the flowers and dry gently on kitchen paper. Lightly beat the egg white in a small bowl and sprinkle some caster sugar on to a plate. Line another plate with kitchen paper.

2 Using a paintbrush, evenly brush both sides of the petals with the egg white. Holding the flower by the stem over the paper-lined plate, sprinkle it evenly with the sugar and shake off any excess.

22

3 Place on a flat board or wire rack covered with kitchen paper and leave to dry in a warm place.

COOK'S TIP: The flower stems are kept long for frosting so that they are easy to hold. They can be trimmed afterwards, if preferred.

SUCCESSFUL COOKIE-MAKING

Many cookies can be made from store-cupboard items, but some will
require fresh ingredients.

Dairy Products and Substitutes

Butter makes the
richest cookies with
the lightest texture.
Use unsalted or lightly

Butter

salted butter for sweet cookies.
Margarine is also good, but tends to
make more brittle biscuits. Low-fat
spreads are suitable for many recipes,
but do lack richness.
They are useful for
healthy eating and for
those on a low-fat diet.
Milk, yogurt, sour cream,

Milk

cream and crème fraîche can
all be used to bind the
dough, giving slightly different flavours
and textures.

Some cookies are filled or
sandwiched together with cream. In
such cases, use whipping or double
(heavy) cream. Soft cheeses
can also be used for
fillings. Grated cheese is a
wonderful flavouring for
savoury biscuits. For best

Parmesan Cheese

results, use hard or semi-
hard cheeses,
such as
Parmesan or Cheddar.
Eggs are also commonly
used for binding the
dough and, for best results,
use free-range, organic eggs.

Eggs

Flour

Plain (all-purpose) flour is the most
commonly used. For best results,
choose organic stone-ground flour.
Wholemeal (whole-wheat) flour is
well-suited to savoury biscuits, while
soft or sponge flour may be used on
its own or mixed with plain flour for
sweet cookies.

Fruit

Dried fruit is featured in
many recipes and includes
sultanas (golden raisins),
raisins and apricots. The
natural sugars add
sweetness and moistness.

Dried Apricots

Glacé (candied) cherries
and candied fruit and peel
may be used for decoration
and also form an

Sultanas

integral part of some
cookies, such as florentines.

Apart from very firm
berries, fresh fruit is rarely
used other than for
decoration, as it tends to
make cookies soggy. Fruit

Glacé Cherries

juices, however, can supply the flavour
and natural sweetness of fresh fruit, so
they are useful for binding the dough
and flavouring fillings. Pear and apple
spread, a concentrated fruit juice, is also
excellent for binding and providing
sweetness and flavour.

Flavourings

Unsweetened cocoa powder, plain (semisweet), milk or white chocolate and chocolate chips are widely used, both for flavouring and decoration. Grated citrus rind and vanilla and almond extracts

Plain Chocolate

White Chocolate

feature in many recipes. Coffee, often as instant powder, is a popular flavouring. Brandy, whisky and liqueurs add sophisticated flavours to cookies.

Vanilla Extract

Grains

Rolled oats and oatmeal feature in many traditional recipes. Cornmeal makes lovely golden cookies. Muesli (granola) and breakfast cereals are also useful.

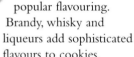

Oats

Herbs and Spices

Chopped fresh herbs may be used to add interest, particularly to savoury cookies. Common spices for sweet cookies are ground cinnamon, nutmeg and ginger. Savoury biscuits may also include spices or curry powder.

Ground Cinnamon

Nuts and Seeds

Traditional favourites are coconut, usually desiccated (dry unsweetened), walnuts, hazelnuts, pecan nuts, almonds and pine nuts. Seeds, such as sesame, sunflower and poppy, may be added to sweet cookies or savoury biscuits. They give additional texture, flavour and nutrients.

Hazelnuts

Sweeteners

Caster (superfine) sugar is easily incorporated into dough, although granulated is sometimes suggested. Unrefined sugars, such as soft dark brown sugar, have more flavour, add colour and contain some minerals. Honey has a strong flavour and is sweeter than sugar, so you can use less of it than the equivalent of sugar.

Muscovado Sugar

Honey

Black treacle (molasses) has a smoky flavour and slightly bitter taste. It goes well with other strong flavours, such as ginger. Malt extract is also distinctive and is a good choice for softer bakes, as it adds moistness. Golden, corn and maple syrup are very sweet with a more subtle flavour. Always use pure maple syrup for the best flavour. Syrup is essential for some very light cookies, such as crisp brandy snaps.

COOKIE-MAKING TECHNIQUES

Stencilling

Use stencils to liven up cookies in a simple and fun way.

Cut a small design out of card and place it over a cookie. Dust with icing (confectioners') sugar or cocoa powder before removing the card.

Grinding Nuts

Using a nut mill or a clean coffee grinder, grind a small batch of nuts at a time to ensure an even texture. As soon as the nuts have a fine texture, stop grinding; if overworked, they will turn to paste. Alternatively, use a food processor. To avoid overworking the nuts add some of the sugar or flour needed in the recipe.

Roasting Nuts

Roasting nuts brings out their flavour and makes them crunchier.

1 To oven-roast or grill (broil) nuts: spread the nuts on a baking sheet. Roast in a 180°C/350°F/Gas 4 oven or under a medium grill (broiler), until golden brown and smelling nutty. Stir the nuts to brown evenly.

2 To dry-roast nuts: put the nuts in a frying pan, with no fat. Roast over moderate heat until golden brown. Stir constantly and watch carefully: nuts can scorch easily.

COOK'S TIP: Set the timer for 3-4 minutes when oven-roasting nuts.

BAKING AND STORING COOKIES

Baking Cookies

Care must be taken when baking cookies. Always preheat the oven. It will take about 15 minutes to reach the required temperature, slightly less if the oven is fan-assisted. Cookies should usually be baked on the middle shelf or just above the middle of the oven. There should be a small gap at either side and at the back of each baking sheet to allow hot air to circulate. If you are baking several sheets of cookies, don't put more than two sheets in the oven at a time or the temperature may drop. Switch the baking sheets round halfway through cooking. If you need to reuse the baking sheets for more cookies, let them cool before adding more cookies, otherwise the residual heat will make the second batch of cookies spread too much.

Baking times

Depending on the efficiency of your oven and whether the dough has been chilled, you may need to make small adjustments to baking times. Check cookies 2–3 minutes before the end of the suggested cooking time; unlike cakes they will not sink if the oven door is opened. Once the oven has heated up, subsequent batches of cookies may take less time to bake. Cookies tend to continue cooking for a minute or two after removing from the oven, so take this into account when judging whether they are done.

Storing Cookies

With few exceptions, cookies are best eaten on the day that they are made. Some, such as American-style soft cookies, are at their most delicious when still slightly warm from the oven, but most cookies need to be cooled to allow them to crisp. Store them as soon as they have cooled. Store crisp and soft cookies separately.

Store soft cookies in an airtight container. Ideally, they should also be stored in the refrigerator. Crisp cookies do not need to be stored in an absolutely airtight container. Ceramic containers and glass jars with cork stoppers are ideal. Cool on a wire rack before storing.

TYPES OF PASTRY

Shortcrust Pastry

One of the easiest and most versatile of pastries, shortcrust consists of flour and fat, with just enough liquid to bind the ingredients together. Always use iced water and, if time permits, wrap the pastry in clear film (plastic wrap) and chill it in the refrigerator for 30 minutes before rolling it out.

Rich or Sweet Shortcrust Pastry

Rich or sweet shortcrust pastry sets to a crisper crust than plain shortcrust. It is often used for fruit pies. Use the shortcrust recipe but use butter and substitute an egg yolk for part of the liquid. For sweet pastry, add 30–45 ml/2–3 tbsp caster (superfine) sugar after rubbing in the fat.

Below: Red Grape and Cheese Tartlets.

Puff Pastry

This is made in such a way that it separates into crisp layers when cooked, thanks to the air trapped in it. A block of butter is wrapped in a basic dough, the pastry is then turned, rolled, folded and chilled several times. If using frozen puff pastry, thaw slowly.

Rough Puff Pastry

Diced fat is mixed with the flour but not rubbed in, so the fat can be seen in the dough. The pastry is rolled and folded several times before being rested and baked. The fat used should be very cold and it helps if the flour is chilled.

Choux Pastry

The butter is melted with water and then the flour added all at once and beaten in before the eggs. It is easy to make, but must be carefully measured.

PASTRY-MAKING TECHNIQUES

Rubbing In

Add the diced fat to the flour. Using the fingertips and thumbs, draw up a small amount of mixture and rub together to break it down into crumbs. Repeat the process lifting the mixture each time to incorporate air, until no large lumps of fat remain. Do not overwork the dough.

Using a Pastry Blender

A pastry blender is a gadget comprising between five and eight arched wires on a wooden handle. Some cooks prefer it for rubbing in as it stops warm hands softening the fat, but it can break down the fat almost too efficiently. Use the blender for half the fat, and add the rest in pea-size pieces.

Rolling Out

A smooth layer of pastry that will not distort or shrink in baking is the desired result. The key to successful rolling out is to handle the dough gently.

1 Using an even pressure, roll out the dough on a lightly floured surface. Start in the centre of the dough and roll out towards the edge.

2 Give the dough a quarter turn from time to time during the rolling, so that it rolls out evenly and does not stick to the surface. Continue the rolling out process until the dough circle is about 5 cm/2 in larger than the size of the tin. It should be about 3 mm/⅛ in thick.

Lining a Tin

Set the rolling pin on the dough, near one side. Fold the outside edge over the pin, then roll the pin to wrap the dough around it. Hold over the tin (pan) and unroll the dough into the tin. Lift and ease the dough gently into the tin, gently pressing the base and side. Turn excess dough over the rim and trim it with a knife or scissors.

Glazing

For a rich, golden crust, brush the pastry with beaten egg, a mixture of beaten egg and water, or milk just before baking. For a sweet pie, you can add a light dusting of caster (superfine) sugar on top of the glaze.

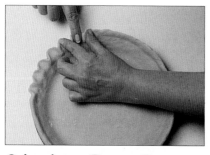

Crimping a Pastry Case

Make a "V" with the thumb and forefinger of one hand, pressing lightly on the pastry. Then use the index finger of your other hand to push between the "V" inwards. Or press the knuckle of one hand against the inner edge, using the other hand to pinch around your finger.

Baking Blind

This refers to the method of partially or fully baking an unfilled pastry case (pie shell). Line it with baking parchment and add an even layer of baking beans (use dried beans kept for the purpose or special china beans). Bake the case for 10 minutes, then remove the paper and baking beans and return the pastry case to the oven for 5 minutes more, or longer if it is not to be cooked again after filling.

Making Shortcrust Pastry

Use half butter or margarine and half white vegetable fat, or all the same fat.

Makes a 23 cm/9 in pastry case

INGREDIENTS
225 g/8 oz/2 cups plain (all-purpose) flour
1.5 ml/¼ tsp salt
115 g/4 oz/½ cup fat, chilled and diced
45–60 ml/3–4 tbsp iced water

1 Sift the flour and salt into a bowl, raising the sieve (strainer) to incorporate as much air as possible. Add the fat. Rub into the flour until the mixture resembles breadcrumbs.

2 Sprinkle 45 ml/3 tbsp water over. Toss the mixture with your fingers to combine and moisten.

3 Press the dough into a ball. If it is too dry, add the remaining water.

4 Shape the dough into an oblong or oval then wrap in clear film (plastic wrap) and chill in the refrigerator for 30 minutes before using.

Making Puff Pastry

Puff pastry has a feather-light texture because of its high butter content.

Makes 500 g/1¼ lb

INGREDIENTS
200 g/7 oz/⅞ cup unsalted (sweet) butter
200 g/7 oz/1½ cups fine plain
   (all-purpose) flour
1.5 ml/1¼ tsp salt
125 ml/4 fl oz/½ cup cold water

1 Cut the butter into 14 pieces and place in the freezer for 30 minutes.

2 Put the flour and salt in a food processor and pulse to combine. Add the butter and pulse three times; there should still be large lumps of butter. Run the machine for 5 seconds while pouring the water through the feed tube, then stop the machine. The dough should look curdy.

3 Turn the mixture on to a lightly floured, cool work surface and gather into a flat ball. If the visible butter is soft, chill the dough for 30 minutes.

4 Roll out the dough on a floured surface to a 40 x 25 cm/16 x 6 in rectangle. Fold in thirds, bringing one end down to cover the middle, then fold the other end over it. Roll out again to a rectangle and fold again. Chill for 30 minutes. Roll and fold twice more then chill for 30 minutes.

TYPES OF FRUIT

The range of fruits available has never been so extensive, and new varieties are appearing all the time.

Apples and Pears

The most popular of all fruits, apples are perfect for eating raw or in hot or cold puddings. Available all

Apples

year round, there are many flavours and textures to choose from.

Sweet and juicy pears have a fine white flesh and are more often enjoyed raw than cooked.

Pears

Citrus Fruits

Lemons and limes are interchangeable in most recipes, but limes have a more aromatic, intense flavour.

Lemons

Grapefruit may have green, yellow or pink-flushed skin, with yellow, green or pink flesh. Kumquats are tiny relatives of oranges and can be eaten whole, either raw or cooked. Oranges, satsumas, tangerines,

Oranges

clementines and numerous other small varieties of citrus fruits are virtually interchangeable in flavour.

Soft Fruits

The most popular of these are probably blackberries, blackcurrants, redcurrants, blueberries, raspberries and strawberries. Do not overlook cranberries. Although too sharp to eat raw, their intense flavour and stunning colour make them very good for cooking. Gooseberries for cooking are small, firm, green and quite sharp, while dessert varieties are larger and sweeter.

Strawberries

Stone Fruits

Apricots, peaches, plums and nectarines may be used raw or lightly poached. White peaches have the sweetest flavour and yellow varieties are more aromatic with a firmer texture. There are many dessert and cooking varieties of plums, ranging from pale gold to black. You can use slightly under-ripe plums for cooking. Sweet dessert cherries are available in

Nectarines

the summer and have white, pink or black skins and a juicy flesh. Choose fruit that is firm and glossy.

Exotic Fruits

Bananas are the most familiar exotic fruit, with a dense texture and sweet taste. Fresh dates are sweet and juicy and more succulent than

Dates

dried. Physalis, or Cape gooseberries, are small, fragrant, pleasantly tart orange berries wrapped in a paper "cape". Kiwi fruit need only peeling and slicing. The flesh, soft when ripe, is a beautiful bright green and has a sweet, slightly tart flavour. Lychees

Kiwi Fruit

are small with a hard pink skin and sweet-smelling, juicy flesh. The purplish brown skin of passion fruit is wrinkled when ripe. Cut the fruit in half and scoop out the juicy seeds. Pineapple, with its knobbly skin, has juicy yellow flesh and is available all year. Star fruit (carambola) falls into pretty five-pointed stars

Passion Fruit

Star Fruit

Pineapples

when sliced. The fruit is ripe when the edges begin to go brown. The skins of mangoes vary in colour, but the flesh should always be golden yellow, sweet and juicy. Papayas have smooth, yellow-orange skins when ripe. The flesh is orange- pink and similar in texture to a melon.

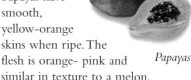

Mangoes

Papayas

Melons, Figs and Grapes

There are many varieties of melons, from small sweet cantaloupes to large juicy red watermelons. Figs are delicious eaten fresh or dried. Black or green grapes are very popular for serving with cheese or in a fruit salad. Muscat grapes are regarded as the finest eating variety.

Watermelons

Fresh Figs

Grapes

33

PREPARING FRUIT

Peeling and Segmenting an Orange

1 Using a serrated knife, cut a thin slice from each end of the orange. Slice off the peel, removing as much of the white pith as possible.

2 Over a bowl to catch the juice, cut each segment between the membranes. Squeeze out the juice.

Peeling a Pineapple

1 Cut the pineapple across into slices of the desired thickness. Use a small, sharp knife to cut off the rind.

2 Hold each slice upright and cut out the "eyes". Remove the central core of each slice with an apple corer.

Preparing a Mango

1 Place the mango stalk end down on a chopping board. Cut a thick lengthways slice from one side, keeping the knife as close to the stone (pit) as possible. Turn the mango round and cut another slice from the other side. Then cut narrower slices from the remaining sides. Cut off the flesh adhering to the stone and scoop out the flesh from the mango slices.

Creating a Hedgehog Effect

1 Prepare the mango as above and score the flesh on each thick slice with criss-cross lines at 1 cm/½ in intervals, taking care not to cut through the skin.

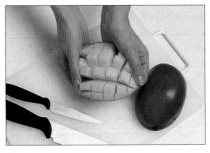

2 Fold the mango halves inside out and serve.

3 When the mango is folded inside out, the cubes can be cut off using a sharp knife, if desired.

Freezing Berries

1 Open-freeze perfect specimens in a single layer on a baking sheet, then pack into rigid containers. Damaged berries can be puréed and strained, then sweetened with sugar and frozen.

Peeling Stone Fruits

Fruits such as peaches, nectarines and apricots can be peeled with a sharp paring knife, but this may waste some of the delicious flesh. The following method removes the skin only.

Make a tiny nick in the skin. Cover with boiling water and leave for 15–30 seconds, depending on the ripeness of the fruit. Remove the fruit with a slotted spoon and peel off the skin, which should come away easily.

Removing Stones and Pips

• To stone (pit) peaches, apricots etc, cut all around the fruit through the seam. Twist the halves in opposite directions, then lever out the stone (pit) with a knife.

• To pit cherries, put the fruit in a cherry pitter and push the bar into the fruit. The pit will be ejected.

• To remove grape pips (seeds), cut the grapes in half, then pick out the pips with the tip of a small sharp knife.

Crystallized Flowers

These pretty decorations add a delightful finishing touch to any light summery dessert. It is best to put them on the dessert just before you are ready to serve it, otherwise the flowers will go soft.

Good flowers and leaves to use are: pansies, violas, herb flowers, variegated mint, carnations and rose petals.

1 Brush flowers and leaves with raw egg white and sprinkle with caster (superfine) sugar.

2 Leave to dry for 1–2 hours on a plate or rack out of direct sunlight. Use on the day of making.

Making Fruit Purée

A wide range of fruit purées are a useful base for many ice creams and sorbets, and they also make good fat-free sauces. They can be cooled and frozen.

1 Remove the stones (pits) and cook the fruit in a pan, with a small amount of water or sugar, until soft. If you are using sugar alone, heat the fruit very gently until the fruit juice begins to run and the sugar dissolves.

2 Tip the cooked fruit into a food processor or blender and process until smooth. The mixture may then need to be sieved.

Strained Fruit

Many recipes call for fruit to be sieved, to remove pips (seeds) or skin. Firmer fruit, such as apples, should be cooked before you strain them; soft fruit, like raspberries, can simple be mashed through a sieve (strainer) to make a delicious sauce that can be spooned straight on to the plate.

1 If the fruit is firm, purée it first in a blender or food processor. Tip it into a sieve over a large bowl.

2 Using a ladle or wooden spoon, rub the purée firmly through the sieve, until all the soft pulp is in the bowl and just the pips or fibrous matter are left in the sieve.

FRUIT AND FLOWER DECORATIONS

Some of the most eyecatching garnishes and decorations used for puddings and desserts are made from real fruit and flowers. These vary from the very simple to the highly elaborate.

Baby Rose Posy

Choose six perfect small roses and trim the stems to 2.5 cm/1 in. Place five of them in a ring on a gâteau so that the stems meet in the centre. Place the remaining rose on top.

Edible Flowers

Colourful edible flowers, such as nasturtiums, can be used to enliven cold soufflés, mousses and ice cream. Simply sprinkle several across the plate.

Flower Bouquet

Gather some fresh flowers together in a small bouquet, tie with a ribbon, if you wish, and place on top of a gâteau or mousse for a fragrant decoration.

Orange Flower

Cut two thin slices from an orange, then cut each slice in half. Cut along the inside of the pith on one half to within 3 mm/⅛ in of the end. Turn the strip of rind in to form a loop that rests against the half slice. Repeat with the remaining half slices. Place them in a ring with the loops on the outside. This looks stunning on chocolate desserts.

Pear Fan

Peel a pear, leaving the stem intact. Poach in a light syrup until tender. Cut in half lengthways and core. Place cut side down and cut about eight thin slices, leaving them intact at the top. Press down gently to fan the slices apart. Use these fans for chocolate and fruit desserts.

Strawberry Fan

Cut a strawberry into thin slices from the pointed end almost to the top. Leave the hull and calyx in place and gently fan out the slices. Use to decorate fruit desserts and mousses.

TYPES OF CHOCOLATE

Plain Dark Chocolate

Often called "bittersweet", "luxury", "bitter" or "continental" chocolate, this has a high percentage of cocoa solids – around 75 per cent – with little or no added sugar. Many people find plain dark chocolate too bitter for eating, but its rich, intense flavour and good dark colour make it an ideal ingredient in desserts or cakes.

Plain Chocolate

Ordinary plain (semisweet) chocolate is the most widely available chocolate for use in cooking. It contains between 30 and 70 per cent cocoa solids, so check the label before you buy. The higher the content of cocoa solids, the better the chocolate flavour will be.

Milk Chocolate

This contains powdered or condensed milk and generally has around 20 per cent cocoa solids. The flavour is mild and sweet. Although this is the most popular eating chocolate, it is not as suitable as plain chocolate for melting and cooking purposes.

White Chocolate

This does not contain any cocoa solids, but gets its flavour from cocoa butter. It is sweet, and the better quality white chocolate is quite rich and smooth. White chocolate must be melted with care as it does not withstand heat as well as plain chocolate and is liable to stiffen if allowed to get too hot.

plain chocolate

organic chocolate

cocoa

plain dark chocolate

milk chocolate

chocolate-flavour cake covering

white chocolate

chocolate chips

chocolate chunks

Cocoa

This is made from the pure cocoa mass after most of the cocoa butter has been extracted. The mass is roasted, then ground to make a powder. It is probably the most economical way of giving puddings and baked goods a chocolate flavour.

Chocolate Chips

These are small pieces of chocolate of uniform size, convenient for stirring directly into cookie dough or cake mixture, or for melting. They are lower in cocoa solids than ordinary chocolate, and are available in plain dark, plain, milk and white.

USING CHOCOLATE

Using chocolate in recipes is easy once you have mastered the basic techniques of melting and manipulating it.

Melting in a Double Boiler

1 Fill the base of a double boiler or a pan about a quarter full with water. Fit the top pan or place a heatproof bowl over the pan. The water should not touch the top container. Boil the water, then lower the heat to the lowest possible setting. It is important that the water is very hot but not bubbling.

2 Break up the chocolate and place in the top pan or bowl. Let it melt completely, without stirring. Keep the water at a very slow simmer.

Melting with Direct Heat

This is only suitable for recipes where the chocolate is melted in plenty of other liquid, such as milk or cream. Break up the chocolate and put it in a pan. Add the liquid, then heat gently, stirring occasionally, until the chocolate has melted and the mixture is smooth.

Melting in the Microwave

Break the chocolate into squares and place them in a microwave-proof bowl. Heat until the chocolate is just softened – remember that chocolate can burn very easily in the microwave, so check it regularly, bearing in mind that the chocolate will retain its shape when it is melted in this way so you will need to check it carefully.

Approximate times for melting plain (semisweet) or milk chocolate in a 650–700 watt microwave oven:	
115 g/4 oz	2 minutes on High (100% power)
200–225 g/7–8 oz	3 minutes on High (100% power)
115 g/4 oz white chocolate	2 minutes on Medium (50% power)

Tips for Melting Chocolate

• Whichever method you use, melt chocolate slowly, as overheating will spoil both the flavour and texture.
• Avoid overheating – dark chocolate should not be heated above 49°C/ 120°F; milk and white chocolate should not go above 43°C/110°F.
• Never allow water or steam to come into contact with melting chocolate as this may cause it to stiffen.
• Do not cover chocolate after it has melted as condensation could cause it to stiffen.

STORING CHOCOLATE:
Chocolate keeps well if stored in a cool, dry place, away from strong-smelling foods. Check "best before" dates on the pack.

Chocolate Decorations

All these decorations can be made using any kind of chocolate.

Grating Chocolate

Using a fine or coarse cheese grater or the grating blade of a food processor, grate a large bar of chocolate. Grated chocolate is useful for sprinkling over desserts or cakes, or coating the sides of gâteaux. If you use a cheese grater, stand it on a sheet of baking parchment for extra convenience. The grated chocolate can then be easily slid or brushed off as required.

Quick Chocolate Curls

Use a swivel-bladed vegetable peeler to shave curls of chocolate from the whole bar. This works best when the chocolate has been allowed to reach room temperature.

Chocolate Curls

This method is for making larger chocolate curls.

1 Spread melted chocolate thinly and evenly over a marble slab or a cool, smooth work surface. Leave until it is just set.

2 Push a metal scraper or cheese slicer across the surface, at a 25° angle, to remove thin shavings of chocolate which should curl gently against the blade. If the chocolate sets too hard it may become too brittle to curl and must be gently melted again.

BREAD INGREDIENTS

Above: A range of flours used for bread.

Flour

White flour has a high gluten content, absorbs water readily and produces an elastic dough when kneaded. Strong white flour, made from hard wheat with a high proportion of gluten, is specifically for bread making. Wholemeal (whole-wheat) flour, containing the complete wheat kernel, produces coarser-textured bread with a high fibre content and a stronger flavour. Rye flour is dark and quite dense. It is often mixed with strong wheat flour to give a lighter loaf. Granary flour is a proprietary name given to a mixture of brown and rye flour and malted wheat grain.

Leavening Agents

These all work on similar principles. When activated, carbon dioxide is produced, making the dough expand, trapping air in tiny pockets throughout. When the bread is baked, the air is locked in, making it light in texture.

Yeast is the traditional leavening agent. Fresh yeast is said to produce the best flavour. It requires warmth to make it work, but over-heating will kill it. Store it in the refrigerator. Dried yeast requires a preliminary mixing with lukewarm liquid. Dough made with fresh or dried yeast requires two sessions of proving (setting aside to increase in bulk). Easy-blend (rapid-rise) dried yeast can be added directly to the dry ingredients for the dough, which requires only a single proving.

Baking powder is an effective raising agent when added to plain (all-purpose) flour. Bicarbonate of soda (baking soda) is activated by acid, such as buttermilk. They both start working immediately they are combined with liquid and the dough does not require proving.

Salt

An vital ingredient in yeast breads to stop the yeast from working too fast.

Sweeteners

Sugar is usually added to fresh yeast to give it a good start. It is not needed with easy-blend dried yeast. As sugar slows down the action of yeast, sweet dough may need extra yeast and longer proving.

Honey may also be used in sweet breads. Malt extract, a sugary by-product of barley, has a strong flavour and adds moistness. Molasses or black treacle, by-products of sugar refining, have a strong, smoky, slightly bitter taste.

Above: Granary (top), wholemeal and white breads make excellent toast.

Liquid

Water is the liquid most often used in bread-making, but milk is also popular. It should be lukewarm for yeast dough. Quantities in recipes are for guidance, as flours vary in how much they will absorb.

Flavourings

Sweet and savoury flavourings may be incorporated in the dough while kneading. These include sautéed onions, celery or courgettes (zucchini), sun-dried tomatoes, fresh or dried herbs, ground spices, cheese, dried fruit, glacé (candied) cherries, candied peel and chopped nuts. Be careful when adding ingredients with a high fat content, such as cheese, as too much will spoil the texture of the bread. Adding oil, butter or margarine to the dough improves the softness of the crumb and delays staleness. Too much, however, impairs the action of the yeast.

Eggs

Used to add flavour and colour and have the benefit of improving the keeping quality of rich breads.

Above: A selection of white breads.

BREAD-MAKING TECHNIQUES

Using Fresh Yeast

Crumble into a small bowl, add a pinch of sugar and cream the mixture with lukewarm water. Set aside in a warm place for 5–10 minutes, until frothy. Add to the dry ingredients.

Using Dried Yeast

Sprinkle on to lukewarm water, and add a pinch of sugar. Stir and set aside for 10–15 minutes, until frothy. Add to the dry ingredients.

Using Easy-blend Dried Yeast

Add straight from the sachet to the dry ingredients. Mix the dough with lukewarm liquid.

Sponging

Dissolve the yeast in more warm water than usual, then mix with some of the flour to make a batter. Set aside for a minimum of 20 minutes, until bubbles appear. Mix with the remaining flour.

A Few Simple Rules

• Warm bowls and equipment.
• For lukewarm water (37–43°C/ 98–108°F), mix two parts cold with one part boiling water.
• Knead the dough for at least 10 minutes to stretch the gluten and produce a light-textured loaf.
• Do not leave the dough to prove in a draught.
• Cover the dough while proving to keep it moist.

Adding Fats

Add diced butter or margarine to the dry ingredients and rub in with the fingertips until the mixture resembles breadcrumbs. Add oil with the liquid.

Kneading by Hand

Turn the dough out on to a lightly floured surface. With floured hands, fold it towards you, pulling and stretching, then push it down firmly with the heel of your hand. Give it a quarter turn and repeat the action for about 10 minutes, until the dough is smooth, elastic and no longer sticky.

Kneading in a Food Processor

Do not try to knead more dough than recommended by the manufacturer. If necessary, knead in batches. Fit the dough blade and blend together the dry ingredients. Add the yeast mixture, lukewarm liquid, oil or butter, if using, and process until the mixture comes together. Knead for 1 minute, or according to the manufacturer's instructions. Turn out and knead by hand for 1–2 minutes.

Kneading in a Mixer

Mix the dry ingredients. Add the yeast mixture, liquid, oil or butter, if using, and mix slowly with the dough hook until the mixture comes together. Continue for 3–4 minutes, or according to the manufacturer's instructions.

Proving

This is the process of setting the dough aside in a warm place to increase in bulk. Keep it moist by covering with a damp dish-towel or lightly oiled clear film (plastic wrap). A loaf or rolls on a baking sheet can be slipped inside a plastic bag, ballooned to trap the air. Set aside in a warm place (24–27°C/ 75–80°F) for an hour or more, until doubled in bulk.

Shaping Rolls To make cottage rolls, shape two-thirds of the dough into rounds the size of golf balls and the remainder into smaller rounds. Make a dent in each large ball and press a small ball on top.

To make knots, roll each dough portion into a fairly thin sausage and knot it like string.

To make twists, twist two strands of dough, dampen the ends and seal.

To make clover-leaf rolls, divide each portion of dough into three equal pieces.

To make braids, divide each portion of dough into three equal pieces and roll them into sausages. Dampen them at one end and press together. Braid loosely, dampen the other end and press together.

To make snipped-top rolls, roll each portion of dough into a smooth ball. Snip the top with kitchen scissors.

Glazing

This gives an attractive finish and introduces moisture during cooking. Bread may be glazed before, during or just after baking. Glazes include egg yolk, egg white, milk, butter, sugar or salt solutions and olive oil. Take care not to brush glazes up the sides of a tin (pan) or drip on a baking sheet, otherwise the bread will stick and crack.

Topping

Roll dough in a topping before the second proving or glaze and sprinkle before baking. Tasty toppings include cheese, oats, cracked wheat, sunflower, sesame, poppy or caraway seeds, herbs, cornmeal and wheat flakes.

Testing Bread

1 At the end of the cooking time, loosen the edges of the loaf with a metal spatula and turn out.

2 Hold the loaf upside down and tap it gently on the base. If it sounds hollow, the bread is ready.

SUCCESSFUL JAM-MAKING

Choosing Containers

Glass jars and bottles are a popular choice for all kinds of preserves because they are durable, versatile and decorative, enhancing the appearance of their contents. Modern recycled glass has many of the qualities of antique glass, such as flaws and colourings, and is inexpensive.

Earthenware jars and pots are also good choices for chutneys and home-made mustards. Specially made preserving jars are best for bottled fruit and vegetables and can be reused, although you should always use fresh seals.

Sterilizing

To ensure that harmful bacteria are eliminated, it is essential to sterilize bottles and jars and their lids, if they have them. This can be done in a variety of ways.

To sterilize in the oven, stand the containers on a baking sheet lined with newspaper or on a wooden board and rest their lids on them, but do not seal. Make sure they are not touching. Place them in a cold oven and then turn it on to 110°C/225°F/ Gas ¼ and leave the containers for 30 minutes. This method has the advantage of ensuring the containers are warm when they are filled with hot jam, syrup or chutney; otherwise they would crack. If you are not going to use them immediately, cover with a clean cloth and make sure they are warmed again before being filled.

An alternative method is to put the containers and their lids in a dishwasher and run it on its hottest setting, including the drying cycle, but without adding any detergent. This, too, ensures the containers are warm when they are filled.

It is also necessary to sterilize a jelly bag before use. Set the bag over a large bowl and pour boiling water through it. Discard the water and replace the bowl with a clean one.

Seals and Labels

The type and effectiveness of the seal required depend on the kind of preserve and the process used. Jams and jellies can be covered with a disc of baking parchment and the top of the jar covered with paper or cellophane held in place with an elastic band. Bottled fruit and vegetables must be sealed with new rubber seals and the lids clipped in place. Chutneys and pickles should be sealed with vinegar-proof lids that will not corrode.

Ideally, all preserves should be labelled with a description of the contents and the date they were made. Self-adhesive labels may be attached to the surface of the container or wooden or metal labels may be tied around the neck.

Setting Point

To test jams and jellies for the setting point, spoon a small quantity on to a chilled saucer. Chill for 3 minutes, then push the jam with your finger. If wrinkles form on the surface, the jam is ready. Alternatively, you could use a sugar thermometer clipped to the side of the pan, but not touching the base. When the temperature reaches 105°C/ 220°F, the jam is ready.

Most jams will benefit if left to stand for about 15 minutes before being ladled into jars. This ensures that the pieces of fruit are evenly distributed. A jam funnel is useful for preventing hot spillages; it can also be used when filling jars with chutney.

FRUITY TREATS

Papaya Skewers with Passion Fruit Coulis

Tropical fruits, full of natural sweetness, make a simple exotic dessert.

Serves 6

INGREDIENTS
3 ripe papayas
10 passion fruit
  or kiwi fruit
30 ml/2 tbsp lime juice
30 ml/2 tbsp icing (confectioners') sugar
30 ml/2 tbsp white rum
toasted coconut and lime, to decorate

COOK'S TIP: If you are short of time, the passion fruit flesh can be used as it is, without puréeing or straining. Simply scoop the flesh from the skins and mix it with the fresh lime juice, sugar and rum. Kiwi fruit, however, will still need to be puréed.

2 Halve eight of the passion fruit or kiwi fruit and scoop out the flesh. Process the flesh for a few seconds in a blender or food processor.

3 Press the pulp through a sieve (strainer) and discard the seeds. Add the lime juice, icing sugar and rum, and then stir well until the sugar has dissolved.

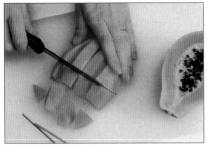

1 Cut the papayas in half and scoop out the seeds. Peel them and cut the flesh into even-size chunks. Thread them on to six bamboo skewers.

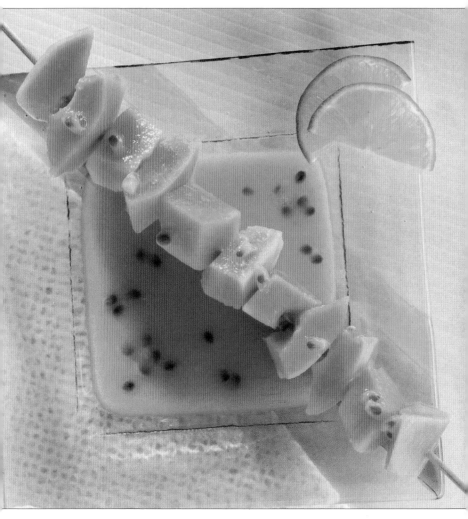

4 Spoon a little of the coulis on to six serving plates. Place the papaya skewers on top. Scoop out the flesh from the remaining passion or kiwi fruit and spoon it over the skewers. Sprinkle with a little toasted coconut, if you like, and garnish with slices of lime before serving.

Cool Green Fruit Salad

A sophisticated yet simple fruit salad for any time of year.

Serves 6

INGREDIENTS
3 Ogen or Galia melons
115 g/4 oz/1 cup green seedless grapes
1 kiwi fruit
1 star fruit (carambola)
1 green-skinned apple
1 lime
175 ml/6 fl oz/¾ cup sparkling grape juice

1 Cut the melons in half and scoop out the seeds. Keeping the shells intact, scoop out the flesh with a melon baller, or scoop it out with a spoon and cut into bite-size cubes. Reserve the melon shells.

2 Remove any stems from the grapes. If the grapes are large, cut them in half. Peel and chop the kiwi fruit. Thinly slice the star fruit. Core and thinly slice the apple and place the slices in a bowl, together with the melon, grapes, kiwi fruit and star fruit.

3 Thinly pare the rind from the lime and cut it into fine strips. Blanch the strips for 30 seconds in boiling water, drain and rinse in cold water. Squeeze the juice from the lime and toss it into the fruit.

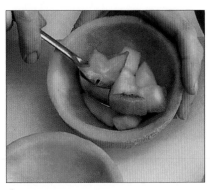

4 Spoon the prepared fruit into the reserved melon shells and chill in the refrigerator until required. Just before serving, spoon the sparkling grape juice over the fruit and scatter it with the lime rind.

COOK'S TIP: If you are serving this dessert on a hot summer day, arrange the melon shells on a platter of crushed ice. This will keep them beautifully cool.

Mandarins in Syrup

Any citrus fruits are suitable for this lovely recipe.

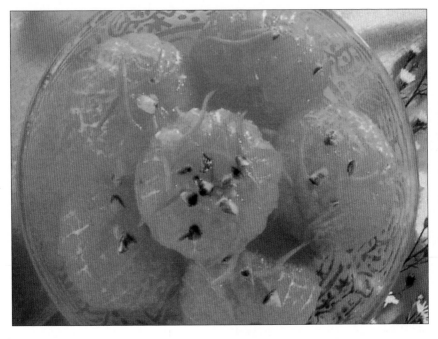

Serves 4

INGREDIENTS
10 mandarins
15 ml/1 tbsp icing (confectioners') sugar
10 ml/2 tsp orange flower water
15 ml/1 tbsp chopped pistachio nuts

1 Thinly pare a little of the zest from one mandarin and cut it into fine shreds for decoration. Squeeze the juice from two of the mandarins and set aside.

2 Peel the remaining fruit, removing as much of the white pith as possible. Arrange the whole fruit in a wide dish.

3 Mix together the mandarin juice, icing sugar and orange flower water and pour it over the fruit. Cover the dish and chill in the refrigerator.

4 Blanch the shreds of mandarin zest in boiling water for 30 seconds. Drain, let cool and sprinkle them over the mandarins with the chopped pistachio nuts before serving.

Figs with Ricotta Cream

Fresh, ripe figs are full of natural sweetness and need little adornment.

Serves 4

INGREDIENTS
4 ripe, fresh figs
115 g/4 oz/½ cup ricotta or cottage cheese
45 ml/3 tbsp low fat, thick natural (plain)
   yogurt or low fat crème fraîche
15 ml/1 tbsp clear honey
2.5 ml/½ tsp vanilla extract
freshly grated nutmeg, to decorate

1 Trim the stalks from the figs. Make four cuts through each fig from the stalk end, cutting them almost through, but leaving them joined at the base.

2 Place the figs on serving plates and open them out.

3 Mix together the ricotta or cottage cheese, yogurt or crème fraîche, honey and vanilla extract.

4 Spoon a little ricotta cream on to each plate and sprinkle with grated nutmeg to serve.

COOK'S TIP: The honey can be replaced with a little artificial sweetener.

Pineapple Flambé

The flavour of alcohol burnt off by flambéing is not too overpowering.

Serves 4

INGREDIENTS
1 large, ripe pineapple
40 g/1½ oz/3 tbsp unsalted (sweet)
   butter
45 ml/3 tbsp brown sugar
60 ml/4 tbsp fresh orange juice
30 ml/2 tbsp brandy
   or vodka
30 ml/2 tbsp flaked (sliced) almonds,
   toasted
low fat crème fraîche or low fat,
   thick natural (plain) yogurt, to serve

2 Cut the pineapple into thin slices and, with an apple corer, remove the hard central core. Prepare to fry the rings, preferably in one batch to avoid cooling.

3 Heat the butter, sugar and orange juice in a large frying pan. Add the pineapple slices and cook for about 1–2 minutes, turning once.

4 Add the brandy or vodka and carefully light with a long taper immediately. Let the flames die down and then sprinkle with the almonds. Serve with low fat crème fraîche or low fat, thick natural yogurt.

1 Cut away the top and base of the pineapple. Then cut down the sides, removing all the dark "eyes", but leaving the pineapple in good shape.

VARIATION: You could substitute 4 thinly sliced apples for the pineapple.

Right: Pineapple Flambé and Warm Pears in Cider.

Warm Pears in Cider

This dessert is simple to make, very attractive and tastes really delicious.

Serves 4

INGREDIENTS
1 lemon
50 g/2 oz/¼ cup caster (superfine) sugar
a pinch of grated nutmeg
250 ml/8 fl oz/1 cup sweet (hard) cider
4 firm, ripe pears
freshly made skimmed-milk custard, low fat
    crème fraîche or low fat, thick natural
    (plain) yogurt, to serve (optional)

1 Carefully remove the rind from the lemon with a vegetable peeler, leaving any white pith behind. Squeeze the juice from the lemon into a pan, add the rind, sugar, nutmeg and cider and heat through to dissolve the sugar.

2 Carefully peel the pears, leaving the stalks intact, and place in the pan of cider. Poach, turning frequently with a spoon, for 10–15 minutes, until almost tender.

3 With a slotted spoon, transfer the pears to individual serving dishes.

4 Simmer the liquid over a high heat until it reduces slightly and becomes syrupy. Pour the warm syrup over the pears and serve as desired.

Hot Bananas with Rum & Raisins

Use bananas that are either all yellow or green-tipped with no black patches.

Serves 4

INGREDIENTS
40 g/1½ oz/¼ cup seedless raisins
75 ml/5 tbsp dark rum
25 g/1 oz/2 tbsp unsalted (sweet) butter
60 ml/4 tbsp soft light brown sugar
1.5 ml/¼ teaspoon grated nutmeg
1.5 ml/¼ tsp ground cinnamon
4 ripe bananas, peeled and halved
  lengthways
30 ml/2 tbsp flaked (sliced) almonds,
  toasted
chilled low fat crème fraîche or low fat, thick
  natural (plain) yogurt, to serve (optional)

1 Soak the raisins in the rum for 10 minutes.

2 Dissolve the sugar in the melted butter and add the spices.

3 Add the bananas and cook until tender.

4 Pour over the rum and raisins and set alight.

5 Sprinkle with the almonds and serve.

Grilled Nectarines with Ricotta & Spice

Use canned peach halves in this easy dessert if fresh fruit is unavailable.

Serves 4

INGREDIENTS
4 ripe nectarines or peaches
15 ml/1 tbsp light muscovado (brown) sugar
115 g/4 oz/½ cup ricotta cheese or low fat
crème fraîche
2.5 ml/½ tsp ground star anise

1 Preheat the grill (broiler) to medium hot. Cut the nectarines or peaches in half and remove the stones (pits).

2 Arrange the nectarines, cut side up, in a wide flameproof dish or on a non-stick baking sheet.

3 Stir the sugar into the ricotta or crème fraîche. Spoon the mixture into the hollow of each nectarine half.

4 Sprinkle with the star anise and grill (broil) for 6–8 minutes, or until the nectarines are hot and the filling is bubbling. Serve warm.

Summer Pudding

Do not reserve this lovely pudding solely for summer. It freezes well and provides a delicious dessert for Christmas Day, as a light and refreshing alternative to the traditional pudding.

Serves 6

INGREDIENTS
8 x 1 cm/½ in thick slices of day-old white bread, crusts removed
800 g/1¾ lb/6–7 cups mixed berry fruits, such as strawberries, raspberries, blackcurrants, redcurrants and blueberries
50 g/2 oz/¼ cup golden caster (superfine) sugar
low fat, thick natural (plain) yogurt or low fat crème fraîche, to serve

1 Trim a slice of the bread to fit in the base of a 1 litre/1¾ pint/4 cup bowl, then trim another 5–6 slices to line the sides of the bowl.

2 Place all the fruit in a heavy-based pan with the sugar. Cook gently, uncovered, for 4–5 minutes, until the juices begin to run – it will not be necessary to add any water. Allow the mixture to cool slightly.

3 Spoon the berries, and juice to moisten, into the bread-lined bowl. Save any leftover juice for serving.

4 Fold over the excess bread, then cover the fruit with the remaining bread slices, trimming to fit. Place a small plate directly on top of the pudding, fitting it inside the bowl. Weight it with a 900 g/2 lb weight, if you have one, or use full cans.

5 Chill in the refrigerator for at least 8 hours or overnight.

6 To serve, run a knife around the pudding and turn on to a plate. Serve with juice and yogurt or crème fraîche.

Tofu Berry "Cheesecake"

This summery "cheesecake" is a very light and refreshing finish to any meal. Strictly speaking it is not a cheesecake at all, as it is based on tofu – but who would guess?

Serves 6

INGREDIENTS

FOR THE BASE
50 g/2 oz/4 tbsp low fat spread
30 ml/2 tbsp apple juice
115 g/4 oz/2½ cups bran flakes or other
high fibre cereal

FOR THE FILLING
275 g/10 oz/1¼ cups tofu or skimmed-milk
soft cheese
200 ml/7 fl oz/⅞ cup low fat,
thick natural (plain) yogurt
15 ml/1 tbsp/1 envelope
powdered gelatine
60 ml/4 tbsp apple juice

FOR THE TOPPING
175 g/6 oz/1¾ cups mixed soft fruit,
such as strawberries, raspberries,
redcurrants and blackberries,
or frozen "fruits of the forest", thawed
30 ml/2 tbsp redcurrant jelly
30 ml/2 tbsp hot water

1 To make the base, place the low fat spread and apple juice in a pan over a low heat. Crush the cereal and stir it into the pan. Spoon into a 23 cm/9 in round flan tin (tart pan) and press down firmly. Chill the base in the refrigerator until set.

2 To make the filling, place the tofu or cheese and yogurt in a food processor and process until smooth. Sprinkle the gelatine in the apple juice to soften, blend until it has completely dissolved, then quickly stir it into the tofu or cheese mixture.

3 Spread the tofu or cheese mixture over the cake base, smoothing it evenly. Chill in the refrigerator until the filling is set.

4 Remove the flan tin and place the "cheesecake" on a serving plate. Arrange the fruits over the top.

5 Melt the redcurrant jelly with the hot water. Let it cool, then spoon it over the fruit before serving.

Banana, Maple & Lime Pancakes

Pancakes are always a treat and can be made in advance and frozen. They take only a few minutes to defrost.

Serves 4

INGREDIENTS
115 g/4 oz/1 cup plain (all-purpose) flour
1 egg white
250 ml/8 fl oz/1 cup skimmed milk
50 ml/2 fl oz/¼ cup water
sunflower oil, for frying

FOR THE FILLING
4 bananas, sliced
45 ml/3 tbsp maple syrup
30 ml/2 tbsp lime juice
strips of lime rind, to decorate

1 Beat together the flour, egg white, milk and water until smooth and bubbly. Chill until required.

2 Heat a little oil in a non-stick frying pan, pour in enough batter to coat the base, cook until golden, loosen with a spatula, and toss. Remove from pan and keep hot.

3 For the filling, simmer the bananas, syrup and lime juice in a pan for one minute. Spoon into the pancakes and fold into quarters. Decorate with lime rind and serve hot.

Lemon & Lime Sauce

A tangy, refreshing sauce, which is delicious with Banana, Maple & Lime
Pancakes or fruit tarts.

Serves 4

INGREDIENTS
1 lemon
2 limes
50 g/2 oz/¼ cup caster (superfine) sugar
25 ml/1½ tbsp arrowroot
300 ml/½ pint/1¼ cups water
lemon balm or mint,
   to decorate

1 Using a citrus zester, thinly pare the
lemon and lime rinds. Squeeze the
juice from the fruit.

2 Place the rind in a pan, cover with
water and bring to the boil. Drain and
set the rind aside.

3 In a small bowl, mix a little of the
sugar with the arrowroot. Blend in
enough of the measured water to make
a smooth paste. Heat the remaining
water in a small pan, pour in the
arrowroot mixture and stir constantly
until the sauce boils and thickens.

4 Stir in the remaining sugar, citrus
juice and rinds. Decorate with the
lemon balm or mint and serve hot.

Fresh Fruit with Mango Sauce

A salad made with fresh fruit is always refreshing and welcome, but it is especially delicious and attractive served with a puréed fruit sauce.

Serves 6

INGREDIENTS

1 large mango, peeled, stoned (pitted)
  and chopped
rind of 1 unwaxed orange
juice of 3 oranges
caster (superfine) sugar, to taste
2 peaches
2 nectarines
1 small mango, peeled
2 plums
1 pear or ½ small melon
juice of 1 lemon
25–50 g/1–2 oz/2 heaped tbsp wild
  strawberries (optional)
25–50 g/1–2 oz/2 heaped tbsp raspberries
25–50 g/1–2 oz/2 heaped tbsp blueberries
small mint sprigs, to decorate

1 In a food processor fitted with the metal blade, process the large mango until smooth. Add the orange rind, juice and sugar to taste and process until smooth. Press through a sieve (strainer) into a bowl and chill the sauce.

2 Peel the peaches, if you like, then stone (pit) and slice the peaches, nectarines, mango and plums. Quarter the pear and remove the core or peel the melon, and slice thinly.

3 Place the sliced fruits on a large plate. Sprinkle with the lemon juice and chill, covered with clear film (plastic wrap), for up to 3 hours before serving. (Some fruits may discolour if left too long.)

4 To serve, arrange the sliced fruits on serving plates, spoon the berries on top, drizzle with a little mango sauce and decorate with mint sprigs. Serve the remaining sauce separately.

Fragrant Fruit Salad

The syrup of this exotic fruit salad is flavoured with lime and coffee liqueur. It can be prepared up to a day before serving.

Serves 6

INGREDIENTS

130 g/4½ oz/⅔ cup sugar
thinly pared rind and juice
    of 1 lime
60 ml/4 tbsp coffee liqueur, such as
    Tia Maria, Kahlúa or Toussaint
1 small pineapple
1 papaya
2 pomegranates
1 medium mango
2 passion fruits
fine strips of lime peel,
    to decorate

2 Using a sharp knife, cut the plume and stalk end from the pineapple. Peel thickly and cut the flesh into bitesize pieces, discarding the woody central core. Add to the bowl.

3 Cut the papaya in half and scoop out the seeds. Peel, cut into chunks and add to the bowl. Cut the pomegranates in half and scoop out the seeds. Break into clusters and add to the bowl.

4 Cut the mango lengthways, along each side of the stone (pit). Peel the skin off the flesh and cut into chunks. Add to the rest of the fruit in the bowl. Stir well.

1 Put the sugar and lime rind in a small pan with 150 ml/¼ pint/⅔ cup water. Heat gently until the sugar dissolves, then bring to the boil and simmer for 5 minutes. Leave to cool, then strain into a large serving bowl, discarding the lime rind. Stir in the lime juice and liqueur.

5 Halve the passion fruits and scoop out the flesh using a teaspoon. Spoon over the salad and serve, decorated with fine strips of lime peel.

COOK'S TIP: To maximize the flavour of the fruit, allow the salad to stand at room temperature for an hour before serving.

Strawberry & Avocado Salad in Ginger & Orange Sauce

Avocado is more often treated as a vegetable, but in the Caribbean it is used as a fruit, which of course it is!

Serves 4

INGREDIENTS
2 firm ripe avocados
3 firm ripe bananas, sliced
12 fresh strawberries, halved,
　or cherries
juice of 1 large orange
shredded fresh root
　ginger (optional)

FOR THE GINGER SYRUP
50 g/2 oz fresh root ginger,
　peeled and chopped
900 ml/1½ pints/3¾ cups water
225 g/8 oz/1 cup demerara
　(raw) sugar
2 cloves

2 Remove the ginger and discard. Leave to cool. Chill in a covered container in the refrigerator.

3 Peel the avocados, cut into slices and place in a bowl with the bananas and strawberries or cherries.

COOK'S TIP: Avocados discolour when exposed to the air, so peel and slice them quickly. The orange juice and ginger syrup will prevent discoloration for some time.

1 First make the ginger syrup: place the ginger, water, sugar and cloves in a pan and bring to the boil. Reduce the heat and simmer for about 1 hour, until well reduced and syrupy.

4 Pour the orange juice over the fruits. Add 60 ml/4 tbsp of the ginger syrup and mix gently, using a metal spoon. Chill for 30 minutes and add a little shredded ginger, if you like. Serve with the remaining ginger syrup. Ginger syrup will keep for two weeks in the refrigerator and can be added to other fruit desserts or ice cream.

Persian Melon

Called *Paludeh Garmac,* this is a typical Persian dessert using delicious, sweet fresh fruits flavoured with rose water and a hint of aromatic mint.

Serves 4

INGREDIENTS
2 small melons
225 g/8 oz/2 cups strawberries
3 peaches, peeled and cut into small cubes
1 bunch of seedless grapes (green or red)
30 ml/2 tbsp caster (superfine) sugar
15 ml/1 tbsp rose water
15 ml/1 tbsp lemon juice
crushed ice (optional)
sprigs of mint, to decorate

1 Cut the melons in half and remove the seeds. Scoop out the flesh with a melon baller, without damaging the skin. Reserve the melon shells. Alternatively, scoop out the flesh using a spoon and cut into bitesize pieces.

2 Reserve four strawberries and slice the others. Place in a bowl and mix with the melon balls, peaches, grapes, sugar, rose water and lemon juice.

3 Pile the fruit into the melon shells and chill for 2 hours.

4 To serve, sprinkle with crushed ice, if you like, decorating each melon with a whole strawberry and a sprig of mint.

VARIATION: If you prefer, nectarines and raspberries could replace the peaches and strawberries.

Fruits of the Tropics Salad

Pineapple, guavas, bananas and mango are combined with ginger and coconut to make this exotic Caribbean dessert.

Serves 4–6

INGREDIENTS
1 medium pineapple
400 g/14 oz can guava halves
    in syrup
2 medium bananas, sliced
1 large mango, peeled, stoned (pitted)
    and diced
115 g/4 oz preserved stem ginger and
    30 ml/2 tbsp of the syrup
60 ml/4 tbsp thick coconut milk
10 ml/2 tsp sugar
2.5 ml/½ tsp freshly
    grated nutmeg
2.5 ml/½ tsp ground cinnamon
strips of coconut,
    to decorate

1 Peel, core and cube the pineapple, and place in a serving bowl. Drain the guavas, reserving the syrup, and chop. Add the guavas to the bowl with one of the bananas and the mango. Chop the stem ginger and add to the pineapple mixture.

2 Pour the ginger syrup and the reserved guava syrup into a blender or food processor and add the other banana, coconut milk, sugar and spices. Process to make a smooth, creamy purée.

3 Pour the banana and coconut mixture over the fruit, add a little nutmeg and cinnamon. Serve chilled, decorated with strips of coconut.

Fresh Fruit Salad

Any fruits in season can be used for this salad.

Serves 6

INGREDIENTS
2 eating apples
2 oranges
2 peaches
16–20 strawberries
30 ml/2 tbsp lemon juice
15–30 ml/1–2 tbsp orange flower water
icing (confectioners') sugar, to taste
a few fresh mint leaves, to decorate

1 Peel, core and thinly slice the apples. Peel the oranges, removing all the pith, and segment them, catching any juice in a bowl.

2 Blanch the peaches for 1 minute in boiling water, then peel away the skin and cut the flesh into thick slices. Hull the strawberries and halve or quarter if large. Place all the fruit in a large serving bowl.

3 Blend together the lemon juice, orange flower water to taste and any orange juice. Add a little icing sugar, if you like. Pour the fruit juice mixture over the fruit salad and serve decorated with mint leaves.

Right: Fresh Fruit Salad (top);
Dried Fruit Salad

Dried Fruit Salad

This is a wonderful combination of fresh and dried fruits.

Serves 4

INGREDIENTS
115 g/4 oz/½ cup dried apricots
115 g/4 oz/½ cup dried peaches
1 pear
1 apple
1 orange
115 g/4 oz/⅔ cup mixed raspberries
   and blackberries
1 cinnamon stick
50 g/2 oz/¼ cup caster (superfine) sugar
15 ml/1 tbsp clear honey
30 ml/2 tbsp lemon juice

1 Soak the apricots and peaches in water for 1–2 hours, until plump, then drain and halve or quarter them.

2 Peel and core the pear and apple and cut into cubes. Peel the orange with a sharp knife, removing all the pith, and cut into wedges. Place all the fruit in a pan with the berries.

3 Add 600 ml/1 pint/2½ cups water, the cinnamon, sugar and honey and bring to the boil. Cover and simmer very gently for 10–12 minutes, then remove the pan from the heat. Stir in the lemon juice. Allow to cool, then pour into a serving bowl and chill for 1–2 hours before serving.

Dried Fruit Compote

Serves 6

INGREDIENTS

350 g/12 oz/2 cups mixed dried fruits, such as
    apples, pears, prunes, peaches or apricots
1 cinnamon stick
300 ml/½ pint/1¼ cups cider or water
65 g/2½ oz/½ cup raisins
30 ml/2 tbsp clear honey
juice of ½ lemon
mint leaves, to decorate

1 Put the mixed dried fruit in a large
pan with the cinnamon and cider or
water. Heat gently until almost boiling,
then cover the pan, lower the heat and
cook gently for 12–15 minutes, to
soften the fruit.

2 Remove the pan from the heat and
stir in the raisins and honey. Cover the
pan and leave to cool. Remove the
cinnamon stick and then stir in the
lemon juice.

3 Transfer the compote to a serving
bowl, cover with clear film and keep
refrigerated until needed. Allow the
fruit compote to come to room
temperature before serving, decorated
with a few mint leaves.

COOK'S TIP: This compote will
keep refrigerated for up to a week.

Citrus Fruit Flambé with Pistachio Praline

Serves 4

INGREDIENTS
oil, for greasing
115 g/4 oz/generous ½ cup caster
  (superfine) sugar
50 g/2 oz/½ cup pistachio nuts
4 oranges
2 ruby grapefruit
2 limes
50 g/2 oz/¼ cup butter
50 g/2 oz/¼ cup light muscovado
  (brown) sugar
45 ml/3 tbsp Cointreau
fresh mint sprigs, to decorate

1 Oil a baking sheet. In a heavy pan, gently cook the sugar and nuts, swirling the pan, until the sugar melts. Cook over a low heat until the nuts pop and the sugar is dark gold.

2 Pour on to the baking sheet and cool. Chop the praline into chunks.

3 Cut off the rind and pith from the citrus fruit. Cut between the membranes so that the segments fall into a bowl, with any juice.

4 Heat the butter and muscovado sugar in a heavy frying pan until the sugar has dissolved. Strain the citrus juices into the pan and cook, stirring occasionally, until reduced and syrupy.

5 Add the fruit segments and warm through without stirring. Pour over the Cointreau and set it alight. When the flames die down, spoon the flambé into serving dishes. Serve sprinkled with praline and decorated with mint.

Fresh Fig, Apple & Date Salad

Sweet Mediterranean figs and dates combine especially well with crisp dessert apples. A hint of almond serves to unite the flavours.

Serves 4

INGREDIENTS
6 large apples
juice of ½ lemon
175 g/6 oz fresh dates
25 g/1 oz white marzipan
5 ml/1 tsp orange flower water
60 ml/4 tbsp natural (plain) yogurt
4 green or purple figs
4 almonds, toasted

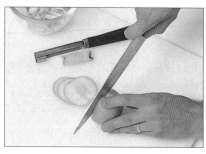

1 Core the apples. Slice thinly, then cut the slices into fine matchsticks. Moisten with lemon juice to stop them from turning brown.

2 Carefully remove the stones (pits) from the fresh dates and cut the flesh into fine strips, then combine with the apple matchsticks.

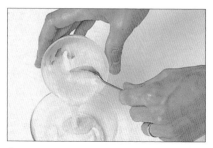

3 Soften the marzipan with the orange flower water in a small bowl and combine with the yogurt. Mix well.

4 Pile the apples and dates in the centre of four plates. Remove the stem from each of the figs and divide the fruit into quarters, without cutting right through the base. Squeeze the base with the thumb and forefinger of each hand to open up the fruit.

5 Place an opened fig in the centre of the apple and date salad and spoon in the yogurt, marzipan and orange flower filling. Decorate the filling with a whole toasted almond.

Clementines with Star Anise & Cinnamon

This fresh dessert, delicately flavoured with mulling spices, makes the perfect ending for a festive meal.

Serves 6

INGREDIENTS
350 ml/12 fl oz/1½ cups sweet dessert wine
75 g/3 oz/⅓ cup caster (superfine) sugar
6 star anise
1 cinnamon stick
1 vanilla pod (bean)
1 strip of thinly pared lime rind
30 ml/2 tbsp Cointreau
12 clementines

1 Put the wine, sugar, star anise and cinnamon in a pan. Split the vanilla pod and add it to the pan with the lime rind.

2 Bring to the boil, lower the heat and simmer for 10 minutes. Allow to cool, then stir in the Cointreau.

3 Peel the clementines, removing all the pith and white membranes. Cut some of the clementines in half and arrange them all in a glass dish. Pour over the spiced wine and chill overnight before serving.

VARIATION: Tangerines or oranges can be used instead of clementines if you prefer.

Grilled Spiced Fruit Kebabs

These colourful, lightly spiced kebabs are a tempting treat and very quick and easy to prepare and cook.

Serves 4–6

INGREDIENTS

4–5 kinds of firm ripe fruit, such as
    pineapple and mango cubes,
    strawberry and pear slices,
    grapes and tangerine segments
25 g/1 oz/2 tbsp unsalted (sweet)
    butter, melted
grated rind and juice of 1 orange
sugar to taste
pinch of ground cinnamon
    or grated nutmeg
yogurt, sour cream or crème fraîche,
    to serve

1 Preheat the grill (broiler) and line a baking sheet with foil. If using wooden skewers, soak them in cold water.

2 Thread the fruit on 4–6 skewers. Arrange the skewers on the prepared baking sheet, spoon over the melted butter, orange rind and juice and sprinkle with sugar to taste, together with a pinch of cinnamon or nutmeg.

3 Grill (broil) the kebabs for 2–3 minutes, turning once, until the sugar begins to caramelize. Serve with yogurt, sour cream or crème fraîche.

Pears in Chocolate Fudge Blankets

Warm poached pears swathed in a rich chocolate fudge sauce – who could resist such a sensual pleasure?

Serves 6

INGREDIENTS
6 ripe eating pears
30 ml/2 tbsp lemon juice
75 g/3 oz/⅓ cup caster (superfine) sugar
300 ml/½ pint/1¼ cups water
1 cinnamon stick

FOR THE SAUCE
200 ml/7 fl oz/scant 1 cup double
   (heavy) cream
150 g/5 oz/scant 1 cup light muscovado
   (brown) sugar
25 g/1 oz/2 tbsp unsalted (sweet) butter
60 ml/4 tbsp golden (light corn) syrup
120 ml/4 fl oz/½ cup milk
200 g/7 oz dark (bittersweet) chocolate,
   broken into squares

1 Peel the pears thinly, leaving the stalks on. Scoop out the cores from the base. Brush the cut surfaces with lemon juice to prevent browning.

2 Place the sugar and water in a large pan. Heat gently until the sugar dissolves. Add the pears and cinnamon stick with any remaining lemon juice, and, if necessary, a little more water, so that the pears are almost covered.

3 Bring to the boil, then lower the heat, cover and simmer gently for 15–20 minutes, or until the pears are just tender.

4 Meanwhile, make the sauce. Place the cream, sugar, butter, golden syrup and milk in a heavy pan. Heat gently until the sugar has dissolved and the butter and syrup have melted, then bring to the boil. Boil, stirring constantly, for about 5 minutes or until thick and smooth.

5 Remove the pan from the heat and stir in the dark chocolate, a few squares at a time, until it has melted.

6 Using a slotted spoon, transfer the poached pears to a dish. Keep hot. Boil the syrup rapidly to reduce to about 45–60 ml/3–4 tbsp. Remove the cinnamon stick and stir the syrup into the chocolate sauce. Serve the pears in individual bowls, with the hot chocolate sauce spooned over.

Fruit Gratin

This out-of-the-ordinary gratin is strictly for grown-ups.

Serves 4

INGREDIENTS
2 tamarillos
½ sweet pineapple
1 ripe mango, peeled
175 g/6 oz/1½ cups blackberries
120 ml/4 fl oz/½ cup sparkling white wine
115 g/4 oz/½ cup caster (superfine) sugar
6 egg yolks

1 Cut the tamarillos in half lengthways and then into thick slices. Cut the rind and core from the pineapple and remove the eyes. Cut the flesh into chunks. Cut the mango in half and slice the flesh from the stone (pit).

2 Divide all the fruit among four gratin dishes set on a baking sheet. Gently heat the wine and sugar in a pan until the sugar has dissolved. Bring to the boil and boil for 5 minutes.

3 Put the egg yolks in a heatproof bowl set over a pan of simmering water and whisk until pale. Slowly pour on the hot sugar syrup, whisking, until thickened. Preheat the grill (broiler).

4 Spoon the mixture over the fruit. Place the baking sheet under the grill until the topping is golden. Serve hot.

Right: Fruit Gratin (top); Hot Pineapple

Hot Pineapple

This dessert is delicious served with the papaya sauce.

Serves 6

INGREDIENTS
1 sweet pineapple
melted butter, for greasing and brushing
2 pieces drained preserved stem ginger, cut into fine matchsticks, plus 30 ml/2 tbsp of the syrup from the jar
30 ml/2 tbsp demerara (raw) sugar
pinch of ground cinnamon
fresh mint sprigs, to decorate

FOR THE SAUCE
1 ripe papaya, peeled and seeded
175 ml/6 fl oz/¾ cup apple juice

1 Peel the pineapple and remove the eyes. Cut it crossways into six slices. Line a baking sheet with foil, rolling up the sides to make a rim, and grease with melted butter. Preheat the grill (broiler).

2 Arrange the pineapple on the foil. Brush with butter, then top with the ginger, syrup, sugar and cinnamon. Grill (broil) for 5–7 minutes.

3 Meanwhile, make the sauce. Cut a few slices from the papaya and set aside, then process the rest with the apple juice in a blender or food processor. Press through a sieve (strainer), then stir in any juices from cooking the pineapple. Serve with the sauce, decorated with papaya and mint.

Stuffed Peaches with Amaretto

Both amaretti and amaretto liqueur have an intense almond flavour, and they make a natural partner for peaches.

Serves 4

INGREDIENTS

4 ripe but firm peaches
50 g/2 oz amaretti
25 g/1 oz/2 tbsp butter, softened, plus extra,
    for greasing
25 g/1 oz/2 tbsp caster (superfine) sugar
1 egg yolk
60 ml/4 tbsp amaretto liqueur
250 ml/8 fl oz/1 cup dry
    white wine
sprigs of mint, to decorate
ice cream or pouring cream,
    to serve (optional)

1 Preheat the oven to 180°C/350°F/ Gas 4. Following the natural indentation line on each peach, cut in half down to the stone (pit), then twist the halves in opposite directions to separate them.

2 Remove the peach stones, then cut away a little of the central flesh to make a larger hole for the stuffing. Chop this flesh finely and set aside.

COOK'S TIP: You might find it easier to crush the amaretti in a knotted, strong plastic bag instead of in a bowl.

3 Put the amaretti in a bowl and crush them to fine crumbs with the end of a rolling pin.

4 Cream the butter and sugar together in a separate bowl until smooth. Stir in the reserved chopped peach flesh, the egg yolk and half the amaretto liqueur with the prepared amaretti crumbs.

5 Lightly butter an ovenproof dish that is just large enough to hold the peach halves in a single layer.

VARIATION: This dish also looks most attractive decorated with tiny sprigs of fresh basil, if available.

6 Spoon the stuffing into the peaches, then stand them in the dish. Mix the remaining liqueur with the wine, pour over the peaches and bake them for 25 minutes, or until they feel tender when tested with a skewer. Decorate with mint sprigs and serve hot, with ice cream or cream, if you like.

Stuffed Apricots

Almonds have a delightful affinity with apricots.

Serves 6

INGREDIENTS

75 g/3 oz/scant ½ cup caster (superfine) sugar
30 ml/2 tbsp lemon juice
115 g/4 oz/1 cup ground almonds
50 g/2 oz/½ cup icing (confectioner's) sugar
    or caster (superfine) sugar
a little orange flower water (optional)
25 g/1 oz/2 tbsp melted butter
2.5 ml/½ tsp almond extract
900 g/2 lb fresh apricots
fresh mint sprigs, to decorate

1 Preheat the oven to 180°C/350°F/Gas 4. Bring the sugar, lemon juice and 300 ml/½ pint/1¼ cups water to the boil and simmer for 5–10 minutes.

2 In a bowl, blend together the ground almonds, icing or caster sugar, orange flower water, if using, melted butter and almond extract to form a smooth paste.

3 Slit each apricot and ease out the stone. Stuff each fruit with a small piece of the almond paste.

4 Put the stuffed apricots in a shallow ovenproof dish and pour over the sugar syrup. Cover the dish with foil and bake the stuffed apricots for 25–30 minutes. Serve with a little of the syrup, if liked, and decorated with sprigs of fresh mint.

Indian Fruit Salad

This is a very appetizing and refreshing salad, with a typically Indian combination of citrus fruits seasoned with salt and pepper.

Serves 6

INGREDIENTS
115 g/4 oz/1 cup seedless green and
    black grapes
225 g/8 oz canned mandarin segments,
    drained
2 navel oranges, peeled and segmented
225 g/8 oz canned grapefruit segments,
    drained
balls from 1 honeydew melon
balls from ½ watermelon
1 fresh mango, peeled and sliced
juice of 1 lemon
2.5 ml/½ tsp sugar
1.5 ml/¼ tsp ground cumin seeds
salt and ground black pepper

1 Place all the fruit in a large serving bowl and add the lemon juice. Toss gently to prevent breaking up the fruit.

2 Mix together the remaining ingredients and sprinkle over the fruit. Gently toss once more, chill thoroughly and serve.

Rich Chocolate & Fruit Fondue

This sumptuous fruit fondue, with its rich, delicious sauce, makes a lavish finish to a party and is fun to share.

Serves 4–6

INGREDIENTS
a selection of mixed fruit, such as kumquats, apple, peach and pear slices, banana slices, clementine segments, seedless grapes, cherries, peeled lychees, mango and papaya cubes, cut figs and plums
lemon juice

FOR THE CHOCOLATE DIP
225 g/8 oz good-quality plain (semisweet) chocolate, chopped
30 ml/2 tbsp golden (light corn) syrup
120 ml/4 fl oz/½ cup whipping cream
30–45 ml/2–3 tbsp brandy or orange liqueur

2 In a medium-sized pan over a medium-low heat, combine the chopped chocolate, golden syrup and whipping cream, folding in well. Carry on stirring until the chocolate is melted and smooth.

3 Remove from the heat and stir in the brandy or orange liqueur.

4 Pour the chocolate mixture into a serving bowl and place in the centre of the serving dish, surrounded by the chilled fruits. Provide cocktail sticks (toothpicks) for your guests to spear and dip the pieces of fruit.

1 Arrange the fruits in an attractive pattern on a large serving dish. Brush any cut-up fruit, such as apples, pears or banana, with lemon juice to prevent discoloration. Cover and refrigerate until ready to serve.

VARIATION: You could also use small cookies for dipping in the chocolate as well as, or instead of, the pieces of fruit.

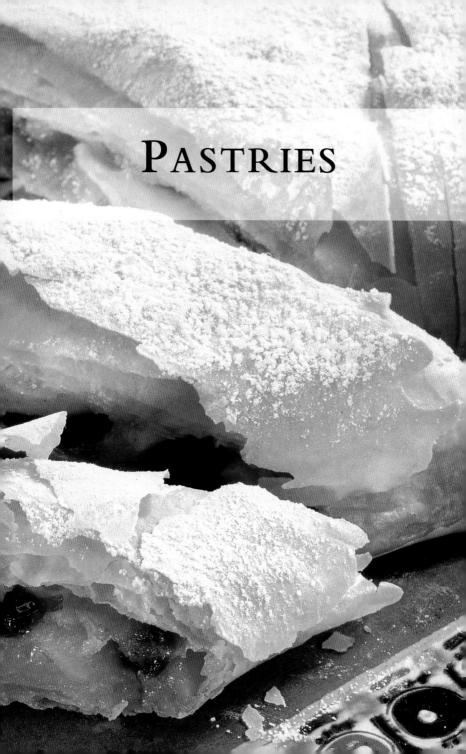

PASTRIES

Apricot & Pear Filo Roulade

This is a very quick way of making a strudel – normally very time consuming to do. It tastes delicious all the same!

Serves 4–6

INGREDIENTS
115 g/4 oz/½ cup ready-to-eat dried
    apricots, chopped
30 ml/2 tbsp apricot conserve
5 ml/1 tsp lemon juice
50 g/2 oz/4 tbsp soft light brown sugar
2 medium-size pears, peeled, cored and
    chopped
50 g/2 oz/½ cup ground almonds
30 ml/2 tbsp flaked (sliced) almonds
8 sheets filo pastry,
    thawed if frozen
25 g/1 oz/2 tbsp butter, melted
icing (confectioners') sugar, to dust
low fat, thick natural (plain) yogurt or
    low fat crème fraîche, to serve

1 Put the apricots, apricot conserve, lemon juice, brown sugar and pears into a pan and heat gently, stirring continuously, for 5–7 minutes.

2 Remove from the heat and cool. Mix in the ground and flaked almonds. Preheat the oven to 200°C/400°F/Gas 6.

COOK'S TIP: This dessert can be frozen before cooking. Defrost the roulade completely on a baking tray.

3 Lightly grease a baking sheet. Layer the pastry on the baking sheet, brushing each layer with melted butter.

4 Spoon the filling down the pastry, just to one side of the centre, and within 2.5 cm/1 in of each end. Lift the other side of the pastry up by sliding a metal spatula underneath.

5 Fold this pastry over the filling, tucking the edges under. Seal the ends neatly and brush all over with melted butter.

6 Bake the roulade for 15–20 minutes, until it is golden. Dust it with icing sugar and serve it hot, in individual portions, with low fat, thick natural yogurt or low fat crème fraîche.

Filo Fruit Baskets

These colourful and light-as-air fruit baskets will just melt in your mouth.

Serves 6

INGREDIENTS

4 large or 8 small sheets of filo pastry,
   thawed if frozen
20 g/¾ oz/1½ tbsp butter or
   margarine, melted
250 ml/8 fl oz/1 cup low fat, thick
   natural (plain) yogurt
65 g/2½ oz/⅓ cup strawberry
   preserve
15 ml/1 tbsp Cointreau or other
   orange liqueur
115 g/4 oz/1 cup seedless red
   grapes, halved
115 g/4 oz/1 cup seedless green
   grapes, halved
115 g/4 oz/1 cup fresh pineapple
   cubes
175 g/6 oz/1 cup raspberries
30 ml/2 tbsp icing (confectioners')
   sugar
6 small sprigs of fresh mint,
   to decorate

1 Preheat the oven to 180°C/350°F/
Gas 4. Lightly grease a 6 cup, deep
tartlet tin (muffin pan).

2 Stack the filo sheets and cut with a
sharp knife or scissors into 11 cm/
4½ in squares.

3 Lay four squares of pastry in each
cup of the tartlet tins, rotating it
slightly to make star-shaped baskets.
Press the pastry firmly into the cups.

4 Brush the pastry baskets lightly
with melted butter or margarine. Bake
for 5–7 minutes, until the pastry is
crisp and golden brown. Transfer to a
wire rack to cool.

5 In a bowl, lightly whip the yogurt
until soft peaks form. Gently fold the
strawberry preserve and Cointreau
into it.

6 Just before serving, spoon a little
of the strawberry preserve mixture
into each pastry basket. Top with the
fruit. Sprinkle with the icing sugar
and decorate each basket with a
small sprig of mint.

Raspberry Millefeuille

Succulent raspberries and luscious confectioner's custard are sandwiched between layers of melt-in-the-mouth puff pastry.

Serves 8

INGREDIENTS
450 g/1 lb rough-puff or puff pastry, thawed
   if frozen
6 egg yolks
65 g/2½ oz/⅓ cup caster (superfine) sugar
45 ml/3 tbsp plain (all-purpose) flour
350 ml/12 fl oz/1½ cups milk
30 ml/2 tbsp Kirsch or cherry liqueur
   (optional)
450 g/1 lb/2⅔ cups raspberries
icing (confectioners') sugar, for dusting
strawberry or raspberry *coulis,* to serve

1 Lightly butter two large baking sheets and sprinkle them very lightly with cold water.

2 On a lightly floured surface, roll out the pastry to a 3 mm/⅛ in thickness. Using a 10 cm/4 in cutter, cut out 12 rounds. Place on the baking sheets and prick each a few times with a fork. Chill for 30 minutes. Preheat the oven to 200°C/400°F/Gas 6.

3 Bake the pastry rounds for about 15–20 minutes, until golden, then transfer to wire racks to cool.

4 Whisk the egg yolks and sugar for 2 minutes, until light and creamy, then whisk in the flour until just blended. Bring the milk to the boil over a medium heat and pour it over the egg mixture, whisking to blend.

5 Return to the pan, bring to the boil and boil for 2 minutes, whisking constantly. Remove from the heat and whisk in the Kirsch or liqueur, if using. Pour into a bowl and press clear film (plastic wrap) on to the surface to prevent a skin forming. Set aside to cool.

COOK'S TIP: To make a raspberry or strawberry *coulis,* crush 225 g/8 oz/ 1¼ cups berries to a purée with a fork, then rub through a fine strainer set over a clean bowl with the back of a spoon. Sweeten with icing sugar.

6 Carefully split the pastry rounds in half. Spread one round at a time with a little custard. Arrange a layer of raspberries over the custard and top with a second pastry round. Spread over a little more custard and a few more raspberries. Top with a third pastry round, flat side up. Dust with icing sugar and serve with the *coulis*.

Donuts

To save time, make the syrup in advance and chill until required, when it can be warmed through quickly.

Serves 6

INGREDIENTS
225 g/8 oz/2 cups plain (all-purpose) flour
2.5 ml/½ tsp salt
5 ml/1 tsp baking powder
15 ml/1 tbsp sugar
1 large (US extra large) egg, beaten
120 ml/4 fl oz/½ cup milk
25 g/1 oz/2 tbsp unsalted (sweet) butter, melted
oil, for frying
sugar, for dusting

FOR THE SYRUP
225 g/8 oz/1⅓ cups soft light brown sugar
750 ml/1¼ pints/3 cups water
2.5 cm/1 in cinnamon stick
1 clove

1 Make the syrup. Combine all the ingredients in a pan. Heat, stirring, until the sugar has dissolved, then simmer until the mixture has reduced to a light syrup. Remove and discard the spices. Keep the syrup warm while you make the dough.

2 Sift the flour, salt and baking powder into a bowl. Stir in the sugar. In a separate mixing bowl, whisk the egg and the milk well together. Gradually stir in the dry mixture, then beat in the melted butter to make a soft dough.

3 Turn the dough on to a lightly floured board and knead until it is smooth and elastic. Divide the dough into 18 even-size pieces. Shape these pieces into balls. With your hands, flatten the balls to disk shapes about 2 cm/¾ in thick.

4 Use the floured handle of a wooden spoon to poke a hole through the centre of each dough ball. Pour oil into a deep frying pan to a depth of 5 cm/2 in. Alternatively, use a deep-fryer. Heat the oil to a temperature of 190°C/375°F or until a cube of day-old bread browns in 30–60 seconds.

5 Add the dough balls to the oil, frying in batches and taking care not to overcrowd the pan or deep-fryer. When the donuts are puffy and golden brown on both sides, lift them out with a slotted spoon and drain them thoroughly on kitchen paper. Dust them with sugar, pour the warm syrup into a small bowl, and serve immediately.

Coffee Crêpes with Peaches & Cream

Juicy golden peaches and cream conjure up the sweet taste of summer. They are delicious as the filling for these light coffee crêpes.

Serves 6

INGREDIENTS
75 g/3 oz/⅔ cup plain (all-purpose) flour
25 g/1 oz/¼ cup buckwheat flour
1.5 ml/¼ tsp salt
1 egg, beaten
200 ml/7 fl oz/scant 1 cup milk
15 g/½ oz/1 tbsp butter, melted
100 ml/3½ fl oz/scant ½ cup strong
    brewed coffee, strained
sunflower oil, for frying

FOR THE FILLING
6 ripe peaches
300 ml/½ pint/1¼ cups double (heavy) cream
15 ml/1 tbsp amaretto liqueur
225 g/8 oz/1 cup mascarpone cheese
65 g/2½ oz/5 tbsp caster (superfine) sugar
icing (confectioners') sugar, for dusting

1 Sift the flours and salt into a mixing bowl. Make a well in the middle and add the egg, half the milk and the melted butter. Gradually mix in the flour, beating until smooth, then beat in the remaining milk and coffee.

COOK'S TIP: To keep the pancakes warm while you make the rest, cover them with foil and place the plate over a pan of barely simmering water.

2 Heat a drizzle of oil in a 15–20 cm/6–8 in crêpe pan. Pour in just enough batter to cover the base of the pan. Cook for 2–3 minutes, until the underneath is golden brown, then flip over and cook the other side.

3 Slide the crêpe out of the pan on to a plate. Continue making crêpes in this way until all the mixture is used, stacking and interleaving with baking parchment.

4 To make the filling, halve the peaches and remove the stones (pits). Cut into thick slices. Whip the cream and amaretto liqueur until soft peaks form. Beat the mascarpone with the caster sugar until smooth. Beat 30 ml/2 tbsp of the cream into the mascarpone, then fold in the remainder.

5 Spoon a little of the amaretto cream on to one half of each pancake and top with peach slices. Gently fold the pancake over and dust with icing sugar. Serve immediately.

Apple Crêpes with Butterscotch Sauce

These wonderful dessert crêpes are flavoured with sweet cider, filled with caramelized apples and drizzled with a rich, smooth butterscotch sauce.

Serves 4

INGREDIENTS
115 g/4 oz/1 cup plain (all-purpose) flour
pinch of salt
2 eggs
175 ml/6 fl oz/¾ cup creamy milk
120 ml/4 fl oz/½ cup sweet cider
butter, for frying

FOR THE FILLING AND SAUCE
4 eating apples
90 g/3½ oz/scant ½ cup butter
225 g/8 oz/1⅓ cups light muscovado
   (brown) sugar
150 ml/¼ pint/⅔ cup double
   (heavy) cream

1 Make the crêpe batter. Sift the flour and salt into a large bowl. Add the eggs and milk and beat until smooth. Stir in the cider and set the batter aside for 30 minutes.

2 Heat a small, heavy non-stick frying pan. Add a little butter and ladle in enough batter to coat the pan thinly. Cook until the crêpe is golden under-neath, then flip it over and cook the other side until golden. Slide the crêpe on to a plate. Repeat with the remaining mixture to make seven more crêpes. Keep warm.

3 Make the filling. Core the apples and cut them into thick slices. Heat 15 g/½ oz/1 tbsp of the butter in a large frying pan. Add the apples and cook until golden on both sides, then transfer the slices to a bowl with a slotted spoon and set them aside.

4 Add the rest of the butter to the pan. As soon as it has melted, add the muscovado sugar. When the sugar has dissolved and the mixture is bubbling, stir in the cream. Continue cooking until it forms a smooth sauce.

5 Fold each pancake in half, then fold in half again to form a cone. Fill each with some of the fried apples. Place two filled pancakes on each dessert plate, drizzle over some of the sauce and serve immediately.

VARIATION: You could just as easily use plums, pears, strawberries or bananas to fill the crêpes. If you like, add a touch of Grand Marnier to the apples towards the end of the cooking time.

Apple Strudel

This classic recipe is usually made with strudel dough, which is wonderful, but can be tricky and time-consuming, especially jelly for a novice. Filo pastry makes a good shortcut.

Serves 8–10

INGREDIENTS
500 g/1¼ lb filo pastry, thawed
  if frozen
115 g/4 oz/½ cup unsalted (sweet) butter,
  melted
icing (confectioners') sugar,
  for dusting

FOR THE FILLING
1 kg/2¼ lb cooking apples, peeled,
  cored and sliced
115 g/4 oz/2 cups fresh white breadcrumbs
150 g/5 oz/¾ cup granulated sugar
5 ml/1 tsp ground cinnamon
75 g/3 oz/generous ½ cup raisins
finely grated rind of 1 lemon
50 g/2 oz/¼ cup butter

1 Preheat the oven to 180°C/350°F/ Gas 4. To make the filling, place the sliced apples in a large mixing bowl. Add the breadcrumbs, sugar, cinnamon, raisins and grated lemon rind and mix well. Melt the butter in a small pan, then stir it in to the mixture.

VARIATION: For extra crunch, add 75 g/3 oz/¾ cup lightly toasted, chopped almonds.

2 Lay a sheet of filo pastry on a lightly floured work surface and brush with a little melted butter. Place another sheet on top and brush with melted butter as before. Continue stacking the sheets and brushing with the butter until there are four or five layers in all.

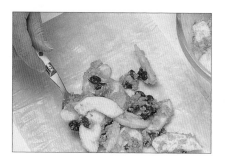

3 Spoon the filling into the centre of the pastry, leaving a 2.5 cm/1 in border all round. Fold in the two shorter sides, then roll up from one long side, Swiss-roll (jelly-roll) style.

4 Place the strudel on a lightly buttered baking sheet, seam side down. Brush the pastry with the remaining melted butter. Bake for 30–40 minutes, or until golden.

5 Remove the strudel from the oven and place on a wire rack to cool. Dust with icing sugar before cutting into slices for serving.

Cherry Strudel

While quite time-consuming to make, cherry strudel, with its light-as-air texture and fruity filling, is well worth the effort.

Serves 8–10

INGREDIENTS
250 g/9 oz/2¼ cups strong white bread flour
75 g/3 oz/⅔ cup plain (all-purpose) flour
1 egg, beaten
150 g/5 oz/10 tbsp butter, melted
100 ml/3½ fl oz/scant ½ cup warm water
sifted icing (confectioners') sugar,
   for dredging

FOR THE FILLING
65 g/2½ oz/generous ½ cup walnuts
115 g/4 oz/generous ½ cup caster
   (superfine) sugar
675 g/1½ lb cherries, pitted
40 g/1½ oz/¾ cup day-old breadcrumbs

1 Preheat the oven to 200°C/400°F/ Gas 6. Sift the flours together into a warm bowl. Make a well in the centre, add the egg, 115 g/4 oz/½ cup of the melted butter and the water. Mix to a smooth, pliable dough, adding a little extra flour if needed. Leave wrapped in clear film (plastic wrap) for 30 minutes.

2 Roughly chop the walnuts and mix with the sugar, cherries and breadcrumbs.

3 Lay out a clean dishtowel and sprinkle it with flour. Carefully roll out the dough until it covers the towel. The dough should be as thin as possible, so that you can see the design on the cloth through it.

4 Dampen the edges with water. Spread the cherry filling over the pastry, leaving a gap all the way around the edge, about 2.5 cm/1 in wide. Roll up the pastry carefully with the side edges folded in over the filling to prevent it from coming out. Use the dishtowel to help you roll the pastry.

5 Brush the strudel with the remaining melted butter. Place on a baking sheet and cook for 30–40 minutes, or until golden brown. Dredge with icing sugar and serve warm or cold.

Upside-down Apple Tart

A special *tarte tatin* – the original French name of this dish – tin is ideal, but an ovenproof frying pan will do very well.

Serves 8–10

INGREDIENTS
225 g/8 oz puff or shortcrust pastry,
   thawed if frozen
10–12 large Golden Delicious apples
lemon juice
115 g/4 oz/½ cup butter, cut into pieces
115 g/4 oz/generous ½ cup caster
   (superfine) sugar
2.5 ml/½ tsp ground cinnamon
crème fraîche or whipped cream, to serve

1 On a lightly floured surface, roll out the pastry into a 28 cm/11 in round less than 5 mm/¼ in thick. Transfer to a lightly floured baking sheet and chill.

2 Peel the apples, cut them in half lengthways and core. Sprinkle the apples generously with lemon juice.

3 In a 25 cm/10 in *tarte tatin* tin (pan), cook the butter, sugar and cinnamon over a medium heat until the butter has melted and the sugar has dissolved, stirring occasionally.

4 Continue cooking for 6–8 minutes, until the mixture turns a medium caramel colour, then remove the tin from the heat and arrange the apple halves, standing on their edges, in the tin, fitting them in tightly since they shrink during cooking.

5 Return the apple-filled tin to the heat and bring to a simmer over a medium heat for 20–25 minutes, until the apples are tender and coloured. Remove the tin from the heat and cool slightly.

6 Preheat the oven to 230°C/450°F/ Gas 8. Place the pastry on top of the apple-filled tin and tuck the edges of the pastry inside the edge of the tin around the apples. Pierce the pastry in two or three places, then bake for 25–30 minutes, until the pastry is golden and the filling is bubbling. Leave to cool in the tin for 10–15 minutes.

7 To serve, run a sharp knife around the edge of the tin to loosen the pastry. Cover with a serving plate and, holding them tightly, invert the tin and plate together (do this carefully, preferably over the sink in case any caramel drips). Lift off the tin and loosen any apples that stick with a metal spatula. Serve warm with cream.

Chocolate Profiteroles

Light-as-air choux pastry puffs are filled with ice cream and coated with a rich chocolate sauce.

Serves 4–6

INGREDIENTS
110 g/3¾ oz/scant 1 cup plain
  (all-purpose) flour
1.5 ml/¼ tsp salt
pinch of freshly grated nutmeg
175 ml/6 fl oz/¾ cup water
75 g/3 oz/6 tbsp unsalted (sweet) butter,
  cut into pieces
3 eggs
750 ml/1¼ pints/3 cups vanilla ice cream

FOR THE CHOCOLATE SAUCE
275 g/10 oz plain (semisweet) chocolate,
  chopped into small pieces
120 ml/4 fl oz/½ cup warm water

1 Preheat the oven to 200°C/400°F/ Gas 6. Grease a baking sheet. Sift the flour, salt and freshly grated nutmeg on to a sheet of baking parchment or foil.

2 Make the sauce. Melt the chocolate with the water in a heatproof bowl placed over a pan of barely simmering water. Stir until smooth. Keep warm until ready to serve, or reheat when required.

3 In a medium pan, bring the water and butter to the boil. Remove from the heat and add the dry ingredients all at once.

4 Beat with a wooden spoon for about 1 minute, until well blended and starting to pull away from the sides of the pan. Set the pan over a low heat and cook the mixture for about 2 minutes, beating constantly. Remove from the heat.

5 Beat 1 egg in a small bowl and set aside. Add the remaining eggs, one at a time, to the flour mixture, beating vigorously after each addition. Beat in just enough of the beaten egg to make a smooth, shiny dough. It should pull away and fall slowly when dropped from a spoon.

6 Using a tablespoon, ease the dough in 12 mounds on to the prepared baking sheet. Bake for 25–30 minutes, until the puffs are golden brown. Remove the puffs from the oven and cut a small slit in the side of each to release the steam. Return to the oven, turn off the heat and leave them to dry out, with the oven door open.

7 Remove the ice cream from the freezer and allow it to soften for about 10 minutes. Split the profiteroles in half and put a small scoop of ice cream in each. Arrange on a serving platter or divide among individual plates. Pour the sauce over the profiteroles and serve immediately.

VARIATION: The profiteroles can be filled with whipped cream instead of ice cream, if you prefer. Either spoon the cream into a piping (pastry) bag and fill the slit profiteroles, or sandwich them together with the whipped cream.

Coffee Cream Profiteroles

Crisp-textured coffee choux pastry puffs are filled with cream and drizzled with a white chocolate sauce.

Serves 6

INGREDIENTS
65 g/2½ oz/9 tbsp plain (all-purpose) flour
pinch of salt
50 g/2 oz/¼ cup butter
150 ml/¼ pint/⅔ cup brewed coffee
2 eggs, lightly beaten
cocoa powder (unsweetened), for dusting

FOR THE WHITE CHOCOLATE SAUCE
50 g/2 oz/¼ cup granulated sugar
100 ml/3½ fl oz/scant ½ cup water
150 g/5 oz white chocolate, broken
    into pieces
25 g/1 oz/2 tbsp unsalted (sweet) butter
45 ml/3 tbsp double (heavy) cream
30 ml/2 tbsp coffee liqueur, such as
    Tia Maria, Kahlúa or Toussaint

TO ASSEMBLE
250 ml/8 fl oz/1 cup double
    (heavy) cream

1 Preheat the oven to 220°C/425°F/ Gas 7. Sift the flour and salt on to a piece of baking parchment. Cut the butter into pieces and put in a pan with the coffee.

2 Bring to a rolling boil, then remove the pan from the heat and add all the flour. Beat until the mixture leaves the sides of the pan. Leave to cool for 2 minutes.

3 Gradually add the eggs, beating well between each addition. Spoon the mixture into a piping (pastry) bag fitted with a 1 cm/½ in plain nozzle.

4 Pipe about 24 small buns on to a dampened baking sheet. Bake for 20 minutes, until the buns are well risen and crisp.

5 Remove the buns from the oven and pierce the side of each with a sharp knife to let out the steam. Cool on a wire rack.

6 To make the sauce, put the sugar and water in a heavy pan and heat gently until dissolved. Bring to the boil and simmer for 3 minutes. Remove from the heat. Add the chocolate and butter, stirring until smooth. Stir in the cream and liqueur.

7 To assemble, whip the cream until soft peaks form. Using a piping bag, fill the choux buns through the slits in the sides. Arrange on plates and pour a little of the sauce over, either warm or at room temperature. Dust with cocoa and serve with the remaining sauce.

Apricot Parcels

These little filo parcels contain a special apricot and mincemeat filling – a good way to use up any mincemeat and marzipan that you have left over from Christmas!

Makes 8

INGREDIENTS
350 g/12 oz filo pastry, thawed if frozen
50 g/2 oz/¼ cup butter, melted
12 ratafia biscuits (almond macaroons)
60 ml/4 tbsp luxury mincemeat
30 ml/2 tbsp grated marzipan
8 apricots, halved and stoned (pitted)
icing (confectioners') sugar, for dusting

1 Preheat the oven to 200°C/400°F/ Gas 6. Cut the filo pastry into 32 x 18 cm/7 in squares. Brush four of the squares with a little melted butter and stack them, giving each layer a quarter turn so that the stack acquires a star shape. Repeat to make eight stars.

2 Crush the ratafias, mix with the mincemeat and marzipan and spoon a little of the mixture into the hollow in each of the apricots. Top with another apricot half.

3 Place a filled apricot in the centre of each pastry star. Bring together the corners of the pastry and squeeze to make a gathered purse.

4 Place the purses on a baking sheet and brush each with a little melted butter. Bake for 15–20 minutes, or until the pastry is golden and crisp. Lightly dust with icing sugar to serve.

COOK'S TIP: Filo pastry dries out quickly, so keep any squares not currently being used covered with a clean, damp dishtowel. Also, try to work as quickly as possible. If the filo should turn dry and brittle, simply brush it with a little melted butter to moisten.

Red Grape and Cheese Tartlets

Fruit and cheese make a natural combination in this simple recipe.

Makes 6

INGREDIENTS
225 g/8 oz/1 cup curd (farmer's) cheese
150 ml/¼ pint/⅔ cup double
    (heavy) cream
2.5 ml/½ tsp vanilla extract
30 ml/2 tbsp icing (confectioners')
    sugar
200 g/7 oz/2 cups red grapes, halved, seeded
    if necessary
60 ml/4 tbsp apricot conserve
15 ml/1 tbsp water

FOR THE PASTRY
200 g/7 oz/1¾ cups plain
    (all-purpose) flour
15 ml/1 tbsp caster (superfine) sugar
150 g/5 oz/⅔ cup butter
2 egg yolks
15 ml/1 tbsp chilled water

1 To make the pastry, sift the flour and sugar into a mixing bowl. Rub or cut in the butter until the mixture resembles fine breadcrumbs.

2 Add the egg yolks and water, mix to a dough. Knead lightly until smooth. Wrap and chill for 30 minutes.

COOK'S TIP: Look out for small, pale, mauve-coloured or red grapes. These are often seedless, and sweeter than large black varieties.

3 Preheat the oven to 200°C/400°F/ Gas 6. Roll out the pastry and use to line six deep 10 cm/4 in fluted tartlet tins (mini quiche pans). Prick the bases and line with foil and baking beans. Bake for 10 minutes, remove the foil and beans, then bake for a further 5 minutes until golden. Remove the pastry cases (pie shells) from the tins and cool.

4 Meanwhile, beat the curd cheese, double cream, vanilla extract and icing sugar in a small bowl. Divide the mixture among the pastry cases. Smooth the surface and arrange the halved grapes attractively on top.

5 Strain the apricot conserve into a pan. Add the water and heat, stirring constantly, until smooth and glossy.

6 Generously spoon the apricot glaze over the grapes. Leave to cool, then chill before serving.

Tia Maria Truffle Tartlets

Sophisticated and indulgent, these mini coffee pastry cases are filled with a chocolate liqueur truffle centre and topped with fresh ripe berries.

Serves 6

INGREDIENTS
300 ml/½ pint/1¼ cups double (heavy) cream
225 g/8 oz/generous ¾ cup seedless
   blackberry or raspberry jam
150 g/5 oz plain (semisweet) chocolate,
   broken up
45 ml/3 tbsp Tia Maria liqueur
450 g/1 lb/4 cups mixed berries

FOR THE PASTRY
225 g/8 oz/2 cups plain (all-purpose) flour
15 ml/1 tbsp caster (superfine) sugar
150 g/5 oz/⅔ cup butter, diced
1 egg yolk
30 ml/2 tbsp very strong brewed coffee,
   chilled

1 Preheat the oven to 200°C/400°F/ Gas 6, placing a large baking sheet in the oven to heat. To make the pastry, sift the flour and sugar into a large bowl. Rub or cut in the butter until the mixture resembles fine breadcrumbs.

2 Blend the egg yolk with the coffee, add to the bowl and mix to a stiff dough. Knead on a floured surface for a few seconds until smooth. Wrap in clear film (plastic wrap) and chill for 20 minutes.

3 Roll out the pastry and use to line six 10 cm/4 in fluted tartlet tins (mini quiche pans). Prick the bases with a fork and line with foil and baking beans. Place on the hot baking sheet and bake for 10 minutes. Remove the foil and beans, and bake for a further 8–10 minutes. Allow to cool in the tins.

4 To make the filling, slowly bring the cream and 175 g/6 oz/generous ½ cup of the jam to the boil, stirring constantly.

5 Remove the pan from the heat, add the chocolate and 30 ml/2 tbsp of the liqueur. Stir until melted. Leave to cool, then spoon the mixture into the cases, and smooth the tops. Place on a baking tray and chill for 40 minutes.

6 Heat the remaining jam and liqueur and stir until smooth. Arrange the berries on top of the tarts, then brush the jam glaze over the fruit. Keep chilled until ready to serve.

Pecan Tartlets

Cream cheese pastry has a rich flavour that goes well with the pecan filling in these tiny tartlets.

Makes 24

INGREDIENTS
2 eggs
175 g/6 oz/¾ cup firmly packed soft dark
  brown sugar
5 ml/1 tsp vanilla extract
large pinch of salt
25 g/1 oz/2 tbsp butter, melted
115 g/4 oz/1 cup pecan nuts

FOR THE PASTRY
115 g/4 oz/½ cup butter
400 g/14 oz/1¾ cups cream cheese
115 g/4 oz/1 cup plain (all-purpose) flour

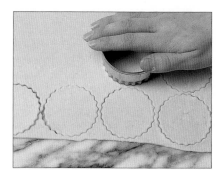

1 Place a baking sheet in the oven and preheat to 180°C/350°F/Gas 4. Grease two 12-cup bun tins or tartlet tins (muffin pans). To make the pastry, cut the butter and cream cheese into pieces and place in a mixing bowl. Sift over the flour and mix to a smooth dough.

2 Roll out the dough thinly, then, using a 6 cm/2½ in fluted pastry cutter, stamp out 24 rounds. Line the bun-tin cups with the rounds and chill.

3 To make the filling, whisk the eggs in a bowl. Whisk in the brown sugar, a few tablespoons at a time, then add the vanilla, salt and butter. Set aside.

4 Reserve 24 undamaged pecan halves for the decoration and chop the rest.

5 Place a spoonful of chopped nuts in each tartlet case and cover with the filling. Set a pecan half on the top of each. Bake on the hot baking sheet for about 20 minutes, until puffed and set. Transfer to a wire rack to cool. Serve at room temperature.

Lemon Curd Tarts

These tasty little tarts are a popular tea-time treat in the north of England. They have a curd cheese and currant filling on a tangy layer of lemon curd.

Makes 24

INGREDIENTS
225 g/8 oz/1 cup curd (farmer's) cheese
2 eggs, beaten
75 g/3 oz/6 tbsp caster (superfine) sugar
5 ml/1 tsp finely grated lemon rind
50 g/2 oz/¼ cup currants
60 ml/4 tbsp lemon curd
thick cream, to serve

FOR THE PASTRY
275 g/10 oz/2½ cups plain (all-purpose) flour
pinch of salt
75 g/3 oz/6 tbsp butter, diced
50 g/2 oz/¼ cup lard or white vegetable fat
60 ml/4 tbsp chilled water

1 To make the pastry, sift the flour and salt into a mixing bowl. Rub or cut in the fat until the mixture resembles fine breadcrumbs. Sprinkle the water over the dry ingredients and mix to a dough. Knead on a lightly floured surface for a few seconds until smooth. Chill.

2 Preheat the oven to 180°C/350°F/ Gas 4. Roll out the pastry thinly, stamp out 24 rounds using a 7.5 cm/3 in plain pastry cutter and use to line bun tins or tartlet tins (muffin pans). Chill until required.

3 Cream the curd cheese with the eggs, sugar and lemon rind in a bowl. Stir in the currants.

4 Place 2.5 ml/½ tsp of the lemon curd in the base of each tartlet case. Spoon on the filling, flatten the tops and bake for 35–40 minutes until just turning golden. Serve warm or cold, topped with thick cream.

COOK'S TIP: The pastry can be made in advance and frozen. Line the tins with pastry, wrap in clear film (plastic wrap) and store.

Peach & Redcurrant Tartlets

Tart redcurrants and sweet peaches make a winning combination in these simple, but very appealing little tartlets.

Serves 4

INGREDIENTS
25 g/1 oz/2 tbsp butter, melted
16 x 15 cm/6 in squares of filo pastry,
   thawed if frozen
icing (confectioners') sugar, for dusting
redcurrant sprigs, to decorate

FOR THE FILLING
150 ml/¼ pint/⅔ cup double (heavy) cream
125 g/4¼ oz carton peach and mango
   fromage frais or yogurt
a few drops of vanilla extract
15 ml/1 tbsp icing (confectioners') sugar, sifted

FOR THE TOPPING
50 g/2 oz/½ cup redcurrants
2 peaches

1 Preheat the oven to 190°C/375°F/
Gas 5. Use a little of the butter to
grease four large bun tins or tartlet tins
(muffin pans). Brush the pastry squares
with butter, stack in fours, then place
in the tins to make four tartlet cases.

2 Bake for 12–15 minutes until
golden. Cool the cases on a wire rack.

3 Whip the cream to form soft peaks,
then fold in the peach and mango
fromage frais or yogurt, vanilla extract
and icing sugar. Divide among the cases.

4 Strip some of the redcurrants from
their stalks by pulling the stalks
through the tines of a fork.

5 Slice the peaches and fan them out
on top of the filling, interspersing with
a few redcurrants. Decorate the tartlets
with redcurrant sprigs and dust with
icing sugar before serving.

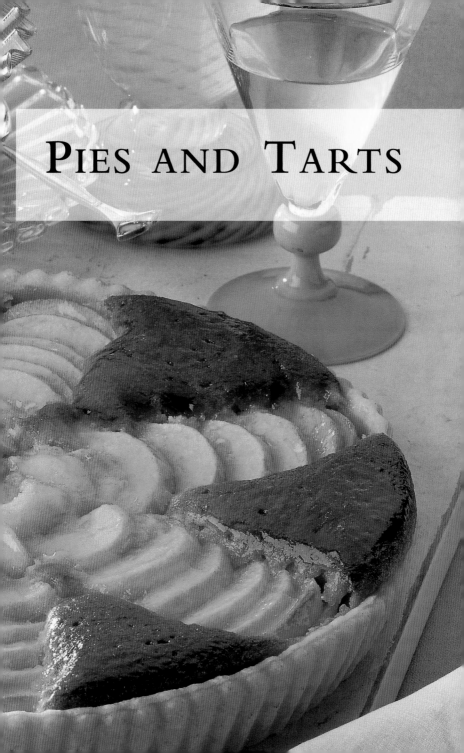

PIES AND TARTS

Pear Tarte Tatin with Cardamom

Crispy puff pastry snugly encloses tasty caramelized pears in this spicy upside-down tart.

Serves 4

INGREDIENTS
50 g/2 oz/¼ cup unsalted (sweet)
  butter, softened
50 g/2 oz/¼ cup caster (superfine) sugar
seeds from 10 cardamoms
225 g/8 oz puff pastry, thawed if frozen
3 ripe pears, peeled, cored and
  halved lengthways

1 Preheat the oven to 220°C/425°F/ Gas 7. Spread the butter over the base of an 18 cm/7 in heavy-based cake tin (pan) or an ovenproof omelette pan. Spread the sugar evenly over the base of the tin or pan. Sprinkle the cardamom seeds over the sugar.

2 On a floured surface, roll out the puff pastry to a round slightly larger than the tin or pan. Prick the pastry lightly, then transfer it to a baking sheet and chill while you prepare the filling.

3 Arrange the pears, rounded side down, on the butter and sugar. Set the cake tin or omelette pan over a medium heat until the sugar melts and begins to bubble. If any areas are browning more than others, move the pan, but do not stir.

4 As soon as the sugar has caramelized, remove the tin or pan carefully from the heat. Place the pastry on top, tucking the edges down the side of the pan. Transfer to the oven and bake for 25 minutes, until well risen and golden.

5 Leave the tart in the tin or pan for 2–3 minutes until the juices have stopped bubbling. Invert the tin over a plate and shake to release the tart. It may be necessary to slide a spatula underneath the pears to loosen them. Serve the tart warm.

Yellow Plum Tart

Glazed yellow plums sit atop a delectable almond filling in a crisp pastry shell. When they are in season, greengages make an excellent alternative to the plums and taste wonderful.

Serves 8

INGREDIENTS
175 g/6 oz/1½ cups plain (all-purpose)
  flour, plus extra for dusting
pinch of salt
75 g/3 oz/6 tbsp butter, chilled
30 ml/2 tbsp caster (superfine) sugar
a few drops of vanilla extract
45 ml/3 tbsp iced water
45 ml/3 tbsp apricot jam, sieved
cream or custard, to serve

FOR THE FILLING
75 g/3 oz/⅓ cup caster (superfine)
  sugar
75 g/3 oz/6 tbsp butter, softened
75 g/3 oz/¾ cup ground almonds
1 egg, beaten
30 ml/2 tbsp plain (all-purpose) flour
450 g/1 lb yellow plums or greengages,
  halved and stoned (pitted)

1 Sift the flour and salt into a bowl, cut the butter in pieces and rub it in until the mixture resembles fine breadcrumbs. Stir in the caster sugar, vanilla extract and enough of the iced water to make a soft dough.

2 Knead the dough gently on a lightly floured surface until smooth, then wrap in clear film (plastic wrap) and chill for 10 minutes.

3 Preheat the oven to 200°C/400°F/ Gas 6. Roll out the pastry and line a 23 cm/9 in fluted flan tin (tart pan), allowing excess pastry to overhang the top. Prick the base with a fork and line with baking parchment and baking beans.

4 Bake blind for 10 minutes, remove the paper and beans, then return the pastry case (pie shell) to the oven for 10 minutes. Remove and allow to cool. Trim off any excess pastry with a sharp knife.

5 To make the filling, whisk together all the ingredients except the plums or greengages. Spread on the base of the pastry case. Arrange the fruit on top, placing it cut side down. Make a glaze by heating the jam with 15 ml/1 tbsp water. Stir well, then brush a little of the jam glaze over the top of the fruit.

6 Bake the tart for 50–60 minutes, until the almond filling is cooked and the plums or greengages are tender. Warm any remaining jam glaze and brush it over the top. Cut into slices and serve with cream or custard.

Fresh Fig Filo Tart

Figs cook wonderfully well and taste superb in this tart – the riper the figs, the better they will taste.

Serves 6–8

INGREDIENTS

five 35 x 25 cm/14 x 10 in sheets filo pastry,
   thawed if frozen
25 g/1 oz/2 tbsp butter, melted, plus extra,
   for greasing
6 fresh figs, cut into wedges
75 g/3 oz/⅔ cup plain (all-purpose) flour
75 g/3 oz/6 tbsp caster (superfine) sugar
4 eggs
450 ml/¾ pint/scant 2 cups creamy milk
2.5 ml/½ tsp almond extract
15 ml/1 tbsp icing (confectioners') sugar
whipped cream or Greek (US strained plain)
   yogurt, to serve

1 Preheat the oven to 190°C/375°F/ Gas 5. Grease a 25 x 16 cm/10 x 6¼ in baking tin (pan) with butter. Brush each filo sheet in turn with melted butter and use to line the prepared tin.

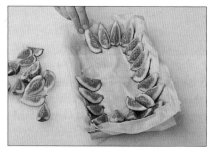

2 Using scissors, cut off any excess pastry, leaving a little overhanging the edge. Arrange the figs in the filo case.

3 Sift the flour into a bowl and stir in the caster sugar. Add the eggs and a little of the milk and whisk until smooth. Gradually whisk in the remaining milk and the almond extract. Pour the mixture over the figs and bake for 1 hour, or until the batter has set and is golden.

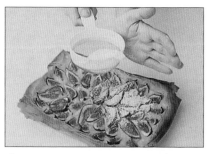

4 Remove the tart from the oven and allow it to cool in the tin on a wire rack for 10 minutes. Dust with the icing sugar and serve with whipped cream or Greek yogurt.

French Apple Tart

This classic tart is delicious served warm or cold, either on its own or with whipped cream for a special treat.

Serves 8

INGREDIENTS
350 g/12 oz sweet shortcrust pastry,
    defrosted if frozen

FOR THE FILLING
115 g/4 oz/½ cup butter, softened
115 g/4 oz/½ cup caster (superfine) sugar
2 large (US extra large) eggs, beaten
115 g/4 oz/1 cup ground almonds
25 g/1 oz/¼ cup plain (all-purpose)
    flour

FOR THE TOPPING
3 eating apples
60 ml/4 tbsp apricot jam
15 ml/1 tbsp water

1 Preheat the oven to 190°C/375°F/ Gas 5. Place a baking sheet in the oven to heat. Roll out the pastry on a lightly floured surface and line a 23 cm/9 in fluted flan tin (tart pan).

2 To make the filling, beat all the ingredients together until light and fluffy. Spoon into the pastry case (pie shell) and level the surface.

> VARIATION: A redcurrant glaze would also look good on this tart. Warm redcurrant jelly with a little lemon juice. Brush over the apples.

3 To make the topping, peel and core the apples and cut in half. Place each half, cut side down, on a board. Using a sharp, fine knife, slice the apples thinly, keeping the shape, then press down lightly to fan each apple half in a row.

4 Using a palette knife or metal spatula, carefully transfer each row of apple slices to the tart, arranging them on top of the filling so that they resemble the spokes of a wheel. You may need to overlap the slices in the middle slightly to fit. Press the slices down well into the filling to secure.

5 Warm the apricot jam with the water, then press the mixture through a sieve (strainer) into a small bowl. Brush half the jam glaze over the apples. Place the tin on the baking sheet and bake the tart for 35 minutes or until the pastry is golden and the apples have started to singe slightly.

6 Rewarm the remaining jam glaze and brush it over the apples. Let the tart cool slightly before serving.

137

Lemon Tart

This is one of the classic French tarts, and it is difficult to beat: a rich lemon curd, encased in crisp pastry.

Serves 6

INGREDIENTS
225 g/8 oz/2 cups plain (all-purpose) flour
115 g/4 oz/½ cup butter, diced
30 ml/2 tbsp icing (confectioners') sugar
1 egg, beaten
5 ml/1 tsp vanilla extract
6 eggs, beaten
350 g/12 oz/1¾ cups caster (superfine) sugar
115 g/4 oz/½ cup unsalted (sweet) butter
grated rind and juice of 4 lemons
icing (confectioners') sugar, for dusting

1 Preheat the oven to 200°C/400°F/ Gas 6. Sift the flour into a bowl, add the diced butter, and work with your fingertips until the mixture resembles fine breadcrumbs. Stir in the icing sugar.

2 Add the egg, vanilla extract and a scant tablespoon of cold water, then work to a dough.

3 Roll out the pastry on a floured surface and use to line a 23 cm/9 in flan tin (tart pan). Line with foil or baking parchment and fill with baking beans. Bake for 10 minutes.

4 For the filling, put the eggs, sugar and butter into a pan and stir over a low heat until the sugar has dissolved. Add the lemon rind and juice, and continue cooking, stirring, until the lemon curd has thickened slightly.

5 Pour the mixture into the pastry case. Bake for 20 minutes, until just set. Transfer to a wire rack to cool. Dust with icing sugar before serving.

Pear & Blueberry Pie

Bursting with fruit and full of flavour, this double-crust pie is the perfect choice for a family supper.

Serves 4

INGREDIENTS
225 g/8 oz/2 cups plain (all-purpose) flour
pinch of salt
50 g/2 oz/¼ cup lard, cubed
50 g/2 oz/¼ cup butter, cubed
675 g/1½ lb/5 cups blueberries
30 ml/2 tbsp caster (superfine) sugar
15 ml/1 tbsp arrowroot
2 ripe, but firm, pears, peeled,
    cored and sliced
2.5 ml/½ tsp ground cinnamon
grated rind of ½ unwaxed lemon
beaten egg, to glaze
caster (superfine) sugar, for sprinkling
crème fraîche, to serve

1 Sift the flour and salt into a bowl and rub in the lard and butter until the mixture resembles fine breadcrumbs. Stir in 45 ml/3 tbsp cold water and mix to a dough. Chill for 30 minutes.

2 Place 225 g/8 oz/2 cups of the blueberries in a pan with the sugar. Cover and cook gently until the blueberries have softened. Press through a nylon sieve (strainer) to remove the seeds.

3 Blend the arrowroot with 30 ml/ 2 tbsp cold water and add to the blueberry purée. Bring to the boil, stirring until thickened. Cool slightly.

4 Place a baking sheet in the oven and preheat to 190°C/375°F/Gas 5. Roll out just over half the pastry on a lightly floured surface and use to line a 20 cm/8 in shallow pie dish or plate.

5 Mix together the remaining blueberries, the pears, cinnamon and lemon rind and spoon into the dish. Pour the blueberry purée over the top.

6 Roll out the remaining pastry and use to cover the pie. Make a small slit in the centre. Brush with egg and sprinkle with caster sugar. Bake the pie on the hot baking sheet, for 40–45 minutes, until golden. Serve warm with crème fraîche.

Exotic Fruit Tranche

This is a good way to make the most of a small selection of exotic fruit and looks simply amazing.

Serves 8

INGREDIENTS

175 g/6 oz/1½ cups plain (all-purpose) flour
50 g/2 oz/¼ cup unsalted (sweet) butter
25 g/1 oz/2 tbsp white vegetable fat
50 g/2 oz/¼ cup caster (superfine) sugar
2 egg yolks
about 15 ml/1 tbsp cold water
115 g/4 oz/scant ½ cup apricot conserve,
    strained and warmed

FOR THE FILLING

150 ml/¼ pint/⅔ cup double (heavy) cream,
    plus extra to serve
250 g/9 oz/generous 1 cup
    mascarpone cheese
25 g/1 oz/¼ cup icing (confectioners')
    sugar, sifted
grated rind of 1 unwaxed orange
450 g/1 lb/3 cups mixed prepared fruits,
    such as mango, papaya, star fruit,
    kiwi fruit and blackberries
90 ml/6 tbsp apricot conserve, strained,
    and 15 ml/1 tbsp white or coconut
    rum, to glaze

1 Sift the flour into a bowl and rub in the butter and white vegetable fat until the mixture resembles fine breadcrumbs. Stir in the caster sugar. Add the egg yolks and enough cold water to make a soft dough.

2 Thinly roll out the pastry between two sheets of clear film (plastic wrap) and use the pastry to line a 35 x 12 cm/14 x 4½ in fluted tranche tin (pan), allowing the excess pastry to hang over the edge. Chill for 30 minutes.

3 Preheat the oven to 200°C/400°F/Gas 6. Prick the base of the pastry case (pie shell) with a fork, and line with baking parchment and baking beans. Bake for 10–12 minutes.

4 Lift out the paper and beans and return the pastry case to the oven for 5 minutes. Trim off the excess pastry and brush the inside of the case with some warmed apricot conserve to form a seal. Leave to cool on a wire rack.

5 Make the filling. Whip the double cream to soft peaks, then stir it into the mascarpone with the icing sugar and orange rind. Spread the mixture inside the cooled pastry case and top with the prepared fruits.

6 Warm the remaining apricot conserve with the rum, and drizzle or brush over the fruits to make a glaze. Serve the tranche with extra cream.

VARIATION: If you don't have a tranche tin, line a 23 cm/9 in flan tin (tart pan) with the pastry.

Pralie Apple Pie with Honey

This deliciously sweet apple pie is made with potato pastry which cooks to a thin crisp crust that melts in the mouth.

Serves 4

INGREDIENTS
225 g/8 oz potatoes
115 g/4 oz/1 cup plain (all-purpose) flour
75 g/3 oz/6 tbsp caster (superfine) sugar
2.5 ml/½ tsp baking powder
pinch of salt
2 cooking apples
1 egg, beaten
30 ml/2 tbsp clear honey,
    to serve

1 Cut the potatoes into even-size chunks. Put into a pan and bring to the boil, then cover and cook for 20 minutes.

2 Drain the potatoes and dry out over a high heat for 1 minute, until all traces of moisture have evaporated. Mash well in a bowl. Preheat the oven to 180°C/350°F/Gas 4.

3 Add the flour, 50 g/2 oz/4 tbsp of the sugar, the baking powder and salt and mix to form a soft dough.

4 Place the dough on a lightly floured surface and divide it in half. Roll out one half to a 20 cm/8 in round. Transfer to a lightly greased baking tray.

5 Peel, core and thinly slice the apples. Arrange them on top of the pastry. Sprinkle with the remaining sugar. Brush the edges of the pastry with beaten egg.

COOK'S TIP: For best results, use a variety of cooking apple, such as Sturmer Pippin or McIntosh, that retains its texture when cooked. Alternatively, use an "all-round" eating apple, such as Egremont Russet, Granny Smith or Jonathan.

6 Roll out the remaining pastry to a 25 cm/10 in round, then lay it over the apples. Seal the pastry edges together and brush with the remaining beaten egg.

7 Bake for 30 minutes, until golden. Serve hot in slices, with a little honey drizzled over each serving.

Pecan Pie

Melt-in-the-mouth pastry encloses the sweet, rich filling of this popular American pie. It's delicious served with cream or ice cream.

Serves 6

INGREDIENTS

200 g/7 oz/1¾ cups plain (all-purpose) flour
115 g/4 oz/½ cup butter
30–60 ml/2–4 tbsp iced water
3 eggs
5 ml/1 tsp vanilla extract
200 g/7 oz/¾ cup soft dark brown sugar
60 ml/4 tbsp golden (light corn) syrup
50 g/2 oz/4 tbsp butter, melted
115 g/4 oz/1 cup chopped pecan kernels, plus 12 pecan halves
salt
whipped cream or vanilla ice cream, to serve

1 Mix the flour with a pinch of salt, then rub in the butter with the fingertips until the mixture resembles fine breadcrumbs. Add iced water a little at a time, mixing first with a fork. Gather into a dough.

2 Wrap the dough in clear film (plastic wrap) and chill in the refrigerator for 30 minutes. Preheat the oven to 190°C/375°F/Gas 5. Grease a 20 cm/8 in loose-based flan tin (tart pan). Roll out the pastry and use to line the tin.

3 Run the rolling pin over the top of the tin to cut off the surplus pastry.

4 Prick the pastry base and line with foil and baking beans. Bake blind for 15 minutes, then remove the foil and bake for a further 5 minutes. Take the pastry case (pie shell) from the oven and lower the temperature to 180°C/350°F/Gas 4.

5 Meanwhile, to make the filling, beat the eggs lightly with a pinch of salt and vanilla extract, then beat in the sugar, syrup and melted butter. Mix in the chopped pecans.

6 Spread the mixture in the pastry case and bake for 15 minutes. Remove from the oven and stud with the pecan halves in a circle.

7 Return to the oven and bake for a further 20–25 minutes until cooked through. Cool the pie for 10–15 minutes and serve warm with whipped

Chocolate Pine Nut Tart

Lemon rind could be used instead of orange and a combination of white and plain chocolate substituted for all plain.

Serves 8

INGREDIENTS
200 g/7½ oz/scant 2 cups plain
    (all-purpose) flour
50 g/2 oz/¼ cup caster (superfine) sugar
pinch of salt
grated rind of ½ orange
115 g/4 oz/½ cup unsalted (sweet) butter
3 egg yolks, lightly beaten
15–30 ml/1–2 tbsp iced water

FOR THE FILLING
2 eggs
40 g/1½ oz/3 tbsp caster (superfine) sugar
grated rind of 1 orange
15 ml/1 tbsp orange-flavour liqueur
250 ml/8 fl oz/1 cup whipping cream
115 g/4 oz plain (semisweet) chocolate,
    chopped
75 g/3 oz/¾ cup pine nuts, toasted

FOR THE DECORATION
1 orange
50 g/2 oz/¼ cup granulated sugar
120 ml/4 fl oz/½ cup water

1 In a food processor, blend the flour, sugar, salt and orange rind. Add the butter and process for 20–30 seconds until it resembles coarse crumbs. Add the yolks and pulse until it begins to combine; do not allow to form a ball. If it is dry, add 15–30 ml/1–2 tbsp iced water, little by little, just until it holds.

2 Turn on to a lightly floured surface. Knead gently until blended. Shape into a disc and wrap in clear film (plastic wrap). Chill for 2–3 hours.

3 Lightly butter a 23 cm/9 in, loose-based flan tin (tart pan). Soften the dough for 5–10 minutes. On a well-floured surface, roll out the dough to a 28 cm/11 in round, about 3 mm/⅛ in thick and line the tin.

4 Roll a rolling pin over the edge to cut off excess dough. Now press the thicker top edge against the side of the tin to form a rim slightly higher than the tin. Prick the base with a fork. Chill for 1 hour. Preheat the oven to 200°C/400°F/Gas 6.

5 Line the pastry with baking parchment and baking beans and bake for 5 minutes. Lift out the paper and beans and bake for 5 more minutes. Cool slightly on a rack. Lower the heat to 180°C/350°F/Gas 4.

6 To make the filling, beat the eggs, sugar, rind and liqueur together. Blend in the cream. Sprinkle the chocolate and pine nuts evenly over the bottom of the pastry. Place the tin on a baking sheet and gently pour the egg mixture into the case. Bake for 20–30 minutes until the pastry is golden and the custard set. Cool slightly then transfer the tart to a wire rack.

7 To make the decoration, remove thin strips of orange rind and cut into julienne strips. Boil for 5–8 minutes with the sugar and water, until the syrup is thickened, then stir in 15 ml/ 1 tbsp cold water to halt the cooking.

8 Carefully brush the tart with the orange-sugar syrup and arrange julienne orange strips over the top.

Italian Chocolate Ricotta Pie

This delectable pie has chocolate in both pastry and filling, and the sherry makes it even more special.

Serves 6

INGREDIENTS
225 g/8 oz/2 cups plain (all-purpose) flour
30 ml/2 tbsp unsweetened cocoa powder,
  plus extra for sprinkling
60 ml/4 tbsp caster (superfine) sugar
115 g/4 oz/½ cup unsalted (sweet) butter
60 ml/4 tbsp dry sherry

FOR THE FILLING
2 egg yolks
115 g/4 oz/generous ½ cup caster
  (superfine) sugar
500 g/1¼ lb/2½ cups ricotta cheese
finely grated rind of 1 lemon
90 ml/6 tbsp dark (bittersweet)
  chocolate chips
75 ml/5 tbsp chopped mixed (candied) peel
45 ml/3 tbsp chopped angelica

1 Preheat the oven to 200°C/400°F/ Gas 6. Sift the flour and cocoa into a bowl, then stir in the sugar. Rub in the butter until the mixture resembles breadcrumbs, then work in the sherry, using your fingertips, until the mixture binds to a firm dough.

2 Roll out three-quarters of the pastry on a lightly floured surface and use it to line a 24 cm/9½ in loose-based flan tin (tart pan).

3 To make the filling, beat the egg yolks and sugar in a bowl, then beat in the ricotta cheese to mix thoroughly. Stir in the lemon rind, chocolate chips, mixed peel and angelica.

4 Scrape the ricotta mixture into the pastry case (pie shell) and level the surface. Roll out the remaining pastry and cut into strips, then arrange these in a lattice over the pie.

VARIATION: Instead of sherry you could use brandy or Amaretto.

5 Bake for 15 minutes, then lower the heat to 180°C/350°F/Gas 4 and cook for a further 30–35 minutes until the pastry is golden brown and the filling is firm. Cool in the tin. Sprinkle with cocoa powder just before serving at room temperature.

COOK'S TIP: This pie is best served at room temperature, so if you make it in advance, chill it when cool, then bring to room temperature for about 30 minutes before serving.

Chocolate Truffle Tart

Try serving this rich tart with cream, for the ultimate indulgence.

Serves 12

INGREDIENTS
150 g/5 oz/1¼ cups plain (all-purpose) flour
25 g/1 oz/¼ cup unsweetened cocoa powder
50 g/2 oz/¼ cup caster (superfine) sugar
2.5 ml/½ tsp salt
115 g/4 oz/½ cup chilled unsalted (sweet)
    butter, cut in pieces
1 egg yolk
15–30 ml/1–2 tbsp iced water
25 g/1 oz white or milk chocolate, melted

FOR THE TRUFFLE FILLING
335 ml/11 fl oz/1⅓ cups double
    (heavy) cream
350 g/12 oz couverture or fine-quality plain
    (semisweet) chocolate, chopped
50 g/2 oz/4 tbsp unsalted (sweet) butter, cut
    in pieces
30 ml/2 tbsp brandy or liqueur

1 Sift the flour and cocoa into a bowl. In a food processor fitted with metal blade, process the flour mixture, sugar and salt to blend. Add the butter and process for 15–20 seconds until the mixture resembles coarse breadcrumbs.

2 In a bowl, lightly beat the yolk with the water. Add to the flour mixture and, using the pulse action, process to a dough. Turn out on to clear film (plastic wrap), shape the dough into a flat disc and wrap tightly. Chill for 1–2 hours until firm.

3 Lightly grease a 23 cm/9 in, loose-based flan tin (tart pan). Soften the dough for 5–10 minutes, then roll out between sheets of baking parchment to a 28 cm/11 in round, about 5 mm/¼ in thick. Peel off the top sheet and invert into the tin. Remove the bottom sheet. Ease the dough on to the base and sides of the tin. Prick the base and chill for 1 hour.

4 Preheat the oven to 180°C/350°F/ Gas 4. Line the pastry with baking parchment and fill with beans. Bake for 5–7 minutes, then lift out the paper and beans and bake for 5–7 minutes until just set. (The pastry may look underdone on the bottom, but it will dry out.) Cool on a wire rack.

5 For the truffle filling bring the double cream to the boil in a pan over medium heat. Remove from the heat and stir in the couverture or plain chocolate until melted. Stir in the butter and liqueur. Strain evenly into the pastry, but avoid touching.

6 Spoon the melted chocolate into a paper cone and cut a tip about 5 mm/ ¼ in in diameter. Drop rounds of chocolate over the surface of the tart and draw the point of a skewer or cocktail stick (toothpick) through the chocolate to produce a marbled effect. Chill for 2–3 hours until set. Allow the tart to soften at room temperature for about 30 minutes before serving.

Mississippi Mud Pie

This open-topped pie has three layers of "mud": dark chocolate, golden, rum-flavoured custard and whipped cream – sheer ecstasy!

Serves 6–8

INGREDIENTS
250 g/9 oz/2¼ cups plain (all-purpose) flour
150 g/5 oz/10 tbsp unsalted (sweet) butter
2 egg yolks
15–30 ml/1–2 tbsp iced water

FOR THE FILLING
3 eggs, separated
20 ml/4 tsp cornflour (cornstarch)
75 g/3 oz/scant ½ cup golden caster
  (superfine) sugar
400 ml/14 fl oz/1⅔ cups milk
150 g/5 oz plain (semisweet) chocolate,
  broken into squares
5 ml/1 tsp pure vanilla extract
1 sachet powdered gelatine
45 ml/3 tbsp water
30 ml/2 tsp dark rum

FOR THE TOPPING
175 ml/6 fl oz/¾ cup double (heavy) or
  whipping cream
chocolate curls

1 Sift the flour into a large bowl and rub in the butter until the mixture resembles coarse breadcrumbs. Stir in the egg yolks with just enough iced water to bind the mixture to a soft pliable dough. Roll out on a lightly floured surface and line a deep, 23 cm/9 in flan tin (tart pan). Chill for about 30 minutes.

2 Preheat the oven to 190°C/375°F/Gas 5. Prick the pastry case (pie shell) all over with a fork, cover with baking parchment weighed down with baking beans and bake blind for 10 minutes. Remove the baking beans and paper, return to the oven and bake for a further 10 minutes until the pastry is crisp and golden. Cool in the tin.

3 To make the filling, mix the egg yolks, cornflour and 30 ml/2 tbsp of the sugar in a bowl. Heat the milk in a pan until almost boiling, then beat into the egg mixture. Return to the clean pan and stir over a low heat until the custard has thickened and is smooth. Pour half the custard into a heatproof bowl.

4 Melt the chocolate in a heatproof bowl over hot water, then stir into the custard in the bowl, with the vanilla extract. Spread in the pastry case, cover closely to prevent the formation of a skin, cool, then chill until set.

5 Sprinkle the gelatine over the water in a small bowl, leave until spongy, then place over simmering water until all the gelatine has dissolved. Stir into the remaining custard, with the rum. Whisk the egg whites in a clean, grease-free bowl until stiff peaks form, whisk in the remaining sugar, then fold quickly into the custard before it sets.

6 Spoon the mixture over the chocolate custard to cover completely. Chill until set, then remove the pie from the tin and place on a large serving plate.

7 Spread whipped cream over the top, sprinkle with the chocolate curls and serve.

Chocolate Pecan Pie

If you thought pecan pie could not be improved upon, just try this gorgeous chocolate one with its rich orange crust.

Serves 6

INGREDIENTS
200 g/7 oz/1¾ cups plain (all-purpose) flour
65 g/2½ oz/5 tbsp caster (superfine) sugar
90 g/3½ oz/scant ½ cup unsalted (sweet) butter, softened
1 egg, beaten
finely grated rind of 1 orange

FOR THE FILLING
200 g/7 oz/¾ cup golden (light corn) syrup
45 ml/3 tbsp light muscovado (brown) sugar
150 g/5 oz plain (semisweet) chocolate, broken into squares
50 g/2 oz/4 tbsp butter
3 eggs, beaten
5 ml/1 tsp vanilla extract
175 g/6 oz/1½ cups pecan nuts

1 Sift the flour into a bowl and stir in the sugar. Rub in the butter evenly with the fingertips until well combined.

2 Beat the egg and orange rind in a bowl, then stir into the mixture to make a firm dough. Add a little water if the mixture is too dry.

3 Roll out the pastry on a lightly floured surface and use to line a deep, 20 cm/8 in loose-based flan tin (tart pan). Chill for 30 minutes.

4 Preheat the oven to 180°C/350°F/Gas 4. Make the pie filling. Mix the golden syrup, muscovado sugar, chocolate and butter in a small pan. Heat the mixture gently, stirring, until it is melted and smooth.

5 Remove the pan from the heat and beat in the eggs and the vanilla extract. Sprinkle the pecan nuts into the chilled pastry case (pie shell) and carefully pour in the melted chocolate mixture.

6 Place the pie on a baking sheet and bake for 50–60 minutes, or until the chocolate mixture is set. Cool completely in the tin.

COOK'S TIP: Make individual tartlets if you prefer – use six 10 cm/4 in flan tins and bake at the same temperature for about 30 minutes. Walnuts or almonds could also be used.

MOUSSES, SOUFFLÉS AND MERINGUES

Cappuccino Coffee Cups

Coffee-lovers will really enjoy this – and it tastes rich and creamy, even though it is very light.

Serves 4

INGREDIENTS
2 eggs
215 g/7½ oz carton evaporated
    semi-skimmed (low fat) milk
25 ml/1½ tbsp instant coffee granules
    or powder
30 ml/2 tbsp sugar
10 ml/2 tsp powdered gelatine
60 ml/4 tbsp low fat, thick natural
    (plain) yogurt
unsweetened cocoa powder or
    ground cinnamon, to decorate

1 Separate one egg and reserve the white. Beat the yolk with the whole of the remaining egg.

2 Put the evaporated milk, coffee granules or powder, sugar and beaten eggs in a pan and whisk until evenly combined.

3 Set the pan over a low heat and stir constantly until the mixture is hot, but not boiling, and is slightly thickened and smooth.

4 Remove the pan from the heat. Sprinkle the gelatine over the mixture and whisk until it has completely dissolved.

5 Spoon the coffee custard into four individual dishes or glasses and chill until well set.

6 Whisk the reserved egg white until it is stiff, adding the low fat yogurt, and then spoon the mixture over each individual glass or dish. Sprinkle the coffee cups with cocoa powder or ground cinnamon and serve.

Fluffy Banana & Pineapple Mousse

This light, low fat mousse looks very impressive, but is really extremely easy to make, especially with a food processor.

Serves 6

INGREDIENTS

2 ripe bananas
225 g/8 oz/1 cup cottage cheese
425 g/15 oz can pineapple chunks or pieces in juice
15 ml/1 tbsp/1 envelope powdered gelatine
2 egg whites

1 Tie a double band of baking parchment around a 600 ml/1 pint/ 2½ cup soufflé dish, to come 5 cm/ 2 in above the rim.

2 Peel and chop one banana and place it in a food processor with the cottage cheese. Process until smooth.

3 Drain the pineapple thoroughly, reserving the juice. Set aside a few chunks or pieces for decoration. Add the rest to the mixture in the food processor and process for a few seconds until finely chopped.

4 Dissolve the gelatine in 60 ml/ 4 tbsp of warmed pineapple juice. Stir the juice and gelatine quickly into the fruit mixture.

5 Whisk the egg whites until they form soft peaks and fold them lightly and evenly into the mixture. Pour the mousse mixture into the prepared dish, smooth the surface and chill in the refrigerator until set.

6 When the mousse is set, carefully remove the paper collar. Decorate the mousse with thin slices of the reserved banana and pineapple chunks.

Lemon Hearts with Strawberry Sauce

These elegant hearts are as light as air. They are best made the day before.

Serves 6

INGREDIENTS

FOR THE HEARTS
175 g/6 oz/¾ cup ricotta cheese
150 ml/¼ pint/⅔ cup low fat crème fraîche
  or sour cream
15 ml/1 tbsp sugar
finely grated rind of ½ lemon
30 ml/2 tbsp lemon juice
10 ml/2 tsp powdered gelatine
2 egg whites

FOR THE SAUCE
225 g/8 oz/2 cups fresh or frozen
  and thawed strawberries
15 ml/1 tbsp lemon juice

1 Beat the ricotta cheese until smooth. Stir in the low fat crème fraîche or sour cream, sugar and lemon rind, until well mixed and thick.

2 Place the lemon juice in a small heatproof bowl and sprinkle the gelatine over it. Place the bowl over a pan of hot water and stir until the gelatine has completely dissolved.

3 Quickly stir the gelatine into the cheese mixture, mixing it in evenly.

4 Beat the egg whites until they form soft peaks. Quickly fold them into the cheese mixture.

5 Spoon the mixture into six lightly oiled, heart-shaped moulds and chill until set.

6 Reserve some strawberries for decoration. Place the remainder with the lemon juice in a blender or food processor and process until smooth. Pour on to serving plates and top with the turned-out hearts.

Currant Apple Mousse

This Romanian recipe uses apples and currants, macerated in red wine, to make a creamy mousse.

Serves 4–6

INGREDIENTS

175 g/6 oz/¾ cup currants
175 ml/6 fl oz/¾ cup red wine,
   plus a little extra for topping up
4 eating apples, cored, peeled and sliced
250 ml/8 fl oz/1 cup water
225 g/8 oz/generous 1 cup caster
   (superfine) sugar
30 ml/2 tbsp cornflour (cornstarch)
few drops of pink food colouring (optional)
3 egg yolks
5 ml/1 tsp vanilla extract
2.5 ml/½ tsp ground cinnamon
2 egg whites
seedless black grapes, a little caster
   (superfine) sugar and mint leaves,
   to decorate

1 Soak the currants in the red wine for 1–1½ hours. Drain and set aside. Strain the wine through a fine sieve (strainer), then top up with more wine as necessary to bring back up to 175 ml/6 fl oz/¾ cup.

2 Meanwhile, put the apples in a pan and cook with the water and three-quarters of the sugar until soft. Cool, then process the apples in a food processor and return the purée to the pan.

3 Blend together the cornflour and red wine and pour it into the purée. Cook for 8–10 minutes, stirring constantly. Add the food colouring, if using.

4 Beat the egg yolks in a bowl with the remaining sugar and the vanilla extract until pale and thick. Whisk the apple mixture slowly into the egg yolks. Add the cinnamon and beat until smooth.

5 Chill until thickened. Reserve 5 ml/ 1 tsp of the egg white for decorating and whisk the remainder until stiff. Fold the currants and the whisked egg whites into the apple mixture, pour into glasses and chill.

6 Meanwhile, make the frosted grapes. Brush the black grapes with a little of the reserved egg white and sprinkle with caster sugar. Leave to dry. Use with the mint leaves to decorate the mousse, and serve.

Caramel Custards

This is a classic dessert in Mexico where it is known simply as *flan*.

Serves 6

INGREDIENTS
275 g/10 oz/1¼ cups granulated sugar
1 litre/1¾ pints/4 cups milk
6 eggs, lightly beaten
5 ml/1 tsp vanilla essence (extract)
pinch of salt

1 Preheat the oven to 180°C/350°F/ Gas 4. To make the caramel, put 115 g/4 oz/½ cup of the sugar into a small heavy pan. Heat, stirring constantly, until the sugar melts. Warm six ramekins by rinsing them in hot water and drying them quickly. Continue to heat the sugar syrup, without stirring, until it turns a deep golden colour. Remove the pan from the heat.

2 Pour some of the caramel into a ramekin and turn it so it coats the bottom and sides. As soon as the caramel sets, turn the ramekin upside down on a baking sheet. Coat the remaining ramekins in the same way.

3 Scald the milk by heating it in a pan to just below boiling point. Pour into a jug and cool.

4 Put the eggs into a bowl and gradually beat in the remaining sugar. Add the cooled milk, vanilla and salt. Mix together well. Strain the egg mixture into the ramekins and put them into a roasting pan filled with enough hot water to come halfway up the sides of the ramekins. Bake for about 40 minutes, or until a knife inserted in the centre of the custard comes out clean.

5 Cool the custards, then chill for several hours in the fridge. Wet a non-serrated knife and run it between the custards and the sides of the ramekins. Put a plate upside down over each ramekin and invert it quickly. The *flan* will easily slide out.

COOK'S TIP: Vary the flavour by adding a little ground cinnamon or rum instead of vanilla.

Passion Fruit Crème Caramels with Dipped Physalis

The aromatic flavour of passion fruit really permeates these delightful crème caramels. Physalis are dipped in some of the caramel to create a unique decoration. These caramels will make an excellent dinner party dessert.

Serves 4

INGREDIENTS
185 g/6½ oz/scant 1 cup caster (superfine) sugar
75 ml/5 tbsp water
4 passion fruits
4 physalis
3 eggs plus 1 egg yolk
150 ml/¼ pint/⅔ cup double (heavy) cream
150 ml/¼ pint/⅔ cup creamy milk

2 Meanwhile, cut each passion fruit in half. Scoop out the seeds into a sieve set over a bowl. Press the seeds against the sieve (strainer) to extract all their juice. Spoon a few of the seeds into each of four 150 ml/¼ pint/⅔ cup ramekins. Set the juice aside.

1 Place 150 g/5 oz/¾ cup of the caster sugar in a heavy pan. Add the water and heat gently until the sugar has dissolved. Increase the heat and boil until the syrup turns a dark golden colour.

COOK'S TIP: Baking the custards in water stops them from curdling.

3 Peel back the papery casing from each physalis and dip the orange berries into the caramel. Place on a sheet of baking parchment and set aside. Pour the remaining caramel carefully into the ramekins.

4 Preheat the oven to 150°C/300°F/ Gas 2. Whisk the eggs, egg yolk and remaining sugar in a bowl. Whisk in the cream and milk, then the passion fruit juice. Strain into each ramekin, then place the ramekins in a baking tin (pan). Pour in hot water to come halfway up the sides of the dishes and bake for 40–45 minutes, or until just set.

5 Remove the custards from the tin and leave to cool, then cover and chill them for 4 hours before serving. Run a knife between the edge of each ramekin and the custard and invert each in turn on to a dessert plate. Shake the ramekins firmly to release the custards. Decorate each with a dipped physalis.

Chocolate Mousse with Chocolate Curls

Dark, white and milk chocolate curls provide a finishing flourish for a sumptuous chocolate mousse with just a hint of ginger.

Serves 6–8

INGREDIENTS
450 g/1 lb plain (semisweet) chocolate, chopped
65 g/2½ oz/5 tbsp butter
200 g/7 oz/scant 1 cup caster (superfine) sugar
6 eggs, separated
60 ml/4 tbsp ginger syrup (from a jar of preserved stem ginger)
100 ml/3½ fl oz/⅓ cup brandy

FOR THE DECORATION
115 g/4 oz plain (semisweet) chocolate or a mixture of plain, milk and white chocolate

1 Melt the chocolate and butter with half the sugar in a bowl set over a pan of hot water. Remove the bowl from the pan and beat in the egg yolks, ginger syrup and brandy.

2 Whisk the egg whites in a large grease-free bowl until soft peaks form. Gradually add the remaining sugar, a spoonful at a time, whisking constantly until stiff and glossy.

3 Beat about a third of the egg whites into the chocolate mixture to lighten it, then fold in the remainder. Pour into 6–8 serving bowls or glasses and chill for 3–4 hours until set.

4 To make the decoration, melt the chocolate, beat it briefly, then pour on to baking parchment. Spread out with a palette knife or metal spatula until about 3 mm/⅛ in thick. Allow to cool until firm but pliable.

5 For a more dramatic effect make light and dark curls, using plain, milk and white chocolate. Pipe the melted chocolate in alternate rows, smooth each in turn with a palette knife and allow to firm before making the multi-coloured curls.

6 Hold a cheese slicer and place it flat against the chocolate. Pull it gently towards you, scraping off a thin layer of chocolate so that it curls into a scroll. Work quickly or the chocolate will harden and splinter. Decorate the mousses just before serving.

COOK'S TIP: This mousse is an ideal choice when you need a dessert that can be prepared in advance. It can be made up to 3 days before it is needed, provided it is kept in the refrigerator.

White Amaretto Mousses with Chocolate Sauce

These little white and dark chocolate desserts are extremely rich, and derive their flavour from Amaretto di Sarone, an almond-flavoured liqueur, and amaretti, little almond-flavoured biscuits.

Serves 8

INGREDIENTS
115 g/4 oz amaretti
350 g/12 oz white chocolate, broken into squares
60 ml/4 tbsp Amaretto di Sarone
15 g/½ oz powdered gelatine, soaked in 45 ml/3 tbsp cold water
450 ml/¾ pint/scant 2 cups double (heavy) cream

FOR THE CHOCOLATE SAUCE
225 g/8 oz dark (bittersweet) chocolate, broken into squares
300 ml/½ pint/1¼ cups single (light) cream
50 g/2 oz/¼ cup caster (superfine) sugar

1 Lightly oil eight individual 120 ml/4 fl oz moulds and line the base of each mould with a small disc of oiled baking parchment. Put the amaretti into a large bowl and crush them finely with the end of a rolling pin.

2 Melt the white chocolate with the Amaretto gently in a bowl over a pan of hot but not boiling water (be very careful not to overheat the chocolate). Stir well until smooth, then remove from the pan and leave to cool.

3 Melt the gelatine over hot water and blend it into the chocolate mixture. Whisk the cream to form soft peaks. Fold in the chocolate mixture, with 60 ml/4 tbsp of the amaretti.

4 Put a teaspoonful of the amaretti into each mould and spoon in the chocolate mixture. Tap to disperse any air bubbles. Level the tops and sprinkle the remaining amaretti on top. Press down and chill for 4 hours.

5 To make the chocolate sauce, put all the ingredients in a small pan and heat gently to melt the chocolate and dissolve the sugar. Simmer for 2–3 minutes. Leave to cool completely.

6 Slip a knife around the sides of each mould, and turn out on to individual plates. Remove the paper, pour a little chocolate sauce around each mousse and serve immediately.

Chilled Chocolate & Espresso Mousse

Heady, aromatic espresso coffee adds a distinctive flavour to this smooth, rich mousse. Serve it in stylish chocolate cups for a special occasion.

Serves 4

INGREDIENTS
small orange, for moulding cups
225 g/8 oz plain (semisweet) chocolate
45 ml/3 tbsp brewed espresso
25 g/1 oz/2 tbsp unsalted (sweet) butter
4 eggs, separated
sprigs of fresh mint,
    to decorate (optional)
mascarpone or clotted cream,
    to serve (optional)

FOR THE CHOCOLATE CUPS
225 g/8 oz plain (semisweet) chocolate

1 For each chocolate cup, cut a double thickness 15 cm/6 in square of foil. Mould it around a small orange, leaving the edges and corners loose to make a cup shape. Remove the orange and press the bottom of the foil case gently on a surface to make a flat base. Repeat to make four foil cups.

2 Break the plain chocolate for the cups into small pieces and place in a heatproof bowl set over a pan of very hot water. Stir occasionally until the chocolate has melted.

3 Spoon the melted chocolate into the foil cups, spreading it up the sides of the cups with the back of a spoon to give a ragged edge. Chill for 30 minutes, or until the chocolate has set hard. Gently peel away the foil cases, starting at the top edge.

4 To make the chocolate mousse, put the chocolate and brewed espresso into a bowl set over a pan of hot water and allow to melt. When the mixture is smooth and liquid, add the butter, a little at a time. Remove the pan from the heat, then stir in the egg yolks.

5 Whisk the egg whites in a bowl until stiff, but not dry, then fold them into the chocolate mixture. Put the bowl into the fridge and chill for at least 3 hours.

6 To serve, scoop the chilled mousse into the chocolate cups. Add a scoop of mascarpone or clotted cream and decorate with a sprig of fresh mint, if you wish.

Frozen Raspberry Mousse

This dessert is like a frozen soufflé. Freeze it in a ring mould, then fill the centre with raspberries flavoured with orange juice or liqueur.

Serves 6

INGREDIENTS

350 g/12 oz/2 cups raspberries, plus
   150 g/5 oz/scant 1 cup extra, for serving
45 ml/3 tbsp icing (confectioners') sugar
2 egg whites
1.5 ml/¼ tsp cream of tartar
90 g/3½ oz/½ cup granulated sugar
25 ml/1½ tbsp lemon juice
250 ml/8 fl oz/1 cup whipping cream
15 ml/1 tbsp *framboise* or orange juice
mint leaves, to decorate

1 Process the raspberries in a food processor until smooth, then press it through a sieve (strainer) or work through the fine blade of a food mill. Pour a third of the purée into a small bowl, stir in the icing sugar, cover and chill. Reserve the remaining purée.

2 Half-fill a medium pan with hot water and set over a low heat (do not allow it to boil). Combine the egg whites, cream of tartar, sugar and lemon juice in a heatproof bowl which just fits into the pan without touching the water.

3 Using an electric mixer, beat at medium speed until the beaters leave tracks on the base of the bowl, then beat at high speed for 7 minutes, until the mixture is thick and forms peaks.

4 Remove the bowl from the pan and beat the mixture for a further 2–3 minutes, until cool. Fold in the reserved raspberry purée.

5 Whip the cream until it forms soft peaks and fold into the raspberry mixture with the liqueur or orange juice. Spoon into a 1.5 litre/2½ pint/6¼ cup ring mould, cover and freeze for at least 4 hours.

6 To unmould, dip the mould in warm water and invert on to a serving plate. Fill the centre of the mousse with raspberries, decorate with mint and serve with the chilled purée.

Country Strawberry Fool

Make this delicious fool on the day you want to eat it, and chill it well, for the best strawberry taste.

Serves 4

INGREDIENTS
300 ml/½ pint/1¼ cups milk
2 egg yolks
90 g/3½ oz/scant ½ cup
    caster (superfine) sugar
few drops of vanilla extract
900 g/2 lb ripe strawberries, plus 4 small
    strawberries, to decorate
juice of ½ lemon
300 ml/½ pint/1¼ cups
    double (heavy) cream
4 sprigs of strawberry leaves or 4 fresh
    mint sprigs, to decorate

3 Gently heat and whisk until the mixture thickens (it should be thick enough to coat the back of a spoon). Lay a wet piece of baking parchment on top of the custard in the pan and leave it to cool.

1 First make the custard by whisking 30 ml/2 tbsp milk with the egg yolks, 15 ml/1 tbsp caster sugar and the vanilla extract.

2 Heat the remaining milk until it is just below boiling point. Stir the milk into the egg mixture. Rinse the pan out and return the mixture to it.

4 Purée the strawberries in a food processor or blender with the lemon juice and the remaining sugar until very smooth.

5 Lightly whip the cream and fold in the fruit purée and custard. Pour into glass dishes and decorate with the whole strawberries and strawberry leaves or mint sprigs.

Apple Mint & Pink Grapefruit Fool

Besides looking particularly attractive, pink grapefruit is usually slightly less tart than the yellow varieties.

Serves 4–6

INGREDIENTS
500 g/1¼ lb tart apples, peeled and sliced
225 g/8 oz pink grapefruit segments
45 ml/3 tbsp clear honey
30 ml/2 tbsp water
6 large sprigs of apple mint,
    plus extra to decorate
150 ml/¼ pint/⅔ cup double (heavy) cream
300 ml/½ pint/1¼ cups custard

1 Place the apples, grapefruit, honey, water and apple mint in a pan, cover and simmer for 10 minutes until soft.

2 Leave in the pan to cool, then discard the apple mint. Process the mixture in a food processor.

3 Whip the double cream until it forms soft peaks, and fold into the custard. Carefully fold the custard cream into the apple and grapefruit mixture, reserving 30 ml/2 tbsp to decorate.

4 Pour into individual glasses. Chill, then decorate with swirls of the remaining custard cream and small sprigs of apple mint.

Lacy Whisky Soufflés

A dusting of icing sugar sets off many desserts and cakes. For a special effect, dust through a doily to create a perfect pattern.

Serves 6

INGREDIENTS

175 g/6 oz plain (semisweet) chocolate
150 g/5 oz/³/4 cup unsalted (sweet) butter,
   plus extra for greasing
4 eggs, separated
30 ml/2 tbsp whisky
50 g/2 oz/¼ cup caster (superfine) sugar
icing (confectioners') sugar, for dusting

1 Preheat the oven to 220°C/425°F/
Gas 7. Grease six ramekins. Melt the
chocolate and butter in a heatproof
bowl over hot but not boiling water.
Allow to cool slightly, then beat in the
egg yolks and whisky.

2 Whisk the egg whites in a large
grease-free bowl until soft peaks form.
Gradually add the caster sugar, continuing to whisk constantly until stiff and
glossy. Beat a third of the whites into
the chocolate mixture to lighten it,
then fold in the rest.

3 Spoon into the ramekins, place on a
baking sheet, and bake for about
10 minutes until well risen.

4 Lay a doily on each individual plate
and dust with icing sugar. Do the same
with the soufflés, then lift off the
doilies and transfer the soufflés to the
plates. Serve immediately.

Hot Blackberry & Apple Soufflés

As the blackberry season is so short and the apple season is so long, it is worth freezing a bag of blackberries to have on hand for treats like this.

Serves 4

INGREDIENTS
low fat spread, for greasing
150 g/5 oz/⅔ cup caster (superfine) sugar
350 g/12 oz/2 cups blackberries
1 large cooking apple, peeled, cored and finely diced
grated rind and juice of 1 orange
3 egg whites
icing (confectioners') sugar, for dusting

1 Preheat the oven to 200°C/400°F/ Gas 6. Put a baking sheet in the oven to heat. Generously grease four 150 ml/¼ pint/⅔ cup individual soufflé dishes with low fat spread and dust with caster sugar, shaking out the excess sugar.

2 Cook the blackberries and diced apple with the orange rind and juice in a pan for 10 minutes, or until the apple has pulped down well. Press through a sieve (strainer), using a wooden spoon or ladle, into a bowl. Stir in 50 g/2 oz/¼ cup of the caster sugar. Set aside to cool.

3 Put a spoonful of the fruit purée into each prepared dish and smooth the surface. Set the dishes aside.

4 Whisk the egg whites until they form stiff peaks. Very gradually whisk in the remaining caster sugar to make a stiff, glossy meringue mixture.

5 Fold in the remaining fruit purée and spoon the flavoured meringue into each prepared dish. Level the tops with a palette knife or metal spatula and run a table knife around the edge of each dish. Place the dishes on the hot baking sheet and bake for 10–15 minutes, until the soufflés have risen well and are lightly browned. Dust the tops with icing sugar and serve immediately.

Cold Mango Soufflés Topped with Toasted Coconut

Fragrant, fresh mango is one of the most delicious exotic fruits around, whether it is simply served in slices or used as the basis for an ice cream or soufflé, as here.

Serves 4

INGREDIENTS

4 small mangoes, peeled, stoned (pitted) and chopped
30 ml/2 tbsp water
15 ml/1 tbsp powdered gelatine
2 egg yolks
115 g/4 oz/generous ½ cup caster (superfine) sugar
120 ml/4 fl oz/½ cup milk
grated rind of 1 unwaxed orange
300 ml/½ pint/1¼ cups double (heavy) cream
toasted flaked coconut, to decorate

1 Place a few pieces of mango in the base of each of four 150 ml/¼ pint/⅔ cup ramekins. Wrap a greased collar of baking parchment around the outside of each dish, extending well above the rim. Secure with adhesive tape, then tie tightly with string.

2 Pour the water into a small heat-proof bowl and sprinkle the powdered gelatine on the surface. Leave for 5 minutes, or until spongy. Place the bowl in a pan of hot water, stirring occasionally, until the gelatine has dissolved.

3 Meanwhile, whisk the egg yolks with the caster sugar and milk in another heatproof bowl. Place the bowl over a pan of simmering water and continue to whisk until the mixture is thick and frothy. Remove from the heat and continue whisking until the mixture cools. Whisk in the liquid gelatine.

4 Process the remaining mango in a food processor or blender, then fold the purée into the egg yolk mixture with the orange rind. Set the mixture aside until starting to thicken.

5 Whip the double cream to soft peaks. Reserve 60 ml/4 tbsp and fold the rest into the mango mixture. Spoon into the ramekins until the mixture is 2.5 cm/1 in above the rim of each dish. Chill for 3–4 hours, or until the mixture is set.

6 Carefully remove the paper collars from the soufflés. Spoon a little of the reserved cream on top of each soufflé and decorate with some toasted flaked coconut.

Apple Soufflé Omelette

This delicious autumn filling is made by sautéing apples until they are
slightly caramelized – you could use fresh berry fruits in the summer.

Serves 2

INGREDIENTS
4 eggs, separated
30 ml/2 tbsp single (light) cream
15 ml/1 tbsp caster (superfine) sugar
15 g/½ oz/1 tbsp butter
icing (confectioners') sugar, for dredging

FOR THE FILLING
1 eating apple, peeled, cored and sliced
25 g/1 oz/2 tbsp butter
30 ml/2 tbsp soft light brown sugar
45 ml/3 tbsp single (light) cream

1 To make the filling, sauté the apple
slices in the butter and sugar in a
heavy pan over a low heat until just
tender. Stir in the cream and keep
warm, while making the omelette.

COOK'S TIP: When whisking egg
whites, make sure that the bowl and
whisk are both grease-free and that
there is no yolk mixed in.

2 Place the egg yolks in a bowl with
the cream and sugar and beat well.
Whisk the egg whites until stiff, then
fold into the yolk mixture using a
figure-of-eight motion.

3 Melt the butter in a large, heavy
frying pan, and pour in the soufflé
mixture evenly. Cook for 1 minute
until golden underneath, then brown
the top under a hot grill (broiler).

4 Slide the omelette on to a plate,
add the apple mixture, then fold over.
Sift the icing sugar over thickly, then
mark in a criss-cross pattern with a
hot metal skewer. Serve immediately.

Chocolate Soufflé Crêpes

Use a non-stick pan if possible, and serve two crêpes per person.

Makes 12 crêpes (serves 6)

INGREDIENTS
75 g/3 oz/⅔ cup plain (all-purpose) flour
10 g/¼ oz/1 tbsp unsweetened cocoa powder
5 ml/1 tsp caster (superfine) sugar
pinch of salt
5 ml/1 tsp ground cinnamon
2 eggs
175 ml/6 fl oz/¾ cup milk
5 ml/1 tsp vanilla extract
50 g/2 oz/4 tbsp unsalted (sweet) butter, melted
icing (confectioners') sugar, for dusting
raspberries, pineapple and mint sprigs,
   to decorate

FOR THE PINEAPPLE SYRUP
½ medium pineapple, peeled, cored and
   finely chopped
120 ml/4 fl oz/½ cup water
30 ml/2 tbsp natural maple syrup
5 ml/1 tsp cornflour (cornstarch)
½ cinnamon stick
30 ml/2 tbsp rum

FOR THE SOUFFLÉ FILLING
250 g/9 oz dark (bittersweet) chocolate
75 ml/3 fl oz/⅓ cup double (heavy) cream
3 eggs, separated
25 g/1 oz/2 tbsp caster (superfine) sugar

1 Prepare the syrup. Bring the pineapple, water, maple syrup, cornflour and cinnamon stick to the boil over a medium heat. Simmer for 2–3 minutes, whisking frequently.

2 When thickened, remove from the heat; discard the cinnamon. Pour into a bowl, stir in the rum and chill.

3 Prepare the crêpes. Sift the flour, cocoa, sugar, salt and cinnamon together. Stir, then make a well in the centre. Beat the eggs, milk and vanilla and mix with the flour mixture until smooth. Stir in half the melted butter and pour into a jug (pitcher). Let stand 1 hour.

4 Heat an 18–20 cm/7–8 in crêpe pan. Brush with butter. Stir the batter and pour 45 ml/3 tbsp into the pan, swirling to thinly cover the base. Cook over a medium heat for 1–2 minutes, until the underside is golden. Turn over and cook for 30–45 seconds. Stack the crêpes between baking parchment.

5 Prepare the filling. Melt the chocolate and cream in a small pan over a medium heat, stirring frequently, until smooth.

6 Using an electric mixer, beat the egg yolks with half the sugar for 3–5 minutes, until creamy. Beat in the chocolate mixture. Beat the whites to soft peaks. Beat in the remaining sugar until stiff peaks form. Beat a spoonful of whites into the cooled chocolate mixture, then fold in the rest.

7 Preheat the oven to 200°C/400°F/ Gas 6. Lay a crêpe on a plate, underside up. Spoon a little soufflé mixture on to the crêpe, spreading it to the edge. Fold the bottom half over the soufflé mixture, then fold in half again to form a filled triangle. Place on a buttered baking sheet. Repeat with the remaining crêpes. Brush the tops with melted butter and bake for 15–20 minutes, until the filling has souffléd. Decorate with raspberries, pineapple, mint and a spoonful of syrup.

Lemon Soufflé with Caramelized Almond Topping

This refreshing soufflé is light and luscious, with a delectable topping.

Serves 6

INGREDIENTS
oil, for greasing
grated rind and juice of 3 large lemons
5 large (US extra large) eggs, separated
115 g/4 oz/½ cup caster (superfine) sugar
25 ml/1½ tbsp powdered gelatine
450 ml/¾ pint/scant 2 cups double
   (heavy) cream

FOR THE DECORATION
75 g/3 oz/¾ cup flaked (sliced) almonds
75 g/3 oz/¾ cup icing (confectioners') sugar
3 physalis

1 Cut a strip of baking parchment long enough to fit around a 900 ml/1½ pint/3¾ cup soufflé dish and wide enough to extend 7.5 cm/3 in above the rim. Fit around the dish, tape, then tie it around the top of the dish with string. Lightly oil the paper.

2 Put the lemon rind and egg yolks in a bowl. Add 75 g/3 oz/⅓ cup of the caster sugar and whisk until light and creamy. Place the lemon juice in a heatproof bowl and sprinkle over the gelatine. Set aside for 5 minutes, then place the bowl in a pan of simmering water. Heat, stirring, until the gelatine has dissolved. Cool slightly, then stir into the egg yolk mixture.

3 In a separate bowl, lightly whip the cream to soft peaks. Fold into the egg yolk mixture and set aside.

4 Whisk the egg whites until stiff peaks form. Gradually whisk in the remaining sugar until the mixture is stiff and glossy. Fold the whites into the yolk mixture. Pour into the prepared dish, smooth the surface and chill for 4–5 hours, or until set.

5 Make the decoration. Brush a baking sheet with oil. Preheat the grill (broiler). Sprinkle the almonds over the sheet and sift the icing sugar over. Grill (broil) until the nuts are golden and the sugar has caramelized. Cool, then remove from the tray with a palette knife or metal spatula and break it into pieces.

6 When the soufflé has set, carefully peel off the paper. Pile the caramelized almonds on top of the soufflé and decorate with the physalis.

Hot Chocolate Delight

These soufflés are easy to make and can be prepared in advance – the filled dishes can wait for up to one hour before baking.

Serves 6

INGREDIENTS

150 g/5 oz/⅔ cup unsalted (sweet) butter, cut in small pieces, plus extra for greasing
175 g/6 oz plain (semisweet) chocolate, chopped
4 large (US extra large) eggs, separated
30 ml/2 tbsp orange liqueur (optional)
1.5 ml/¼ tsp cream of tartar
45 ml/3 tbsp caster (superfine) sugar, plus extra for sprinkling
icing (confectioners') sugar, for dusting
redcurrants and white chocolate curls, to decorate

FOR THE WHITE CHOCOLATE SAUCE

75 g/3 oz white chocolate, chopped
90 ml/6 tbsp whipping cream
15–30 ml/1–2 tbsp orange liqueur
finely grated rind of ½ orange

1 Generously butter six 150 ml/
¼ pint/⅔ cup ramekins. Sprinkle with caster sugar and tap out any excess. Place the ramekins on a baking sheet.

2 In a heavy pan over a very low heat, melt the chocolate and butter, stirring until smooth.

VARIATION: Instead of orange liqueur, try using coffee liqueur or brandy in the soufflés and sauce.

3 Cool slightly, then beat in the egg yolks and orange liqueur, if using. Set aside, stirring occasionally.

4 Preheat the oven to 220°C/425°F/ Gas 7. In a grease-free bowl, whisk the egg whites slowly until frothy. Add the cream of tartar, increase the speed and whisk to soft peaks. Sprinkle over the sugar, 15 ml/1 tbsp at a time, whisking until stiff and glossy.

5 Stir a third of the whites into the cooled chocolate mixture, then pour over the remaining whites. Gently fold the chocolate mixture into the whites. Spoon into the prepared dishes.

6 For the sauce, gently heat the chocolate and cream in a pan, stirring constantly, until melted and smooth. Off the heat, stir in the liqueur and orange rind. Keep warm.

7 Bake the soufflés for 10–12 minutes, until risen and set, but still slightly wobbly. Dust with icing sugar and serve with the sauce, decorated with redcurrants and chocolate curls.

Soft Fruit Pavlova

This is the queen of desserts and is ideal for a special occasion.

Serves 4

INGREDIENTS
4 egg whites
175 g/6 oz/¾ cup caster (superfine) sugar
30 ml/2 tbsp redcurrant jelly
15 ml/1 tbsp rose water
300 ml/½ pint/1¼ cups low fat,
 thick natural (plain) yogurt or
 low fat crème fraîche
450 g/1 lb/4½ cups mixed soft fruits,
 such as blackberries, blueberries
 redcurrants, raspberries or loganberries
10 ml/2 tsp icing (confectioners')
 sugar, sifted
pinch of salt

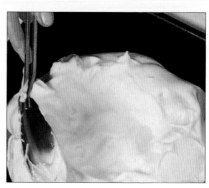

2 Spoon the meringue into a 25 cm/ 10 in round on the baking sheet, making a slight indentation in the centre and soft crests around the edge.

3 Bake for 1–1½ hours until the meringue is firm. Check it frequently, as the meringue can easily overcook and turn brown. Transfer the meringue to a serving plate.

4 Melt the redcurrant jelly in a small bowl set over a pan of hot water. Cool slightly, then spread the jelly in the centre of the meringue.

1 Preheat the oven to 140°C/275°F/ Gas 1. Lightly oil a baking sheet. Whisk the egg whites with a pinch of salt in a grease-free bowl until they are white and standing in firm peaks. Gradually whisk in the caster sugar and continue to whisk until the mixture is stiff and glossy.

5 Mix the rose water with the yogurt or crème fraîche and spoon into the centre of the meringue. Place the fruits on top and dust with icing sugar.

Raspberry Vacherin

Meringue rounds with an orange-flavoured filling combined with fresh raspberries make a perfect dinner party dessert.

Serves 6

INGREDIENTS
3 egg whites
175 g/6 oz/¾ cup caster (superfine) sugar
5 ml/1 tsp chopped almonds
icing (confectioners') sugar, for dusting
raspberry leaves, to decorate

FOR THE FILLING
175 g/6 oz/¾ cup low fat soft cheese
15 ml/1 tbsp clear honey
15 ml/1 tbsp Cointreau or other
    orange-flavoured liqueur
120 ml/4 fl oz/½ cup low fat, thick natural
    (plain) yogurt or low fat crème fraîche
225 g/8 oz/1⅓ cups raspberries

1 Preheat the oven to 140°C/275°F/ Gas 1. Draw a 20 cm/8 in circle on two pieces of baking parchment. Turn the paper over so the marking is on the underside and use it to line two heavy baking sheets.

2 Whisk the egg whites in a grease-free bowl until very stiff. Gradually whisk in the caster sugar until the mixture is stiff and glossy.

> COOK'S TIP: Whisk the egg whites until they are so stiff that you can turn the bowl upside down without them falling out.

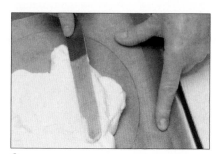

3 Spoon the mixture into the circles on the baking sheets, spreading the meringue evenly to the edges. Sprinkle one meringue round with the chopped almonds.

4 Bake for 1½–2 hours, then carefully lift the meringue rounds off the baking sheets, peel away the paper and cool on wire racks.

5 To make the filling, cream the soft cheese with the honey and liqueur in a bowl. Fold in the yogurt or low fat crème fraîche and most of the raspberries, reserving the three best ones for decoration.

6 Place the plain meringue on a board, spread with the filling and top with the nut-covered round. Dust with icing sugar, transfer to a plate and decorate with the reserved raspberries and a sprig of raspberry leaves.

Floating Islands in Hot Plum Sauce

An unusual dessert that is simpler to make than it looks. The sauce can be made in advance and reheated just before you cook the meringues.

Serves 4

INGREDIENTS
450 g/1 lb red plums
300 ml/½ pint/1¼ cups apple juice
2 egg whites
30 ml/2 tbsp concentrated apple juice syrup
freshly grated nutmeg

1 Cut the plums in half and remove the stones (pits). Place them in a wide pan with the apple juice.

2 Bring to the boil, cover and simmer gently over a low heat until the plums are tender, but still retain their shape. Test with the tip of a sharp knife for softness.

3 While the plums are cooking, whisk the egg whites in a clean, grease-free bowl until soft peaks form.

4 Gradually whisk in the apple juice syrup and continue whisking until the meringue forms quite firm peaks.

5 Using a tablespoon, scoop the meringue into the simmering sauce. You will need to do this in two batches.

6 Cover and simmer for about 2–3 minutes, until the meringues are just set. Serve immediately, sprinkled with a little freshly grated nutmeg.

COOK'S TIP: If you cannot obtain apple juice syrup, use clear honey.

Coffee Pavlova with Exotic Fruits

You can use virtually any fruit in season to decorate the meringue base – let your imagination run riot.

Serves 6–8

INGREDIENTS
30 ml/2 tbsp ground coffee, e.g. mocha
30 ml/2 tbsp near-boiling water
3 egg whites
2.5 ml/½ tsp cream of tartar
175 g/6 oz/scant 1 cup caster (superfine) sugar
5 ml/1 tsp cornflour (cornstarch), sifted

FOR THE FILLING
150 ml/¼ pint/⅔ cup double (heavy) cream
5 ml/1 tsp orange flower water
150 ml/¼ pint/⅔ cup crème fraîche
500 g/1¼ lb sliced exotic fruits, such as mango, papaya and kiwi

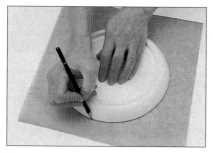

1 Preheat the oven to 140°C/275°F/ Gas 1. Draw a 20 cm/8 in circle on baking parchment. Place pencil side down on a baking sheet.

2 Put the coffee in a small bowl and pour the hot water over. Leave to steep for 4 minutes, then strain through a very fine sieve (strainer).

3 Whisk the egg whites with the cream of tartar until stiff, but not dry. Gradually whisk in the sugar until the meringue is stiff and shiny, then quickly whisk in the cornflour and coffee.

4 Using a long knife or spatula, spread the meringue mixture on to the prepared baking sheet to an even 20 cm/ 8 in round. Make a slight hollow in the middle. Bake in the oven for 1 hour, then turn off the heat and leave in the oven until cool.

VARIATION: 450 g/1 lb soft fruit, such as wild or cultivated strawberries, raspberries or blueberries, may be used instead of the exotic fruits.

5 Peel off the lining paper and transfer the meringue to a serving plate. To make the filling, whip the double cream with the orange flower water until soft peaks form. Fold in the crème fraîche. To assemble, spoon the cream mixture into the centre of the meringue. Arrange the exotic fruits over the cream and serve.

Chocolate Pavlova with Chocolate Curls & Fruits

The addition of chocolate makes this popular dessert even harder to resist.

Serves 8–10

INGREDIENTS
275 g/10 oz/2¼ cups icing
   (confectioners') sugar
10 g/¼ oz/1 tbsp unsweetened cocoa
   powder
5 ml/1 tsp cornflour (cornstarch)
5 egg whites, at room temperature
pinch of salt
5 ml/1 tsp cider vinegar or lemon juice

FOR THE CHOCOLATE CREAM
175 g/6 oz dark (bittersweet)
   chocolate, chopped
120 ml/4 fl oz/½ cup milk
25 g/1 oz/2 tbsp unsalted (sweet) butter,
   cut into pieces
30 ml/2 tbsp brandy
475 ml/16 fl oz/2 cups double (heavy) or
   whipping cream

FOR THE TOPPING
chocolate curls
450 g/1 lb/2 cups mixed berries or cut-up
   fresh fruits, such as mango, papaya,
   lychees and pineapple
icing (confectioners') sugar

1 Preheat the oven to 160°C/325°F/
Gas 3. Draw a 20 cm/8 in circle
on a sheet of baking parchment and
place it, pencil side down, on a large
baking sheet.

2 In a bowl, sift 15 ml/3 tbsp icing
sugar with the cocoa and cornflour.
Using an electric mixer, beat the egg
whites until frothy. Add the salt and
beat until stiff peaks form. Gradually
sprinkle in the remaining icing sugar,
pausing to let it dissolve. Fold in the
cocoa mixture, then the vinegar or
lemon juice.

3 Spoon the mixture on to the circle
on the paper, building up the sides.
Bake in the centre of the oven for
1 hour, until set. Turn off the oven and
allow the meringue to stand in the
oven for 1 hour (it may crack or sink).
Remove and cool.

4 Melt the chocolate and milk in a
pan over a low heat, stirring until
smooth. Off the heat, whisk in the
butter and brandy and cool for 1 hour.

5 Using a palette knife or metal spatula, transfer the meringue to a serving plate. Cut a circle around the centre, about 5 cm/2 in from the edge to allow it to sink. When the chocolate mixture has cooled, but is not too firm, beat the cream until soft peaks form. Stir half the cream into the chocolate, then fold in the rest. Spoon into the centre of the meringue. Arrange chocolate curls and berries or fruits on top. Dust lightly with icing sugar.

Fresh Berry Pavlova

Pavlova is the simplest of desserts, but it can also be the most stunning. Fill with a mix of berry fruits if you like – raspberries and blueberries make a marvellous combination.

Serves 6–8

INGREDIENTS

4 egg whites, at room temperature
225 g/8 oz/1 cup caster (superfine) sugar
5 ml/1 tsp cornflour (cornstarch)
5 ml/1 tsp cider vinegar
2.5 ml/½ tsp vanilla extract
300 ml/½ pint/1¼ cups double
    (heavy) cream
150 ml/¼ pint/⅔ cup crème fraîche
175 g/6 oz/1 cup raspberries
175 g/6 oz/1½ cups blueberries
fresh mint sprigs, to decorate
icing (confectioners') sugar, for dusting

1 Preheat the oven to 140°C/275°F/Gas 1. Line a baking sheet with baking parchment.

2 Whisk the egg whites until they form stiff peaks. Gradually whisk in the sugar to make a stiff, glossy meringue. Sift the cornflour over and fold it in with the vinegar and vanilla.

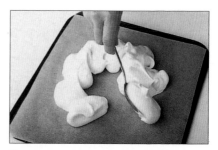

3 Spoon the meringue mixture on to the paper-lined sheet, using a circle drawn on the paper as a guide, if you like (see Cook's Tip). Spread into a round, swirling the top, and bake for 1¼ hours or until the meringue is crisp and very lightly golden.

4 Switch off the oven, keeping the door closed, and allow the meringue to cool gradually for 1–2 hours.

5 Carefully peel the paper from underneath the meringue and transfer it to a serving plate.

COOK'S TIP: To begin, invert a 23 cm/9 in plate on the baking parchment and draw round it with a pencil. Turn the paper over and use the circle as a guide for the shape of the meringue.

6 Whip the double cream in a large mixing bowl until it forms soft peaks. Fold in the crème fraîche, then spoon the mixture into the centre of the meringue case.

7 Top with the raspberries and blueberries and decorate with the mint sprigs. Sift icing sugar over the top and serve immediately.

Meringue Gâteau with Chocolate Mascarpone

This superb gâteau makes the perfect centrepiece for a celebration buffet table, and most of the preparation can be done in advance.

Serves 10

INGREDIENTS
4 egg whites
pinch of salt
175 g/6 oz/¾ cup caster (superfine) sugar
5 ml/1 tsp ground cinnamon
75 g/3 oz dark (bittersweet) chocolate, grated
icing (confectioners') sugar and rose petals,
    to decorate

FOR THE FILLING
115 g/4 oz plain (semisweet) chocolate,
    broken into squares
5 ml/1 tsp vanilla extract or rose water
115 g/4 oz/½ cup mascarpone

1 Preheat the oven to 150°C/300°F/ Gas 2. Line two baking sheets. Whisk the egg whites with the salt in a bowl to form stiff peaks.

2 Gradually whisk in half the sugar, then add the rest and whisk until the meringue is very stiff and glossy. Add the cinnamon and chocolate and whisk lightly to mix.

COOK'S TIP: The unfilled meringues can be stored for up to a week in an airtight container.

3 Draw a 20 cm/8 in circle on the lining paper on one of the baking sheets, replace it upside-down and spread the marked circle evenly with about half the meringue. Spoon the remaining meringue into 28–30 small neat heaps on both baking sheets. Bake for 1–1½ hours, or until crisp.

4 Make the filling. Melt the chocolate in a heatproof bowl over a pan of gently simmering water. Cool slightly, then add the vanilla extract or rose water and Mascarpone. Cool the mixture until it holds its shape.

5 Spoon the chocolate mixture into a large piping (pastry) bag and sandwich the meringues together in pairs, reserving a little filling for the gâteau.

6 Arrange the filled meringues on top of the meringue circle on a serving platter, piling them up in a pyramid and securing them with a few well-placed dabs of the reserved filling. Dust the gâteau with icing sugar, sprinkle with the rose petals and serve.

Apricot & Hazelnut Meringue Roll with Apricot Brandy

A soft nutty meringue, rolled around a creamy apricot filling spiked with apricot brandy, makes a superb dinner party dessert.

Serves 6

INGREDIENTS
5 egg whites
150 g/5 oz/¾ cup caster (superfine) sugar
5 ml/1 tsp cornflour (cornstarch)
50 g/2 oz/½ cup toasted hazelnuts, chopped
icing (confectioners') sugar, for dusting
apricot slices and mint sprigs,
   to decorate

FOR THE FILLING
300 ml/½ pint/1¼ cups double (heavy) cream
30 ml/2 tbsp apricot brandy
60 ml/4 tbsp apricot conserve, any large
   chunks chopped
6 apricots, stoned (pitted) and thinly sliced

1 Preheat the oven to 110°C/225°F/ Gas ¼. Grease a 30 x 20 cm/12 x 8 in Swiss roll tin (jelly roll pan) and line it with baking parchment. Whisk the egg whites until stiff but not dry. Whisk in half the sugar and then continue to whisk until the mixture is stiff. Fold in the remaining sugar.

> VARIATION: You can add extra texture and flavour by turning the baked meringue on to a sheet of baking parchment dusted with ground hazelnuts.

2 Fold in the cornflour and hazelnuts and spoon the mixture into the tin. Bake for about 45 minutes, or until set. Leave the meringue in the tin to cool, uncovered, for 1 hour.

3 Whip the cream lightly in a bowl, then stir in the apricot brandy and conserve. Fold in the apricot slices.

4 Dust a sheet of baking parchment with icing sugar and turn the meringue on to it. Peel away the lining paper and spread the filling over the top of the meringue.

5 With the aid of the parchment, and working from a short end, roll the meringue over the filling. Place the roll on a serving plate, dust with more icing sugar and decorate with apricot slices and mint sprigs.

Grilled Peaches with Meringues

These mini meringues, made with brown sugar, make a perfect accompaniment for the sweet grilled peaches.

Serves 6

INGREDIENTS

2 egg whites
115 g/4 oz/½ cup soft light brown sugar,
   reserving 5 ml/1 tsp for
   the peaches
pinch of ground cinnamon
6 ripe peaches, or nectarines
15–30 ml/1–2 tbsp orange juice
5 ml/1 tsp finely grated orange rind, to serve
crème fraîche, to serve

1 Preheat the oven to 140°C/275°F/
Gas 1. Line two large baking trays
with non-stick baking parchment.

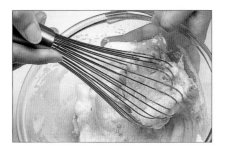

2 Whisk the egg whites until they
form stiff peaks. Gradually whisk in
the sugar and ground cinnamon until
the mixture is stiff and glossy. Pipe 18
very small meringues on to the trays
and bake for 40 minutes. Leave in the
oven to cool.

3 Meanwhile, halve and stone the
peaches. Brush the cut sides with
orange juice and sprinkle on a little
sugar. Grill for 4–5 minutes until
just beginning to caramelize.

4 Stir the orange rind into the
crème fraîche with 15 ml/1 tbsp
orange juice. Serve the peaches
topped with a little crème fraîche
and three meringues.

COOK'S TIP: Use leftover egg
whites to make these little
cinnamon-flavoured meringues.
The meringues can be stored in
an airtight container for about
2 weeks. Serve them after dinner
with coffee or with desserts in
place of biscuits (cookies).

Mint Chocolate Meringues

Omit the alcohol and these mini meringues are perfect for a child's party.

Makes 50

INGREDIENTS
2 egg whites
115 g/4 oz/generous ½ cup caster (superfine)
    sugar
50 g/2 oz chocolate mint sticks, chopped
unsweetened cocoa powder, sifted
    (optional)

FOR THE FILLING
150 ml/¼ pint/⅔ cup double (heavy)
    or whipping cream
5–10 ml/1–2 tsp crème de menthe,
    or mint essence

1 Preheat the oven to 110°C/225°F/
Gas ¼. Line two or three baking sheets
with baking parchment.

2 Whisk the egg whites until stiff,
then gradually whisk in the sugar until
it is thick and glossy.

VARIATION: For delicious
tangy-flavoured meringues: omit
the cocoa powder, replace the
mint sticks with orange-flavoured
dark (bittersweet) chocolate
pieces, and use an orange
flavoured liqueur or essence in
place of the crème de menthe or
mint essence.

3 Fold in the chopped mint sticks
and then place teaspoons of the
mixture on the prepared baking sheets.

4 Bake for 1 hour or until crisp.
Remove from the oven and allow to
cool, then dust with cocoa, if using.

5 Lightly whip the cream until it
stands in soft peaks and stir in the
crème de menthe or mint essence. Use
the cream to sandwich the meringues
together in pairs just before serving.

Coconut Meringues

Make these meringues tiny to serve with a fruit salad, or make the bigger ones and sandwich with cream or crème fraîche.

Makes 16 larger or 32 tiny meringues

INGREDIENTS
3 egg whites, at room temperature
175 g/6 oz/scant 1 cup caster (superfine) sugar
50 g/2 oz/½ cup desiccated (dry unsweetened) coconut
whipped cream or crème fraîche, and lemon curd (optional), to serve

2 Carefully fold in the remaining sugar and the coconut with a metal spoon. When well blended, place tablespoonfuls well apart on non-stick baking parchment on baking sheets.

1 Preheat the oven to 160°C/325°F/ Gas 3. Whisk the egg whites in a large, clean bowl, until stiff. Whisk in half the sugar until smooth and glossy.

COOK'S TIP: You could use this mixture to make one large meringue gateau. Spread out the mixture in two 18 cm/7 in rounds and bake as above, then sandwich with one of the suggested fillings.

3 Bake the meringues for 20 minutes, then change the baking sheets over and reduce the temperature to 140°C/275°F/Gas 1 for a further 40 minutes, or until the meringues are crisp and slightly golden.

4 Remove the meringues from the paper while they are still warm. Transfer them to a wire rack and leave to cool.

5 When the meringues are completely cool, sandwich them together with whipped cream, crème fraîche, or a mixture of whipped cream and lemon curd.

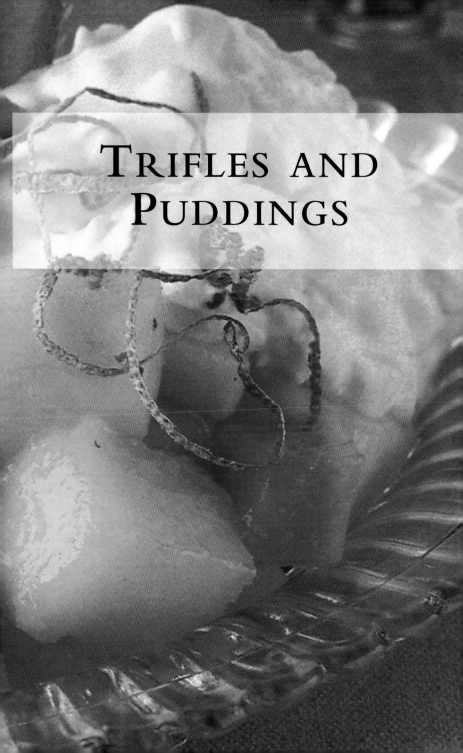

TRIFLES AND PUDDINGS

Sherry Trifle

There are many versions of sherry trifle, ranging from the everyday to the exquisite. This one falls into the latter category.

Serves 6–8

INGREDIENTS
75 g/3 oz ratafia biscuits (almond macaroons)
90 ml/6 tbsp raspberry jam
175 ml/6 fl oz/¾ cup sherry
175 g/6 oz/1 cup fresh raspberries
225 g/8 oz/2 cups seedless black grapes, halved
300 ml/½ pint/1¼ cups double (heavy) cream, whipped
crystallized (candied) fruit and icing sugar, to decorate

FOR THE CUSTARD
25 g/1 oz/¼ cup cornflour (cornstarch)
600 ml/1 pint/2½ cups milk
3 egg yolks
2.5 ml/½ tsp vanilla extract
25 g/1 oz/2 tbsp caster sugar

1 Make the custard. In a heatproof bowl, blend the cornflour with a little milk. Stir in the egg yolks, vanilla extract and sugar. Bring the remaining milk to the boil. Pour on to the cornflour mixture, stirring constantly.

2 Return to the heat and, continuing to stir, bring to the boil again, then lower the heat and simmer for 3 minutes. Remove from the heat, cover the surface with baking parchment and leave to cool.

3 Sandwich the ratafia biscuits together with the raspberry jam, then arrange them in a deep glass bowl and sprinkle over the sherry.

4 Spoon over half the custard. Level the surface and arrange the fruit on top. Cover with the remaining custard, ensuring that the layers are visible through the side of the bowl. Swirl or pipe the cream on top of the trifle and decorate with pieces of crystallized fruit. Dust with a little icing sugar just before serving.

VARIATION: Vary the fruit used for the filling to make the most of seasonal availability.

Italian Trifle

Known in Italy as "English Soup", this is nonetheless an Italian classic.

Serves 6–8

INGREDIENTS

475 ml/16 fl oz/2 cups milk
grated rind of ½ lemon
4 egg yolks
75 g/3 oz/⅓ cup caster (superfine) sugar
50 g/2 oz/½ cup flour, sifted
15 ml/1 tbsp rum or brandy
25 g/1 oz/2 tbsp butter
200 g/7 oz savoyard biscuits or 300 g/11 oz
    sponge cake, cut into 1 cm/½ in slices
75 ml/3 fl oz/5 tbsp Alchermes liqueur
    or cherry brandy
75 ml/3 fl oz/5 tbsp Strega liqueur
45 ml/3 tbsp apricot jam

TO DECORATE
fresh whipped cream
chopped toasted nuts

1 Heat the milk and lemon rind in a pan. Remove from the heat when small bubbles form on the surface.

2 Whisk the egg yolks. Gradually add the sugar and beat until pale yellow. Beat in the flour. Stir in the milk, through a sieve (strainer), and pour into a heavy pan.

3 Bring to the boil, whisking constantly. Simmer, stirring constantly, for 5 minutes. Off the heat, add the rum or brandy and the butter. Allow to cool, stirring to avoid a skin.

4 Brush the biscuits or cake with the Alchermes liqueur or cherry brandy on one side, and the Strega liqueur on the other.

5 Spread a thin layer of the custard over the base of a serving dish. Line with a layer of biscuits or cake. Cover with some of the custard. Add another layer of biscuits.

6 Heat the jam in a small pan with 30 ml/2 tbsp water. When hot, pour or brush it evenly over the biscuits or cake slices. Continue with layers of custard and liqueur-brushed biscuits or cake slices. End with custard. Cover with clear film (plastic wrap) or foil, and refrigerate for at least 2–3 hours. Serve, decorated with cream and nuts.

Jamaica Fruit Trifle

A deliciously light version of a traditional Caribbean dessert contains plenty of fruit and is made with crème fraîche, as well as cream.

Serves 8

INGREDIENTS

1 large sweet pineapple, peeled and cored,
    about 350 g/12 oz, leaves reserved
300 ml/½ pint/1¼ cups double
    (heavy) cream
200 ml/7 fl oz/scant 1 cup crème fraîche
60 ml/4 tbsp icing (confectioners')
    sugar, sifted
10 ml/2 tsp vanilla extract
30 ml/2 tbsp white or coconut rum
3 papayas, peeled, seeded and chopped
3 mangoes, peeled, stoned (pitted)
    and chopped
thinly pared rind and juice of 1 lime
25 g/1 oz/⅓ cup coarsely shredded or
    flaked coconut, toasted (optional)

1 Cut the pineapple into large chunks, place in a food processor or blender and process briefly until chopped. Transfer to a sieve (strainer) placed over a bowl and leave for 5 minutes so that the juice drains from the fruit.

COOK'S TIP: It is important to allow the chopped pineapple to drain thoroughly, otherwise the pineapple cream will be watery. Don't throw away the drained pineapple juice – mix it with fizzy mineral water for a refreshing drink.

2 Whip the double cream to very soft peaks, then lightly but thoroughly fold in the crème fraîche, sifted icing sugar, vanilla extract and rum.

3 Fold the drained, chopped pineapple into the cream mixture. Place the chopped papayas and mangoes in a large bowl and pour over the lime juice. Gently stir the fruit mixture to combine. Shred the pared lime rind.

4 Divide the fruit mixture and the pineapple cream among eight dessert plates. Decorate with the lime shreds, toasted coconut, if using, and small pineapple leaves, and serve immediately.

Chocolate Mandarin Trifle

Trifle is always a tempting treat, but when a rich chocolate and mascarpone custard is combined with Amaretto and mandarin oranges, it becomes sheer delight.

Serves 6–8

INGREDIENTS
4 trifle sponges
14 amaretti
60 ml/4 tbsp amaretto liqueur or
    sweet sherry
8 mandarin oranges
250 g/9 oz/generous 1 cup fromage frais
    or ricotta, softened
chocolate shapes and mandarin slices,
    to decorate

FOR THE CUSTARD
200 g/7 oz plain (semisweet) chocolate,
    broken into squares
25 g/1 oz/2 tbsp cornflour (cornstarch)
    or custard powder
25 g/1 oz/2 tbsp caster (superfine) sugar
2 egg yolks
200 ml/7 fl oz/scant 1 cup milk
250 g/9 oz/generous 1 cup mascarpone

1 Break up the trifle sponges and place them in a large glass serving dish. Crumble the amaretti over and then sprinkle with amaretto liqueur or sweet sherry.

2 Squeeze the juice from two mandarins and sprinkle into the dish. Segment the rest of the mandarins and put in the dish in an even layer.

3 Make the custard. Melt the chocolate in a heatproof bowl over hot water. In a separate bowl, mix the cornflour or custard powder, sugar and egg yolks to a paste.

4 Heat the milk in a small pan until almost boiling, then pour on to the egg yolk mixture, stirring constantly. Return to the clean pan and keep stirring over a low heat until the custard has thickened slightly and is smooth.

5 Stir in the mascarpone until melted, then add the melted chocolate, mixing it evenly. Spread evenly over the trifle, cool, then chill until set.

6 To finish, spread the fromage frais or ricotta over the custard, then decorate with chocolate shapes and mandarin slices just before serving.

Sultana & Couscous Puddings

Most couscous on the market now is the pre-cooked variety, which needs only the minimum of cooking, but check the pack instructions first to make sure. Serve these puddings hot, with low fat, thick natural yogurt or skimmed-milk custard.

Serves 4

INGREDIENTS
50 g/2 oz/⅓ cup sultanas
  (golden raisins)
475 ml/16 fl oz/2 cups apple juice
90 g/3½ oz/¾ cup couscous
2.5 ml/½ tsp mixed (apple pie) spice

3 Add the couscous and mixed spice to the pan and bring back to the boil, stirring. Cover and cook over a low heat for 8–10 minutes, or until the liquid has been absorbed.

1 Lightly grease four 250 ml/8 fl oz/ 1 cup heatproof bowls and set aside. Place the sultanas and apple juice in a small pan.

2 Bring the apple juice to the boil. Cover and simmer over a low heat for 2–3 minutes to plump up the fruit. Using a slotted spoon, lift out about half the fruit and place it in the bottom of the bowls.

4 Spoon the couscous into the bowls, spread it level and then cover the bowls tightly with foil. Place the bowls in a steamer over boiling water, cover and steam for about 30 minutes. Run a knife around the edges, carefully turn out the puddings and serve immediately.

Chocolate, Date & Walnut Pudding

"Proper" puddings are not totally taboo when you are cutting down on fat or calories – this one stays within the rules. Serve hot with low fat, thick natural yogurt or skimmed-milk custard.

Serves 4

INGREDIENTS
15 g/½ oz/1 tbsp chopped walnuts
25 g/1 oz/2 tbsp chopped dates
1 egg, separated, plus 1 egg white
5 ml/1 tsp vanilla extract
30 ml/2 tbsp golden caster
  (superfine) sugar
20 g/¾ oz/3 tbsp wholemeal
  (whole-wheat) flour
15 ml/1 tbsp unsweetened cocoa powder
30 ml/2 tbsp skimmed milk

2 Place the egg yolk in a heatproof bowl with the vanilla and sugar. Place the bowl over a pan of hot water and whisk until the mixture is thick and pale. Remove the bowl from the heat.

3 Sift the flour and cocoa into the mixture and fold them in with a metal spoon. Stir in the milk to soften the mixture slightly. Whisk the egg whites until they form soft peaks and fold them in.

1 Preheat the oven to 180°C/350°F/ Gas 4. Grease a 1.2 litre/2 pint/ 5 cup ovenproof bowl and place a small circle of baking parchment in the base. Spoon in the walnuts and dates.

4 Spoon the mixture into the ovenproof bowl and bake for 40–45 minutes, or until the pudding is well risen and firm to the touch. Run a knife around the pudding to loosen it and then turn it out. Serve.

Fruit & Spice Bread Pudding

An easy-to-make fruity dessert with a hint of spice, which is delicious served either hot or cold.

Serves 4

INGREDIENTS
6 slices wholemeal (whole-wheat)
   bread
50 g/2 oz/⅓ cup jam
50 g/2 oz/⅓ cup sultanas
   (golden raisins)
50 g/2 oz/¼ cup ready-to-eat dried
   apricots, chopped
50 g/2 oz/4 tbsp soft light brown sugar
5 ml/1 tsp ground mixed (apple pie)
   spice
2 eggs
600 ml/1 pint/2½ cups skimmed milk
finely grated rind of 1 lemon

2 Mix together the sultanas, apricots, sugar and spice and sprinkle half the fruit mixture over the bread in the ovenproof dish.

3 Top with the remaining bread and jam triangles and then sprinkle them with the remaining fruit mixture.

1 Preheat the oven to 160°C/325°F/ Gas 3. Remove the crusts from the bread, spread with jam and cut into small triangles. Place half the triangles in a lightly greased ovenproof dish.

4 Beat the eggs, milk and lemon rind together and pour the mixture over the bread. Set aside for about 30 minutes to allow the bread to absorb some of the liquid. Bake for 45–60 minutes, until lightly set and golden brown. Serve hot or cold.

Steamed Chocolate & Fruit Puddings with Chocolate Syrup

Some things always turn out well, including these wonderful little puddings. Dark, fluffy chocolate sponge is topped with tangy cranberries and apple, and served with a honeyed chocolate syrup.

Serves 4

INGREDIENTS
115 g/4 oz/⅔ cup muscovado (molasses) sugar
1 eating apple
75 g/3 oz/¾ cup cranberries, thawed if frozen
75 g/3 oz/⅔ cup plain (all-purpose) flour
2.5 ml/½ tsp baking powder
45 ml/3 tbsp unsweetened cocoa powder
115 g/4 oz/½ cup soft margarine
2 eggs

FOR THE CHOCOLATE SYRUP
115 g/4 oz plain (semisweet) chocolate,
    broken into squares
30 ml/2 tbsp clear honey
15 g/½ oz/1 tbsp unsalted (sweet) butter
2.5 ml/½ tsp vanilla extract

1 Prepare a steamer or half fill a pan with water and bring it to the boil. Grease four individual heatproof bowls and sprinkle each one with a little of the muscovado sugar to coat well all over.

2 Peel and core the apple. Dice it into a bowl, add the cranberries and mix well. Divide among the prepared heatproof bowls.

3 Sift the flour with the baking powder and cocoa into a large bowl. Add the remaining sugar, margarine and eggs and beat until combined and smooth.

4 Spoon the mixture into the bowls and cover each with a double thickness of foil. Steam for about 45 minutes, topping up the boiling water as required, until the puddings are well risen and firm.

5 Make the syrup. Mix the chocolate, honey, butter and vanilla in a small pan. Heat gently, stirring, until melted and smooth.

6 Run a knife around the edge of each pudding to loosen it, then turn out on to individual plates. Serve immediately, with the chocolate syrup.

Chocolate Chip & Banana Pudding

Hot and steamy, this superb light pudding has a beguiling banana and chocolate flavour that is sure to make it a family favourite.

Serves 4

INGREDIENTS
200 g/7 oz/1¾ cups self-raising
   (self-rising) flour
75 g/3 oz/6 tbsp unsalted (sweet) butter
2 ripe bananas
75 g/3 oz/⅓ cup caster (superfine) sugar
60 ml/4 tbsp milk
1 egg, beaten
60 ml/4 tbsp plain (semisweet) chocolate
   chips or chopped chocolate
chocolate sauce and whipped cream, to serve

1 Half fill a pan with water and bring it to the boil. Grease a 1 litre/1¾ pint/4 cup heatproof bowl Sift the flour into a bowl and rub in the butter until the mixture resembles coarse breadcrumbs.

2 Mash the bananas in a bowl. Stir them into the flour and butter mixture, with the caster sugar.

3 Whisk the milk with the egg in a bowl, then beat into the pudding mixture. Stir in the chocolate.

4 Spoon into the prepared bowl, cover closely with a double thickness of foil and steam for 2 hours, topping up the water as required.

5 Run a knife around the top of the pudding, turn out on to a dish and serve hot, with the sauce and cream.

COOK'S TIP: To make chocolate sauce, gently heat 115 g/4 oz/½ cup caster (superfine) sugar with 60 ml/ 4 tbsp water in a pan, stirring occasionally, until dissolved. Stir in 175 g/6 oz plain (semisweet) chocolate, until melted. Stir in 25 g/1 oz/2 tbsp butter, a little at a time, until melted. Stir in 30 ml/ 2 tbsp brandy or orange juice.

Steamed Ginger & Cinnamon Syrup Pudding

A traditional and comforting steamed pudding, best served with custard on a chilly winter's evening.

Serves 4

INGREDIENTS
120 g/4$^{1}/_4$ oz/9 tbsp softened butter
45 ml/3 tbsp golden (light corn) syrup
115 g/4 oz/$^{1}/_2$ cup caster (superfine) sugar
2 eggs, lightly beaten
115 g/4 oz/1 cup plain (all-purpose) flour
5 ml/1 tsp baking powder
5 ml/1 tsp ground cinnamon
25 g/1 oz preserved stem ginger, finely chopped
30 ml/2 tbsp milk

2 Cream the remaining butter and sugar until light and fluffy. Gradually beat in the eggs until the mixture is glossy. Sift the dry ingredients together and fold into the mixture with the ginger. Add the milk to make a dropping consistency.

1 Set a full steamer or pan of water on to boil. Lightly grease a 600 ml/ 1 pint/2½ cup heatproof bowl with 15 g/½ oz/1 tbsp butter. Pour the golden syrup into the bowl.

3 Spoon the batter into the bowl and smooth the top. Cover with a pleated piece of baking parchment to allow for expansion. Tie with string and steam for 1½–2 hours, topping up the water level. Turn out to serve.

Bread Pudding

This moist fruit pudding is delicious served hot or cold, cut into slices.

Serves 4–6

INGREDIENTS
450 g/1 lb stale white bread, thickly sliced
225 g/8 oz/1⅓ cups dried fruit
175 g/6 oz/¾ cup brown sugar
grated rind of 1 lemon
5 ml/1 tsp mixed (apple pie) spice
3 eggs, beaten
15 g/½ oz/1 tbsp butter
single (light) cream and brown sugar, to serve

1 Grease a 20 cm/8 in round cake tin. Put the bread into a bowl and soak in plenty of water (about 1.2 litres/2 pints/5 cups) for 30 minutes. Drain off the water and squeeze out the excess moisture from the bread. Preheat the oven to 180°C/350°F/Gas 4.

2 Mash the bread with a fork and stir in the dried fruit, sugar, lemon rind, mixed spice and eggs, mixing well.

3 Spoon the mixture into the cake tin. Dot the top of the pudding with butter, then bake for 1½ hours. Serve warm or leave until completely cool and cut into slices. Serve with single cream and brown sugar.

Marmalade Pudding

Use a thick-cut peel marmalade for this delicious steamed pudding.

Serves 4–6

INGREDIENTS
115 g/4 oz/1 cup self-raising (self-rising) flour
pinch of salt
5 ml/1 tsp ground ginger
115 g/4 oz/1 cup shredded suet (US chilled, grated shortening)
115 g/4 oz/2 cups fresh white breadcrumbs
75 g/3 oz/6 tbsp dark brown sugar
175 g/6 oz/generous ½ cup marmalade, plus 60 ml/4 tbsp to serve
30 ml/2 tbsp milk
single cream and orange slices, to serve

1 Grease a 900 ml/1½ pint/3¾ cup pudding bowl. Sift the flour, salt and ginger into a large bowl. Add the shredded suet, fresh breadcrumbs and sugar and mix thoroughly.

2 Add the marmalade and milk, mixing thoroughly to form a wet, dough-like mixture. Pour into the pudding bowl. The mixture should three-quarters fill the bowl. Cover with a double layer of baking parchment and secure with string.

3 Steam the pudding for 2½ hours in a double boiler with a tight-fitting lid. Check the water after 1¼ hours.

4 Lift out the bowl and remove the paper. Run a knife around the edge of the bowl, invert on to a plate and turn out. Warm the remaining marmalade in a small pan with 30 ml/2 tbsp water and serve with the pudding with cream and orange slices.

Cornflake-topped Peach Bake

A golden, crisp-crusted family pudding that is made in minutes from easily available ingredients.

Serves 4

INGREDIENTS
415 g/14½ oz can peach slices in juice
30 ml/2 tbsp sultanas (golden raisins)
1 cinnamon stick
strip of fresh orange rind
30 ml/2 tbsp butter or margarine
50 g/2 oz/1½ cups cornflakes
15 ml/1 tbsp sesame seeds

1 Preheat the oven to 200°C/400°F/ Gas 6. Drain the peaches, reserving the juice, and arrange the slices in a shallow ovenproof dish.

2 Place the juice, sultanas, cinnamon stick and orange rind in a pan and bring to the boil. Simmer, uncovered, for 3–4 minutes, until reduced by about half. Remove the cinnamon stick and orange rind.

3 Spoon the syrup over the drained peach slices and set aside while you prepare the topping.

4 Melt the butter or margarine in a small pan and stir in the cornflakes and sesame seeds. Mix well to coat thoroughly.

5 Spread the cornflake mixture over the fruit filling. Bake for 15–20 minutes, or until the topping is crisp and golden. Serve hot.

Peach & Raspberry Crumble

A quick and easy, tasty dessert, this crumble is good served hot or cold, on its own, or with custard.

Serves 4

INGREDIENTS
75 g/3 oz/⅔ cup wholemeal (whole-wheat) flour
75 g/3 oz/¾ cup medium oatmeal
75 g/3 oz/6 tbsp butter
50 g/2 oz/¼ cup soft light brown sugar
2.5 ml/½ tsp ground cinnamon
400 g/14 oz can peach slices in fruit juice
225 g/8 oz/1⅓ cups raspberries
30 ml/2 tbsp clear honey
sprig of fresh mint, to garnish

1 Preheat the oven to 180°C/350°F/ Gas 4. Put the flour and oatmeal in a bowl and mix together.

2 Rub in the butter until the mixture resembles breadcrumbs, then stir in the sugar and cinnamon.

3 Drain the peach slices and reserve the juice. Chop the peach slices to about the same size as the raspberries.

4 Arrange the chopped peaches evenly over the base of an ovenproof dish, then sprinkle over the raspberries.

5 Mix together the reserved peach juice and honey, pour the mixture over the fruit and stir.

VARIATION: For a tasty change, use other combinations of fruit, such as apples and blackberries, rhubarb and orange, or strawberries and pineapple. If using all fresh fruit, add a little fruit juice.

6 Spoon the crumble mixture over the fruit, pressing it down lightly. Bake for about 45 minutes, until golden brown on top. Garnish with fresh mint and serve hot or cold.

Spiced Apple Crumble

In this version of an ever-popular dessert, hazelnuts and cardamom seeds add a spicy crunchiness to the golden topping.

Serves 4–6

INGREDIENTS
butter, for greasing
450 g/1 lb cooking apples
115 g/4 oz/1 cup blackberries
grated rind and juice of 1 orange
50 g/2 oz/¼ cup light muscovado (molasses)
    sugar
custard, to serve

FOR THE TOPPING
175 g/6 oz/1½ cups plain (all-purpose) flour
75 g/3 oz/⅓ cup butter
75 g/3 oz/⅓ cup caster (superfine) sugar
25 g/1 oz/¼ cup chopped hazelnuts
2.5 ml/½ tsp crushed cardamom seeds

2 Set the fruit mixture aside while you make the topping. Sift the flour into a large bowl and rub in the butter until the mixture resembles coarse breadcrumbs.

3 Stir in the sugar, hazelnuts and cardamom seeds. Sprinkle the topping over the top of the fruit.

4 Press the topping around the edges of the dish to seal in the juices. Bake for 30–35 minutes, or until the crumble is golden brown. Serve hot, with custard.

VARIATION: This crumble can be made with other types of fruit, as preferred. Rhubarb with banana, pears, gooseberries and apricots would all be delicious.

1 Preheat the oven to 200°C/400°F/ Gas 6. Generously butter a 1.2 litre/ 2 pint/5 cup ovenproof dish. Peel and core the apples, then slice into the dish. Level the surface, then sprinkle the blackberries and orange rind on top. Mix the muscovado sugar and the orange juice and pour over the fruit.

Apricot Panettone Pudding

Slices of light-textured panettone are layered with dried apricots and cooked in a creamy coffee custard for a satisfyingly warming dessert.

Serves 4

INGREDIENTS
50 g/2 oz/4 tbsp unsalted (sweet) butter
6 x 1 cm/½ in thick slices (about 400 g/
    14 oz) panettone containing candied fruit
175 g/6 oz/¾ cup ready-to-eat dried
    apricots, chopped
400 ml/14 fl oz/1⅔ cups milk
250 ml/8 fl oz/1 cup double (heavy) cream
60 ml/4 tbsp mild-flavoured
    ground coffee
90 g/3½ oz/½ cup caster (superfine) sugar
3 eggs
30 ml/2 tbsp demerara (raw) sugar
pouring cream or crème fraîche,
    to serve

2 Pour the milk and cream into a pan and heat until almost boiling. Pour the milk mixture over the coffee and leave to steep for 10 minutes. Strain through a fine sieve (strainer), discarding the coffee grounds.

3 Lightly beat the caster sugar and eggs together, then whisk in the warm coffee-flavoured milk. Slowly pour the mixture over the panettone. Leave to soak for 15 minutes.

4 Sprinkle the top of the pudding with demerara sugar and place the dish in a large roasting pan. Pour in enough boiling water to come halfway up the sides of the dish.

1 Preheat the oven to 160°C/325°F/ Gas 3. Soften the butter and use 15 g/ ½ oz/1 tbsp to grease a 2 litre/ 3½ pint/8 cup oval ovenproof dish. Spread the panettone with the remaining butter and arrange in the dish. Cut to fit, and sprinkle the apricots among and over the layers.

5 Bake for 40–45 minutes, until the top is golden and crusty, but the middle still slightly wobbly. Remove from the oven, but leave the dish in the hot water for 10 minutes. Serve the pudding warm with pouring cream or crème fraîche.

Peachy Chocolate Bake

"I can resist everything except temptation", said Oscar Wilde. When it comes to this delicious, hot chocolatey pudding, it's best not to even try!

Serves 6

INGREDIENTS
200 g/7 oz dark (bittersweet) chocolate,
   broken into squares
115 g/4 oz/½ cup unsalted (sweet) butter
4 eggs, separated
115 g/4 oz/½ cup caster (superfine) sugar
425 g/15 oz can peach slices, drained
cream or yogurt, to serve (optional)

1 Preheat the oven to 160°C/325°F/ Gas 3. Butter a wide ovenproof dish. Melt the chocolate with the butter in a heatproof bowl over barely simmering water. Remove the bowl from the heat.

2 Whisk the egg yolks with the sugar until thick and pale. In a grease-free bowl, whisk the whites until stiff.

3 Beat the melted chocolate into the whisked egg yolk mixture until well combined.

4 Fold in large spoonfuls of whisked egg whites, then add the remainder lightly and evenly.

5 Fold the peach slices into the mixture, then scrape it carefully into the prepared dish.

6 Bake for 35–40 minutes, or until risen and just firm. Serve hot, with cream or yogurt if you like.

COOK'S TIP: Do not level the mixture as it looks more interesting if the surface is rough and uneven.

Cherry Clafoutis

When fresh cherries are in season this makes a deliciously simple dessert for any occasion. Serve warm with a little yogurt or pouring cream.

Serves 6

INGREDIENTS
50 g/2 oz/¼ cup butter, melted
675 g/1½ lb fresh cherries
50 g/2 oz/½ cup plain (all-purpose) flour
pinch of salt
4 eggs, plus 2 egg yolks
115 g/4 oz/½ cup caster (superfine) sugar,
    plus extra for dusting (optional)
600 ml/1 pint/2½ cups milk
yogurt or pouring cream,
    to serve

2 Sift the flour and salt into a large bowl. Add the eggs, egg yolks, caster sugar and a little of the milk and, using a balloon whisk, beat to a smooth batter ensuring that all the flour is incorporated.

1 Preheat the oven to 190°C/375°F/ Gas 5. Lightly butter the base and sides of a shallow ovenproof dish. Pit the cherries and place in the dish.

VARIATION: Use two 425 g/ 15 oz cans pitted black cherries, thoroughly drained, if fresh cherries are not available. For a special dessert, add 45 ml/3 tbsp kirsch to the batter.

3 Gradually whisk in the remaining milk and the rest of the butter, then strain the batter over the cherries.

4 Bake for 40–50 minutes, until the topping is golden and just set. Dust with caster sugar and serve while still warm, with yogurt or pouring cream.

Lemon Surprise Pudding

This is a much-loved dessert many of us remember from childhood. The surprise is the unexpected sauce concealed beneath the delectable sponge.

Serves 4

INGREDIENTS

50 g/2 oz/¼ cup butter, plus extra
   for greasing
grated rind and juice of 2 lemons
115 g/4 oz/½ cup caster (superfine) sugar
2 eggs, separated
50 g/2 oz/½ cup self-raising
   (self-rising) flour
300 ml/½ pint/1¼ cups milk

1 Preheat the oven to 190°C/375°F/
Gas 5. Butter a 1.2 litre/2 pint/5 cup
ovenproof dish.

2 Beat together the lemon rind,
butter and caster sugar in a bowl until
pale and fluffy. Add the egg yolks and
flour and beat together well. Gradually
whisk in the lemon juice and milk.

3 In a grease-free bowl whisk the egg
whites until they form stiff peaks. Fold
the egg whites lightly into the lemon
mixture, then pour into the prepared
ovenproof dish.

4 Place the dish in a roasting tin pan
and pour enough hot water into the
tin to come halfway up the side of the
dish. Bake for about 45 minutes, until
golden. Serve immediately.

COOK'S TIP: When whisking the
lemon juice and milk into the
pudding mixture, don't be alarmed
if the mixture curdles. This is
perfectly normal and will not affect
the finished pudding.

Magic Chocolate Mud Pudding

A popular favourite, which magically separates into a light and luscious sponge and a velvety chocolate sauce.

Serves 4

INGREDIENTS
50 g/2 oz/¼ cup butter
200 g/7 oz/generous 1 cup light muscovado (brown) sugar
475 ml/16 fl oz/2 cups milk
90 g/3½ oz/scant 1 cup self-raising (self-rising) flour
5 ml/1 tsp ground cinnamon
75 ml/5 tbsp unsweetened cocoa powder
Yogurt or vanilla ice cream, to serve

1 Preheat the oven to 180°C/350°F/ Gas 4. Lightly grease a 1.5 litre/ 2½ pint/6¼ cup ovenproof dish and place on a baking sheet.

2 Place the butter in a pan. Add 115 g/4 oz/¾ cup of the sugar and 150 ml/¼ pint/⅔ cup of the milk. Heat gently, stirring occasionally, until the butter has melted and all the sugar has dissolved. Remove from the heat.

3 Sift the flour, ground cinnamon and 15 ml/1 tbsp of the cocoa into the pan and stir into the mixture, mixing evenly. Pour the mixture into the prepared dish and level the surface.

4 Sift the remaining cocoa powder into a bowl, mix with the remaining sugar, then sprinkle over the pudding mixture in the dish. Pour the remaining milk over the pudding.

5 Bake for 45–50 minutes, or until the sponge has risen to the top and is firm to the touch. Serve the pudding hot, with the Greek yogurt or vanilla ice cream.

COOK'S TIP: A soufflé dish or similar straight-sided ovenproof dish is ideal for this pudding, since it supports the sponge as it rises above the sauce below.

Sticky Pear Pudding

Cloves add a distinctive fragrant flavour to this melt-in-the-mouth hazelnut, pear and coffee pudding.

Serves 6

INGREDIENTS
30 ml/2 tbsp ground coffee
15 ml/1 tbsp near-boiling water
50 g/2 oz/½ cup toasted skinned hazelnuts
4 ripe pears
finely grated rind and juice of ½ orange
115 g/4 oz/½ cup butter, softened, plus
 extra, for greasing
115 g/4 oz/generous ½ cup golden caster
 (superfine) sugar, plus an extra 15 ml/
 1 tbsp, for sprinkling
2 eggs, beaten
50 g/2 oz/½ cup self-raising (self-rising)
 flour, sifted
pinch of ground cloves
8 whole cloves
45 ml/3 tbsp maple syrup
300 ml/½ pint/1¼ cups whipping cream
15 ml/1 tbsp icing (confectioners')
 sugar, sifted
fine strips of orange rind,
 to decorate

1 Preheat the oven to 180°C/350°F/ Gas 4. Lightly grease a 20 cm/8 in loose-based cake tin (pan). Put the coffee in a small bowl with the water. Leave for 4 minutes, then strain.

2 Finely grind the hazelnuts. Peel, halve and core the pears. Thinly slice across the pear halves part of the way through. Brush with orange juice.

3 Beat the softened butter and the 115 g/4 oz/generous ½ cup caster sugar together in a bowl until light and fluffy. Gradually beat in the eggs, then fold in the flour, ground cloves, hazelnuts and coffee. Spoon the mixture into the tin and level the surface.

4 Pat the pears dry on kitchen paper, and press one clove into the hollow of each half, then arrange in the sponge mixture, flat side down. Brush the pears with 15 ml/1 tbsp maple syrup.

5 Sprinkle the pears with the 15 ml/ 1 tbsp caster sugar. Bake the pudding for 45–50 minutes, until firm and risen.

6 Meanwhile, make the orange cream. Whip the cream, icing sugar and orange rind until soft peaks form. Spoon into a serving dish and chill until needed.

7 Allow the sponge to cool for about 10 minutes in the tin, then remove and place on a serving plate. Brush with the remaining maple syrup before decorating with orange rind and serving warm with the orange cream.

Blackberry Charlotte

A classic pudding, perfect for cold days. Serve with low fat, thick yogurt or skimmed-milk custard.

Serves 4

INGREDIENTS
40 g/1½ oz/3 tbsp unsalted (sweet) butter
175 g/6 oz/3 cups fresh white breadcrumbs
50 g/2 oz/4 tbsp soft light brown sugar
60 ml/4 tbsp golden (light corn) syrup
finely grated rind and juice of 2 lemons
50 g/2 oz/⅔ cup walnut halves
450 g/1 lb/4 cups blackberries
450 g/1 lb cooking apples, peeled, cored and finely sliced

1 Preheat the oven to 180°C/350°F/Gas 4. Grease a 450 ml/¾ pint/2 cup dish with 15 g/½ oz/1 tbsp of the butter. Melt the remaining butter. Add the breadcrumbs and sauté for 5–7 minutes, until crisp and golden. Leave to cool slightly.

2 Place the sugar, syrup, lemon rind and juice in a small pan and warm gently. Stir in the crumbs.

3 Process the walnuts until they are finely ground.

4 Arrange a thin layer of blackberries in the prepared dish. Top with a thin layer of crumbs. Add a thin layer of apple and cover it with another thin layer of crumbs.

5 Repeat with another layer of berries, followed by another layer of crumbs, until you have used up all the ingredients, finishing with crumbs. The mixture should be piled well above the top edge of the dish because it shrinks during cooking. Bake for 30 minutes, until the crumbs are golden brown and the fruit is soft.

COOK'S TIP: If blackberries are not available, raspberries and blueberries are just as delicious.

COOKIES

Ladies' Kisses

These old-fashioned Italian cookies are just the thing for a special tea party.

Makes 20

INGREDIENTS
150 g/5 oz/10 tbsp butter, softened
115 g/4 oz/½ cup caster (superfine) sugar
1 egg yolk
2.5 ml/½ tsp almond extract
115 g/4 oz/1 cup ground almonds
175 g/6 oz/1½ cups plain (all-purpose) flour
50 g/2 oz plain (semi-sweet) chocolate

1 Cream the butter and sugar together with an electric mixer until light and fluffy, then beat in the yolk, almond extract, almonds and flour until evenly mixed. Chill until firm.

2 Preheat the oven to 160°C/325°F/Gas 3. Line three to four baking sheets with non-stick baking parchment. Break off small pieces of dough and roll into 40 balls. Place well apart on the baking sheets.

3 Bake for 20 minutes, or until golden. Remove the baking sheets from the oven, lift off the paper with the cookies on, then place on wire racks to cool.

4 Lift the cold cookies off the paper. Melt the chocolate and use it to sandwich the cookies in pairs. Leave to cool and set before serving.

Tea Cookies

If you don't want to pipe the mixture, spoon it on to the baking sheets and press with a fork.

Makes 20

INGREDIENTS
150 g/5 oz/10 tbsp butter, softened
75 g/3 oz/¾ cup icing (confectioners') sugar, sifted
1 egg, beaten
a few drops of almond extract
225 g/8 oz/2 cups plain (all-purpose) flour
2–3 large pieces of candied peel

1 Preheat the oven to 230°C/450°F/Gas 8. Line two baking sheets with baking parchment. Cream the butter and sugar with an electric mixer until light and fluffy, then beat in the egg, almond extract and flour until evenly mixed.

2 Spoon the mixture into a piping (pastry) bag fitted with a star nozzle and pipe ten rosette shapes on each of the baking sheets.

3 Cut the candied peel into small diamond shapes and press one diamond into the centre of each cookie. Bake for 5 minutes, or until golden. Transfer the cookies on the baking sheet to a wire rack to cool completely. Lift the cookies off the paper when cool.

Right: Ladies' Kisses (top); Tea Cookies

Mocha Viennese Swirls

Some temptations just can't be resisted. Put out a plate of these melt-in-the-mouth marvels and watch them vanish.

Makes about 20

INGREDIENTS
200 g/7 oz/scant 1 cup unsalted (sweet)
   butter, softened, plus extra for greasing
50 g/2 oz/½ cup icing (confectioners') sugar
115 g/4 oz plain (semisweet) chocolate
30 ml/2 tbsp strong black coffee
200 g/7 oz/scant 2 cups plain
   (all-purpose) flour
50 g/2 oz/½ cup cornflour (cornstarch)

FOR THE DECORATION
about 20 blanched almonds
150 g/5 oz plain (semisweet) chocolate

1 Preheat the oven to 190°C/375°F/Gas 5. Lightly grease two large baking sheets. Break the chocolate into squares and melt in a bowl over hot water. Cream the butter with the icing sugar in a bowl until smooth and pale. Beat in the melted chocolate, then the coffee. Sift the plain flour and cornflour over the mixture. Fold in lightly to make a soft mixture.

2 Spoon the mixture into a piping (pastry) bag fitted with a large star nozzle and pipe about 20 swirls on the baking sheets, allowing room for spreading during baking.

3 Press an almond into the centre of each swirl. Bake for about 15 minutes, or until the biscuits are firm and just beginning to brown. Leave to cool for about 10 minutes on the baking sheets, then transfer to a wire rack to cool completely.

4 When cold, melt the plain chocolate for the decoration, and dip the base of each swirl to coat. Place the coated biscuits on a sheet of baking parchment and leave to set.

COOK'S TIP: If the mixture is too stiff to pipe, soften it with a little more black coffee.

Vanilla Crescents

These attractive little almond and vanilla–flavoured biscuits are absolutely irresistible.

Makes 36

INGREDIENTS
175 g/6 oz/1 cup unblanched almonds
115 g/4 oz/1 cup plain (all-purpose) flour
2.5 ml/½ tsp salt
225 g/8 oz/1 cup butter, at room temperature, plus extra for greasing
90 g/3½ oz/½ cup sugar
5 ml/1 tsp vanilla extract
icing (confectioners') sugar, for dusting

1 Put the almonds and a few tablespoons of the flour in a food processor or blender, and process.

2 Sift the remaining flour with the salt. Set aside. With an electric mixer, cream the butter and sugar together in a bowl until light and fluffy.

3 Add the almonds, vanilla extract and the flour mixture. Stir to mix well. Gather the dough into a ball, wrap in baking parchment and chill in the refrigerator for at least 30 minutes.

4 Preheat the oven to 160°C/325°F/ Gas 3. Lightly grease two baking sheets. Break off walnut-size pieces of dough and roll into small cylinders about 1 cm/½ in diameter. Bend into small crescents and place on the prepared baking sheets.

5 Bake for about 20 minutes, until dry but not brown. Transfer to a rack to cool slightly. Set the rack over a baking sheet and dust with an even layer of icing sugar.

COOK'S TIPS: Chilling the dough makes it firmer and therefore easier to shape.

Bake cookies at or just above the centre of the oven. If you are using two baking sheets, place one above the other and swap them over halfway through the cooking time, so that they brown evenly.

Chocolate Chip Cookies

Keep a supply of these favourite cookies stored in the freezer.

Makes 16

INGREDIENTS

75 g/3 oz/6 tbsp soft margarine, plus extra
    for greasing
50 g/2 oz/¼ cup soft light brown sugar
50 g/2 oz/¼ cup caster (superfine) sugar
1 egg, beaten
few drops of vanilla extract
75 g/3 oz/¾ cup rice flour
75 g/3 oz/¾ cup cornmeal
5 ml/1 tsp baking powder
115 g/4 oz/⅔ cup plain (semisweet) chocolate
    chips, or a mixture of milk and white
    chocolate chips
salt

1 Preheat the oven to 190°C/375°F/
Gas 5. Lightly grease two baking
sheets. Cream the margarine and
sugars together until light and fluffy.

2 Beat in the egg and vanilla extract.
Fold in the rice flour, cornmeal,
baking powder and a pinch of salt,
then fold in the chocolate chips.

3 Place spoonfuls of the mixture on
the baking sheets, spaced well apart.
Bake for 10–15 minutes, until the
cookies are lightly browned. Leave on
the baking sheets for a few minutes,
then cool on a wire rack.

Cherry Munchies

You'll find it hard to stop at just one of these munchies.

Makes 20

INGREDIENTS

2 egg whites
115 g/4 oz/1 cup icing (confectioners')
    sugar, sifted
115 g/4 oz/1 cup ground almonds
115 g/4 oz/generous 1 cup desiccated (dry
    unsweetened shredded) coconut
few drops of almond extract
75 g/3 oz/½ cup glacé (candied) cherries,
    finely chopped

1 Preheat the oven to 150°C/300°F/
Gas 2. Line two baking sheets with
non-stick baking paper. Place the egg
whites in a bowl and whisk until stiff.

2 Fold in the icing sugar, then fold in
the ground almonds, coconut and
almond extract to form a sticky
dough. Fold in the chopped cherries.

3 Place heaped teaspoonfuls of the
mixture on the prepared baking sheets.
Bake for 25 minutes, or until pale
golden. Cool on the baking sheets for
a few minutes, then transfer to a wire
rack until cold.

*Right: Chocolate Chip Cookies (top);
Cherry Munchies*

Chunky Chocolate Cookies

Do not allow these cookies to cool completely on the baking sheet or they will become too crisp and will break when you try to lift them.

Makes about 18

INGREDIENTS
175 g/6 oz plain (semisweet) chocolate
115 g/4 oz/½ cup unsalted (sweet) butter,
   cut into pieces
2 eggs
90 g/3½ oz/½ cup sugar
50 g/2 oz/¼ cup (packed) soft light
   brown sugar
40 g/1½ oz/⅓ cup plain (all-purpose) flour
25 g/1 oz/¼ cup unsweetened cocoa powder
5 ml/1 tsp baking powder
10 ml/2 tsp vanilla extract
pinch of salt
115 g/4 oz/1 cup pecans, toasted and
   coarsely chopped
175 g/6 oz/1 cup plain chocolate chips
115 g/4 oz fine quality white chocolate,
   chopped into 5 mm/¼ in pieces
115 g/4 oz fine quality milk chocolate,
   chopped into 5 mm/¼ in pieces

1 Preheat the oven to 160°C/325°F/ Gas 3. Grease two large baking sheets. Melt the plain chocolate and butter in a pan over a low heat, stirring frequently. Leave to cool slightly.

2 Using an electric mixer, beat the eggs and sugars for 2–3 minutes. Gradually beat in the melted chocolate. Beat in the flour, cocoa, baking powder, vanilla and salt. Stir in the nuts, chocolate chips and pieces.

3 Drop heaped tablespoons of the mixture on to the baking sheets 10 cm/4 in apart and flatten each to a round about 7.5 cm/3 in across.

4 Bake for 8–10 minutes, until the tops are shiny and cracked and the edges look crisp; do not over-bake or the cookies will break when removed from the baking sheet.

5 Remove the baking sheets to a wire rack to cool for 2 minutes, until just set, then remove the cookies to the wire rack to cool completely. Continue to bake in batches. Store in airtight containers.

Lavender Heart Cookies

Serve these fragrant cookies on any romantic anniversary.

Makes 16–18

INGREDIENTS
115 g/4 oz/½ cup unsalted (sweet) butter
90 ml/6 tbsp caster (superfine) sugar
175 g/6 oz/1½ cups plain (all-purpose) flour,
    plus extra for dusting
30 ml/2 tbsp fresh lavender florets
    or 15 ml/1 tbsp dried culinary lavender,
    roughly chopped

1 Cream the butter and 60 ml/4 tbsp of sugar together until fluffy. Stir in the flour and lavender and bring the mixture together in a soft ball. Cover and chill for 15 minutes.

2 Preheat the oven to 200°C/400°F/ Gas 6. Roll out the dough on a lightly floured surface and stamp out about 18 cookies, using a 5 cm/2 in heart-shaped cutter. Place on a heavy baking sheet and bake for about 10 minutes, or until golden.

3 Leave the cookies standing for 5 minutes, then transfer them carefully to a wire rack to cool.

COOK'S TIP: These cookies would make an unusual gift, contained in an airtight jar decorated with ribbon.

Chocolate Crackle-tops

Makes about 38 cookies

INGREDIENTS

200 g/7 oz dark (bittersweet) or plain
  (semisweet) chocolate, chopped
90 g/3½ oz/7 tbsp unsalted (sweet) butter,
  plus extra for greasing
115 g/4 oz/⅔ cup caster (superfine) sugar
3 eggs
5 ml/1 tsp vanilla extract
215 g/7½ oz/2 cups plain (all-purpose) flour
25 g/1 oz/¼ cup unsweetened cocoa powder
2.5 ml/½ tsp baking powder
pinch of salt
175 g/6 oz/1½ cups icing (confectioners')
  sugar

1 Melt the chocolate and butter in a pan over low heat, stirring frequently. Remove from heat. Add the sugar, stirring for 2–3 minutes until dissolved. Add the eggs, one at a time, beating after each addition. Stir in the vanilla.

2 Sift the flour, cocoa, baking powder and salt into a bowl. Gradually stir into the chocolate mixture until blended. Cover and chill for at least 1 hour.

3 Preheat the oven to 160°C/325°F/ Gas 3. Grease two baking sheets. Place the icing sugar in a small bowl. Take teaspoonfuls of dough and roll into 4 cm/1½ in balls.

4 Drop the balls, one at a time, into the icing sugar and roll until heavily coated. Remove with a slotted spoon and tap against the side of the bowl to remove any excess sugar. Place on baking sheets 4 cm/1½ in apart.

5 Bake the cookies for 10–15 minutes, or until slightly firm when touched. Leave on the baking sheet for 2–3 minutes to set then cool on a wire rack.

Coffee Sponge Drops

Low-fat cheese and stem ginger make a delicious filling for these lovely light sponge drops.

Makes 12

INGREDIENTS
50 g/2 oz/½ cup plain (all-purpose) flour
15 ml/1 tbsp instant coffee powder
2 eggs
75 g/3 oz/scant ½ cup caster (superfine) sugar

FOR THE FILLING
115 g/4 oz/¼ cup low-fat soft cheese
40 g/1½ oz/¼ cup chopped preserved stem
    ginger

2 Combine the eggs and caster sugar in a bowl. Beat with a hand-held electric whisk until thick and mousse-like (when the whisk is lifted a trail should remain on the surface of the mixture for at least 15 seconds).

1 Preheat the oven to 190°C/375°F/ Gas 5. Line two baking sheets with non-stick baking parchment. Make the filling by beating together the soft cheese and stem ginger. Chill until required. Sift the flour and instant coffee powder together.

3 Carefully add the sifted flour and coffee mixture and gently fold in with a metal spoon.

4 Spoon the mixture into a piping (pastry) bag fitted with a 1 cm/½ in plain nozzle. Pipe 4 cm/1½ in rounds on the baking sheets. Bake for 12 minutes. Cool on a wire rack. Sandwich together with the filling.

VARIATION: If liked, use the rind of one orange in place of the stem ginger and add 15 ml/1 tbsp caster (superfine) sugar.

Flapjacks

Low in fat and sugar, high in crunch factor and flavour – what better for teatime?

Makes 16

INGREDIENTS
oil, for brushing
115 g/4 oz/½ cup low-fat spread
60 ml/4 tbsp rice syrup
50 g/2 oz/½ cup wholemeal
 (whole-wheat) flour
225 g/8 oz/generous 2 cups rolled oats
50 g/2 oz/⅓ cup pine nuts

1 Preheat the oven to 180°C/350°F/Gas 4. Line a 20 cm/8 in shallow baking tin (pan) with oiled foil. Melt the low-fat spread and rice syrup in a small pan over a low heat, then stir in the flour, oats and pine nuts until well mixed.

2 Turn the mixture into the tin and pat it out evenly with your fingers. Press the mixture down lightly. Bake for 25–30 minutes, until the flapjacks are lightly browned and crisp. Mark into squares while still warm. Cool slightly, then transfer to a wire rack.

COOK'S TIP: Do not let the syrup mixture boil or the flapjacks will be tacky rather than crisp.

Right: Flapjacks (top); Ginger Figures

Ginger Figures

Surprisingly, each of these charming, plump little figures contains less than 2 grams of fat.

Makes 8

INGREDIENTS
115 g/4 oz/1 cup plain (all-purpose) flour,
 sifted, plus extra for dusting
7.5 ml/1½ tsp ground ginger
grated rind of 1 orange and 1 lemon
75 ml/5 tbsp pear and apple spread or
 maple syrup
25 g/1 oz/ 2 tbsp low-fat spread
16 currants and 8 raisins, to decorate

1 Preheat the oven to 180°C/350°F/Gas 4. Mix the flour, ginger and grated orange and lemon rind in a bowl. Melt the pear and apple spread and the low-fat spread in a pan over a low heat.

2 As soon as the pear and apple spread mixture has melted, stir it into the dry ingredients. Mix to a firm dough in the bowl, then wrap the dough in clear film (plastic wrap) and chill for 2–3 hours.

3 Roll out the dough on a lightly floured surface to a thickness of about 5 mm/¼ in. Cut out figures, using a cutter or a template.

4 Use currants for eyes and raisins for noses. Draw a mouth using the point of a knife. Place the figures on a lightly floured baking sheet and bake for 8–10 minutes. Cool on a wire rack.

Almond Tuiles

These cookies are named after the French roof tiles they resemble. Making them is a little fiddly, so bake only four at a time until you get the knack.

Makes about 24

INGREDIENTS

40 g/1½ oz/3 tbsp unsalted (sweet) butter, plus extra for greasing
65 g/2½ oz/½ cup whole blanched almonds, lightly toasted
65 g/2½ oz/⅓ cup caster (superfine) sugar
2 egg whites
2.5 ml/½ tsp almond extract
35 g/1¼ oz/scant ⅓ cup plain (all-purpose) flour, sifted
50 g/2 oz/½ cup flaked (sliced) almonds

1 Preheat the oven to 200°C/400°F/ Gas 6. Butter two heavy baking sheets.

2 Place the almonds and 30 ml/2 tbsp of the sugar in a food processor and pulse until finely ground, but not pasty.

3 With an electric mixer, beat the butter until creamy, then add the remaining caster sugar and beat for 12 minutes, until light and fluffy. Gradually beat in the egg whites, then beat in the almond extract. Sift the flour over the mixture and fold in, then fold in the ground almond mixture.

COOK'S TIP: If the cookies flatten or go soft, reheat them on a baking sheet at 180°C/350°F/Gas 4, until completely flat, then reshape.

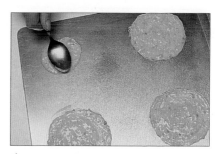

4 Drop tablespoons of mixture on to the baking sheets about 15 cm/6 in apart. With the back of a wet spoon, spread each mound into a paper-thin 7.5 cm/3 in round. (Don't worry if holes appear, they will fill in.) Sprinkle each round with a few flaked almonds.

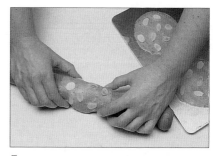

5 Bake the cookies, one sheet at a time, for 5–6 minutes, or until the edges are golden and the centres still pale. Remove the baking sheet to a wire rack and, working quickly, use a thin metal spatula to loosen the edges of one cookie. Carefully place the cookie over a rolling pin, then press down the sides of the cookie to curve it.

6 Continue shaping the cookies, transferring them to a wire rack as they cool and crisp. If the cookies become too crisp to shape, return the baking sheet to the hot oven for 15–30 seconds to soften them, then continue as before.

VARIATION: A few chopped glacé (candied) fruits could be sprinkled over the top of the cookies with the almonds, if liked.

Raspberry Shortcake

Rose water cream and fresh raspberries form the filling for this delectable dessert, which is actually quite easy to make.

Serves 6

INGREDIENTS
115 g/4 oz/½ cup unsalted (sweet)
    butter, softened
50 g/2 oz/¼ cup caster (superfine) sugar,
    plus extra for dusting
½ vanilla pod (bean), split, seeds reserved
115 g/4 oz/1 cup plain (all-purpose) flour
50 g/2 oz/⅓ cup semolina
12 miniature roses, unsprayed
1 egg white, beaten
icing (confectioners') sugar, for dusting
6 mint sprigs, to decorate

FOR THE FILLING
300 ml/½ pint/1¼ cups double
    (heavy) cream
15 ml/1 tbsp icing (confectioners') sugar
2.5 ml/½ tsp rose water
450 g/1 lb/2⅔ cups raspberries

1 Cream the butter, caster sugar and vanilla seeds until pale and fluffy. Sift the flour and semolina together, then gradually work into the creamed mixture to make a firm dough.

2 Knead the dough on a lightly floured surface until smooth. Roll out quite thinly and prick all over with a fork. Using a 7.5 cm/3 in fluted cutter, cut out 12 rounds. Place on a baking sheet and chill for 30 minutes.

3 Meanwhile, make the filling. Whisk the cream with the icing sugar until soft peaks form. Fold in the rose water and chill until required.

4 Preheat the oven to 180°C/350°F/ Gas 4. Paint the miniature roses and their leaves with the egg white. Dust with caster sugar, then leave to dry on a wire rack.

5 Bake the shortcakes for 15 minutes, or until lightly golden. Lift them off the baking sheet with a metal spatula and cool on a wire rack.

6 To assemble the shortcakes, spoon the rose water cream on to half the biscuits. Add a layer of raspberries, then top with a second shortcake. Dust with icing sugar. Decorate with the frosted roses and mint sprigs.

COOK'S TIP: For best results, serve the shortcakes as soon as possible after assembling them. Otherwise, they are likely to turn soggy from the berries' liquid.

Gingersnaps

Crisp and crunchy, gingersnaps are firm favourites with all the family.

Makes 60

INGREDIENTS
115 g/4 oz/½ cup butter, at room
    temperature, plus extra for greasing
275 g/10 oz/2½ cups plain (all-purpose) flour
5 ml/1 tsp bicarbonate of soda (baking soda)
7.5 ml/1½ tsp ground ginger
1.5 ml/¼ tsp ground cinnamon
1.5 ml/¼ tsp ground cloves
300 g/11 oz/generous 1½ cups sugar
1 egg, lightly beaten
60 ml/4 tbsp molasses or black treacle
5 ml/1 tsp lemon juice

1 Preheat the oven to 180°C/350°F/ Gas 4. Grease four baking sheets. Sift the flour, bicarbonate of soda and spices into a bowl. Set aside.

2 With an electric mixer, cream the butter and 200 g/7 oz/1 cup of the sugar together. Stir in the egg, molasses or treacle and lemon juice. Add the flour mixture and mix thoroughly with a wooden spoon to make a soft dough.

3 Shape into 2 cm/¾ in balls. Roll in the remaining sugar and place 5 cm/2 in apart on the baking sheets. Bake for 12 minutes, or until just firm. Leave to cool for a few minutes, then transfer to a wire rack.

Right: Gingersnaps (top); Cowboy Bakes

Cowboy Bakes

There'll be no need to corral the kids at teatime for these tasty treats.

Makes 60

INGREDIENTS
115 g/4 oz/½ cup butter, plus extra
    for greasing
115 g/4 oz/1 cup plain (all-purpose) flour
2.5 ml/½ tsp bicarbonate of soda
    (baking soda)
1.5 ml/¼ tsp baking powder
1.5 ml/¼ tsp salt
90 g/3½ oz/½ cup granulated sugar
115 g/4 oz/½ cup brown sugar
1 egg
2.5 ml/½ tsp vanilla extract
90 g/3½ oz/1 cup rolled oats
175 g/6 oz/1 cup milk chocolate chips

1 Preheat the oven to 160°C/325°F/ Gas 3. Grease three or four baking sheets. Sift the flour, bicarbonate of soda, baking powder and salt into a mixing bowl. Set aside.

2 With an electric mixer, cream the butter and sugars together. Add the egg and vanilla and beat until light and fluffy. Add the flour mixture and beat on low speed until blended. Stir in the oats and chocolate, mixing well. The dough should be crumbly.

3 Drop heaped teaspoons on to the baking sheets, 2.5 cm/1 in apart. Bake for 15 minutes, or until just firm around the edge. Cool on a wire rack.

Apricot Yogurt Cookies

You can afford to indulge yourself with these low-fat, low-cholesterol, flavour-packed fruity cookies.

Makes 16

INGREDIENTS

45 ml/3 tbsp sunflower oil, plus extra
   for brushing
175 g/6 oz/1½ cups plain (all-purpose) flour
5 ml/1 tsp baking powder
5 ml/1 tsp ground cinnamon
75 g/3 oz/scant 1 cup rolled oats
75 g/3 oz/scant ½ cup light muscovado
   (brown) sugar
115 g/4 oz/½ cup chopped ready-to-eat
   dried apricots
15 ml/1 tbsp flaked (sliced) almonds or
   chopped hazelnuts
150 ml/¼ pint/⅔ cup natural (plain) yogurt
demerara (raw) sugar,
   for sprinkling

2 Beat together the yogurt and oil, then stir evenly into the mixture to make a firm dough. If necessary, add a little more yogurt.

3 Use your hands to roll the mixture into about 16 small balls, place on the baking sheet and flatten with a fork. Sprinkle with demerara sugar.

1 Preheat the oven to 190°C/375°F/ Gas 5. Lightly oil a large baking sheet. Stir together the flour, baking powder and cinnamon. Stir in the oats, sugar, apricots and nuts.

VARIATIONS: If liked, use unsulphured dried apricots, as these have a richer flavour. Dried dates could replace the apricots.

4 Bake for 15–20 minutes, or until firm and golden brown. Transfer to a wire rack to cool.

COOK'S TIP: These cookies do not keep well, so it is best to eat them within two days, or to freeze them. Pack into a plastic bag and freeze for up to four months.

Sultana Cookies

Makes about 48

INGREDIENTS
75 g/3 oz/½ cup sultanas (golden raisins)
225 g/8 oz/1 cup butter, plus extra
   for greasing
115 g/4 oz/1 cup finely ground
   yellow cornmeal
175 g/6 oz/1½ cups plain (all-purpose) flour
7.5 ml/1½ tsp baking powder
2.5 ml/½ tsp salt
225 g/8 oz/generous 1 cup
   granulated sugar
2 eggs
15 ml/1 tbsp Marsala or 5 ml/1 tsp vanilla
   extract

1 Soak the sultanas in a small bowl
of warm water for 15 minutes. Drain.
Preheat the oven to 180°C/350°F/
Gas 4. Grease two baking sheets.

2 Sift the cornmeal, flour, baking
powder and salt into a bowl. Cream
the butter and sugar together until
light and fluffy. Beat in the eggs, one at
a time. Beat in the Marsala or vanilla
extract. Add the dry ingredients to the
batter, beating until well blended. Stir
in the sultanas.

3 Drop heaped teaspoons of batter
on to the baking sheets in rows about
5 cm/2 in apart. Bake for 7–8 minutes,
or until golden brown at the edges.
Transfer to a wire rack to cool.

Right: Sultana Cookies (top); Amaretti

Amaretti

Makes about 36

INGREDIENTS
200 g/7 oz/1¼ cups blanched almonds
225 g/8 oz/generous 1 cup caster
   (superfine) sugar
2 egg whites
2.5 ml/½ tsp almond extract
flour, for dusting
icing (confectioners') sugar, for dusting

1 Preheat the oven to 160°C/325°F/
Gas 3. Spread out the almonds on a
baking sheet and place in the oven for
10–15 minutes without browning.
Remove from the oven and allow to
cool. Turn the oven off. Finely grind
the almonds with half the sugar in a
food processor.

2 Beat the egg whites until they form
soft peaks. Sprinkle half the remaining
sugar over them and continue beating.
Fold in the remaining sugar, the
almond extracts and almonds.

3 Spoon the mixture into a pastry
bag with a smooth nozzle. Line a
baking sheet with baking parchment.
Dust with flour. Pipe the mixture in
walnut-size rounds. Sprinkle with
icing sugar and set aside for about
2 hours. Preheat the oven to 180°C/
350°F/Gas 4.

4 Bake for 15 minutes, or until pale
gold. Cool on a wire rack.

Black & White Ginger Florentines

These crunchy florentines can be stored in an airtight container in the refrigerator for up to one week.

Makes about 30

INGREDIENTS
120 ml/4 fl oz/½ cup double (heavy) cream
50 g/2 oz/4 tbsp unsalted (sweet) butter
90 g/3½ oz/½ cup sugar
30 ml/2 tbsp clear honey
150 g/5 oz/1⅔ cups flaked
    (sliced) almonds
40 g/1½ oz/⅓ cup plain (all-purpose) flour
2.5 ml/½ tsp ground ginger
50 g/2 oz/⅓ cup diced candied orange peel
65 g/2½ oz/½ cup diced preserved
    stem ginger
50 g/2 oz plain (semisweet) chocolate,
    chopped
150 g/5 oz dark (bittersweet) chocolate,
    chopped
150 g/5 oz fine quality white chocolate,
    chopped

1 Preheat the oven to 180°C/350°F/ Gas 4. Lightly grease two large non-stick baking sheets. Stir the cream, butter, sugar and honey in a pan over a medium heat, until the sugar dissolves completely.

2 Bring to the boil, stirring constantly. Remove from the heat and stir in the almonds, flour, ground ginger, orange peel, stem ginger and plain chocolate.

3 Drop teaspoons of mixture on to the sheets at least 7.5 cm/3 in apart. Dip a spoon in water and use to spread as thinly as possible.

4 Bake in batches for 8–10 minutes, or until bubbling, and golden brown at the edges. Be careful not to under- or over-bake. If you wish, neaten the edges with a 7.5 cm/3 in cookie cutter.

5 Remove from the oven and allow to cool for 10 minutes, until firm. Using a palette knife or metal spatula, transfer to a wire rack to cool completely.

6 Melt the dark chocolate in a pan over a very low heat, until smooth; then cool. In the top of a double boiler over low heat, melt the white chocolate until smooth, stirring frequently. Remove from the heat and cool, stirring occasionally, for about 5 minutes, until thickened.

7 Using a palette knife, spread half the florentines with the dark chocolate on the flat side, swirling to create a decorative surface, and place on a wire rack, chocolate side up. Spread the remaining florentines with the white chocolate and place on a rack. Chill for 10–15 minutes.

Glazed Gingerbread Cookies

Look for interesting-shaped cutters to make these cookies special.

Makes about 20

INGREDIENTS

175 g/6 oz/1½ cups plain (all-purpose) flour,
  plus extra for dusting
1.5 ml/¼ tsp bicarbonate of soda
  (baking soda)
5 ml/1 tsp ground ginger
5 ml/1 tsp ground cinnamon
65 g/2½ oz/5 tbsp unsalted (sweet) butter, cut
  into pieces, plus extra for greasing
75 g/3 oz/scant ½ cup caster (superfine) sugar
30 ml/2 tbsp maple syrup
1 egg yolk, beaten
red and green food colouring
175 g/6 oz white marzipan
salt

FOR THE ICING GLAZE

30 ml/2 tbsp lightly beaten egg white
30 ml/2 tbsp lemon juice
175–225 g/6–8 oz/1½–2 cups icing
  (confectioners') sugar

1 Sift together the flour, bicarbonate
of soda, spices and a pinch of salt into a
large bowl. Rub in the butter. Add the
sugar, syrup and egg yolk and mix to a
firm dough. Knead lightly, wrap and
chill for 30 minutes.

2 Preheat the oven to 180°C/350°F/
Gas 4. Grease a large baking sheet.
Roll out the dough on a floured
surface and stamp out decorative
shapes with novelty cookie cutters.

3 Transfer to the prepared sheet and
bake for 8–10 minutes, until the
cookies are beginning to colour
around the edges. Leave on the baking
sheet for 2 minutes until the cookies
begin to harden, then transfer to a
wire rack to cool.

4 To make the glaze, mix the egg
white and lemon juice in a bowl.
Gradually beat in the icing sugar until
the mixture is smooth and has the
consistency of thin cream. Place the
wire rack over a tray or plate. Spoon
the icing glaze over the cookies until
they are completely covered. Leave in
a cool place to dry for several hours.

5 Knead red food colouring into half
the marzipan and green into the other
half. Roll a thin length of each piece
and then twist together into a rope.
Secure a rope of marzipan around
a cookie, dampening the icing with a
little water, if necessary, to hold the
marzipan twist in place. Repeat on
about half the cookies.

6 Dilute a little of each food colouring with water. Using a fine brush, paint decorations on the plain cookies. Leave to dry.

COOK'S TIP: These biscuits can be made to suit the occasion, such as Christmas, as here, or birthdays.

Christmas Cookies

These festive cookies would make a lovely present – as well as a special teatime treat on Christmas day.

Makes about 12

INGREDIENTS
75 g/3 oz/6 tbsp butter, plus extra
    for greasing
50 g/2 oz/½ cup icing (confectioners') sugar
finely grated rind of 1 small lemon
1 egg yolk
175 g/6 oz/1½ cups plain (all-purpose) flour,
    plus extra for dusting
salt

TO DECORATE
2 egg yolks
red and green food colouring

1 In a large bowl, beat the butter, sugar and lemon rind together until pale and fluffy. Beat in the egg yolk, and then sift in the flour and a pinch of salt. Knead together to form a smooth dough. Wrap in clear film (plastic wrap) and chill for 30 minutes.

2 Preheat the oven to190°C/375°F/ Gas 5. Lightly grease two baking sheets. On a lightly floured surface, roll out the dough to 3 mm/⅛ in thick.

3 Using a 6 cm/2½ in fluted cutter, stamp out as many cookies as you can, with the cutter dipped in flour to prevent it from sticking to the dough. Transfer the cookies to the prepared sheets.

4 For the decoration, mark the cookies lightly with a 2.5 cm/1 in holly leaf cutter and use a 5 mm/¼ in plain piping (icing) nozzle for the berries. Chill for 10 minutes.

5 Put each egg yolk for the decoration into a small cup. Mix red food colouring into one and green food colouring into the other. Using a small brush, paint the colours on to the cookies. Bake for 10–12 minutes, or until they begin to colour around the edges. Cool slightly on the baking sheets, then transfer to a wire rack.

Mini Florentines with Grand Marnier

Orange liqueur adds a luxury note to these ever-popular nut and dried fruit cookies. The are just as good made with raisins or walnuts.

Makes about 24

INGREDIENTS
50 g/2 oz/¼ cup soft light brown sugar
15 ml/1 tbsp clear honey
15 ml/1 tbsp Grand Marnier
50 g/2 oz/¼ cup butter
40 g/1½ oz/⅓ cup plain (all-purpose) flour
25 g/1 oz/¼ cup hazelnuts,
  roughly chopped
50 g/2 oz/½ cup flaked (sliced)
  almonds, chopped
50 g/2 oz/¼ cup glacé
  cherries, chopped
115 g/4 oz dark (bittersweet) chocolate,
  melted, for coating

2 Remove the pan from the heat and add the flour, hazelnuts, almonds and cherries. Stir well.

3 Spoon small heaps of the mixture on to the baking sheets. Bake for about 10 minutes, until golden brown. Leave the cookies on the baking sheet until the edges begin to harden a little, then transfer to a wire rack to cool.

1 Preheat the oven to 180°C/350°F/ Gas 4. Line four baking sheets with baking parchment. Combine the sugar, honey, Grand Marnier and butter in a small pan and melt over a low heat.

VARIATION: You could use melted white chocolate for the zigzag decoration, if you like.

4 Spread the melted chocolate over one side of each florentine, using a kitchen knife. When it begins to set, drag a fork through to form wavy lines. Leave to set completely. Fill a piping (pastry) bag with the remaining melted chocolate, snip off the end and pipe zigzag lines over the plain side of the florentines.

Brandy Snaps

The combination of the crisp, light-as-air cookie and rich, brandy-flavoured creamy filling is magical.

Makes 16

INGREDIENTS
50 g/2 oz/¼ cup butter, at room temperature, plus extra for greasing
130 g/4½ oz/⅔ cup sugar
20 ml/4 tsp golden (light corn) syrup
40 g/1½ oz/⅓ cup plain (all-purpose) flour
2.5 ml/½ tsp ground ginger

FOR THE FILLING
250 ml/8 fl oz/ 1 cup whipping cream
30 ml/2 tbsp brandy

1 With an electric mixer, cream together the butter and sugar until light and fluffy, then beat in the syrup. Sift over the flour and ginger and mix to a rough dough.

2 Transfer the dough to a work surface and knead until smooth. Cover and chill in the refrigerator for 30 minutes.

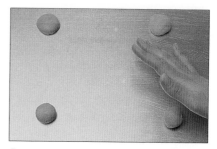

3 Preheat the oven to 190°C/375°F/ Gas 5. Grease a baking sheet. Working in batches of four, form walnut-size balls of dough. Place far apart on the prepared sheet and flatten the balls slightly. Bake for about 10 minutes, or until golden and bubbling.

4 Remove from the oven and cool for a few moments. Working quickly, slide a metal spatula under each one, turn over and wrap around the handle of a wooden spoon (have four spoons ready). If they firm up too quickly, reheat for a few seconds to soften. When firm, slide the snaps off and place on a rack to cool.

5 When all the brandy snaps are cool, prepare the filling. Whip the cream and brandy until soft peaks form. Fill a piping (pastry) bag with the brandy cream. Pipe into each end of the brandy snaps just before serving.

Mini Chocolate Marylands

These tasty little cookies are perfect for any age group. They're easy to make and even young children can get involved with helping to press the chocolate chips into the unbaked dough.

Makes 40–45

INGREDIENTS

125 g/4¼oz/generous ½ cup unsalted (sweet) butter, at room temperature, diced
90 g/3½ oz/½ cup caster (superfine) sugar
1 egg
1 egg yolk
5 ml/1 tsp vanilla extract
175 g/6 oz/1½ cups self-raising (self-rising) flour
90 g/3½ oz/generous ½ cup milk
90 g/3½ oz/generous ½ cup chocolate chips

1 Preheat the oven to 180°C/350°F/Gas 4. Grease two baking sheets.

2 In a large bowl, beat together the butter and sugar until pale and creamy. Add the egg, egg yolk, vanilla extract, flour, milk and half the chocolate chips and stir well until thoroughly combined.

3 Using two teaspoons, place small mounds of the mixture on the baking sheets, spacing them slightly apart to allow room for spreading.

4 Press the remaining chocolate chips on to the mounds of cookie dough and press down gently.

5 Bake for 10–15 minutes until pale golden. Leave the cookies on the baking sheet for 2 minutes to firm up, then transfer to a wire rack to cool completely.

COOK'S TIP: This recipe makes quite a large quantity. If you like, you can freeze half of the cookies for another time. Simply thaw, then return to the oven for a few minutes to re-crisp before serving.

Chocolate Cookie Slice

These rich, dark chocolate refrigerator cookies are perfect served with strong coffee, either as a mid-morning treat or even in place of dessert.

Makes 10

INGREDIENTS
275 g/10 oz fruit and nut plain (semisweet) chocolate
130 g/4½ oz/½ cup unsalted (sweet) butter, diced
90 g/3½ oz digestive biscuits (graham crackers)
90 g/3½ oz white chocolate

1 Grease and line the base and sides of a 450 g/1 lb loaf tin (pan) with baking parchment.

2 Break the fruit and nut chocolate into even-size pieces and place in a heatproof bowl along with the diced unsalted butter.

3 Set the bowl over a pan of simmering water and stir gently until melted. Cool for 20 minutes.

4 Break the digestive biscuits into small pieces with your fingers. Finely chop the white chocolate.

5 Stir the broken biscuits and white chocolate into the cooled, melted fruit and nut chocolate until combined. Turn the mixture into the prepared tin and pack down gently. Chill for 2 hours, or until set.

6 To serve, turn out the mixture and remove the lining paper. Cut into slices with a sharp knife.

> VARIATION: You can use this simple, basic recipe for all kinds of variations. Try different kinds of chocolate, such as ginger, hazelnut, honey and almond, peanut or mocha.

Chocolate Marzipan Cookies

These crisp cookies – with a little almond surprise inside – are perfect for those with a sweet tooth.

Makes about 36

INGREDIENTS
200 g/7 oz/scant 1 cup unsalted (sweet) butter, softened, plus extra for greasing
200 g/7 oz/scant 1 cup light muscovado (brown) sugar
1 egg
300 g/11 oz/2⅔ cups plain (all-purpose) flour, plus extra for dusting
60 ml/4 tbsp unsweetened cocoa powder
200 g/7 oz white marzipan
115 g/4 oz white chocolate, broken into squares

3 Roll out about half the dough on a lightly floured surface to about 5 mm/¼ in thick. Using a 5 cm/2 in biscuit cutter, cut out rounds, re-rolling the dough as required until you have about 36 rounds.

1 Preheat the oven to 190°C/375°F/Gas 5. Lightly grease two large baking sheets. Cream the butter with the sugar in a bowl until pale and fluffy. Add the egg and beat well.

2 Sift the flour and cocoa over the mixture. Stir in, first with a wooden spoon, then with clean hands, pressing the mixture together to make a fairly soft dough.

4 Cut the marzipan into about 36 equal pieces. Roll into balls, flatten slightly and place one on each round of dough. Roll out the remaining dough, cut out more rounds, then place on top of the almond paste. Press the dough edges to seal.

5 Bake for 10–12 minutes, or until the cookies have risen well and are beginning to crack on the surface. Leave on the baking sheet to cool slightly for about 2–3 minutes, then transfer to a wire rack to cool completely.

6 Melt the white chocolate, then either drizzle it over the biscuits to decorate or spoon into a paper piping bag and quickly pipe a design on them.

COOK'S TIP: If the dough is too sticky to roll, chill it for about 30 minutes, then try again.

Fudgy Glazed Chocolate Bars

For a simpler bar, omit the fudge glaze and dust with icing sugar instead.

Serves 8–10

INGREDIENTS

115 g/4 oz/½ cup unsalted (sweet) butter, cut
 into pieces, plus extra for greasing
250 g/9 oz dark (bittersweet) or plain
 (semisweet) chocolate, chopped
25 g/1 oz unsweetened chocolate, chopped
90 g/3½ oz/scant ½ cup light brown sugar
50 g/2 oz/¼ cup granulated sugar
2 eggs
15 ml/1 tbsp vanilla extract
65 g/2½ oz/9 tbsp plain (all-purpose) flour
115 g/4 oz/⅔ cup pecan nuts or walnuts,
 toasted and chopped
150 g/5 oz fine quality white chocolate,
 chopped into 5 mm/¼ in pieces
pecan halves, to decorate (optional)

FOR THE FUDGY CHOCOLATE GLAZE

175 g/6 oz plain (semisweet) or dark
 (bittersweet) chocolate, chopped
50 g/2 oz/¼ cup unsalted (sweet) butter
30 ml/2 tbsp corn or golden (light corn) syrup
10 ml/2 tsp vanilla extract
5 ml/1 tsp instant coffee powder

1 Preheat the oven to 180°C/350°F/
Gas 4. Invert a 20 cm/8 in square cake
tin (pan) and mould a piece of foil
over it. Turn it over and line with the
moulded foil. Lightly grease the foil.

2 In a medium pan over a low heat,
melt the dark chocolates and butter
until smooth, stirring frequently.

3 Remove the pan from the heat.
Stir in the sugars and continue stirring
for 2 more minutes, until they dissolve.
Beat in the eggs and vanilla and stir in
the flour until just blended. Stir in the
pecan nuts or walnuts and white
chocolate. Pour the batter into the
prepared tin.

4 Bake for 20–25 minutes, or until
a cocktail stick (toothpick) inserted
5 cm/2 in from the centre comes out
with just a few crumbs attached (do
not overbake or it will be dry).
Remove the tin to a wire rack to cool
for about 30 minutes. Using the foil to
lift, remove the "cake" from the tin and
cool on the rack for at least 2 hours.

5 Prepare the glaze. In a medium pan over a medium heat, melt the chocolate, butter, syrup, vanilla extract and coffee powder, stirring frequently, until smooth. Remove from the heat. Chill for 1 hour, or until thickened and spreadable.

6 Invert the "cake" on to the wire rack and remove the foil. Turn top-side up. Using a palette knife or metal spatula, spread a thick layer of fudgy glaze over the top. Chill for 1 hour, until set. Cut into bars. If you wish, top each with a pecan half.

Nut & Chocolate Chip Brownies

Moist, dark and deeply satisfying – meet the ultimate chocolate brownie.

Makes 16

INGREDIENTS
120 ml/4 fl oz/½ cup sunflower oil
215 g/7½ oz/1 cup light muscovado
   (brown) sugar
2 eggs
5 ml/1 tsp vanilla extract
150 g/5 oz plain (semisweet)
   chocolate, melted
65 g/2½ oz/9 tbsp self-raising
   (self-rising) flour
60 ml/4 tbsp unsweetened cocoa powder
75 g/3 oz/¾ cup chopped walnuts
50 g/2 oz/4 tbsp milk chocolate chips

1 Preheat the oven to 180°C/350°F/
Gas 4. Lightly grease a shallow 19 cm/
7½ in square cake tin (pan).

2 Beat the oil, sugar, eggs and vanilla
extract together thoroughly in a large
mixing bowl.

3 Stir in the melted chocolate,
then beat the mixture well until
it is evenly blended.

4 Sift the flour and cocoa powder
into the bowl containing the wet
ingredients and fold in thoroughly.
Stir in the chopped nuts and milk
chocolate chips, scrape the mixture
into the prepared cake tin and spread
it evenly to the edges.

5 Bake for 30–35 minutes, or until
the top is firm and crusty. Allow
to cool in the tin before cutting
into 16 squares.

COOK'S TIP: These brownies will
freeze for up to 3 months in an
airtight container.

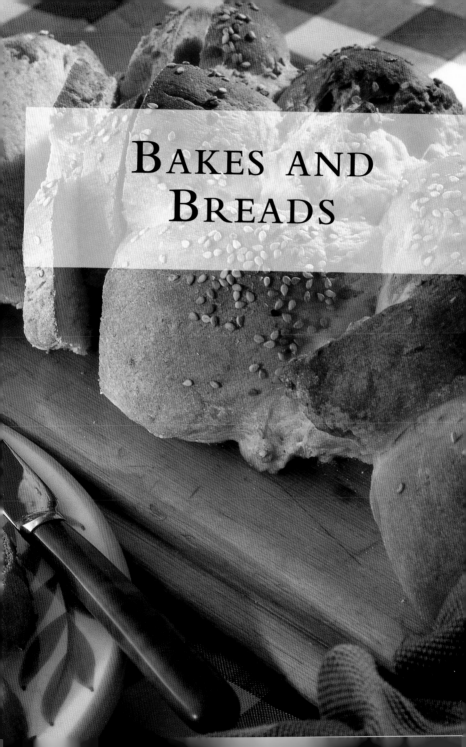

BAKES AND BREADS

Double Chocolate Chip Muffins

The generous pieces of white and plain chocolate in these muffins make them particularly delectable.

Makes 16

INGREDIENTS
400 g/14 oz/3½ cups plain (all-purpose) flour
15 ml/1 tbsp baking powder
30 ml/2 tbsp unsweetened cocoa powder
115 g/4 oz/¾ cup muscovado
  (molasses) sugar
2 eggs
150 ml/¼ pint/⅔ cup sour cream
150 ml/¼ pint/⅔ cup milk
60 ml/4 tbsp sunflower oil
175 g/6 oz white chocolate
175 g/6 oz plain (semisweet) chocolate
cocoa powder, for dusting

2 In a separate bowl, beat the eggs with the sour cream, milk and oil, then stir into the centre of the dry ingredients. Beat well, gradually incorporating the flour mixture to make a thick and creamy batter.

3 Chop both the white and the plain chocolate into small pieces, then stir into the batter mixture.

4 Spoon the mixture into the muffin cases, filling them almost to the top. Bake for 25–30 minutes, until they are well risen and firm to the touch. Cool on a wire rack, then dust with cocoa powder.

1 Preheat the oven to 190°C/375°F/ Gas 5. Place 16 paper muffin cases in muffin tins (pans) or deep bun tins. Sift the flour, baking powder and cocoa into a bowl and stir in the sugar. Make a well in the centre.

COOK'S TIP: If sour cream is not available, sour 150 ml/¼ pint/ ⅔ cup single (light) cream by stirring in 5 ml/1 tsp lemon juice and letting it stand until thickened.

Fresh Blueberry Muffins

Make these popular American treats in paper cases for moister muffins.

Makes 12

INGREDIENTS
275 g/10 oz/2½ cups plain (all-purpose) flour
15 ml/1 tbsp baking powder
75 g/3 oz/scant ½ cup caster
    (superfine) sugar
250 ml/8 fl oz/1 cup milk
3 eggs, beaten
115 g/4 oz/½ cup butter, melted
few drops of vanilla extract
225 g/8 oz/2 cups fresh or
    frozen blueberries

FOR THE TOPPING
50 g/2 oz/½ cup pecan nuts,
    coarsely chopped
30 ml/2 tbsp demerara (raw) sugar

1 Preheat the oven to 200°C/400°F/
Gas 6. Stand 12 paper muffin cases
in a muffin tin (pan) or simply grease
the tin thoroughly.

2 Sift the flour and baking powder
into a large bowl. Stir in the caster
sugar. Mix the milk, eggs, melted
butter and vanilla extract in a jug
(pitcher) and whisk lightly. Add to the
flour mixture and fold together lightly.

3 Fold in the blueberries, then divide
the mixture among the muffin cases.
Sprinkle a few nuts and a little demerara
sugar over the top of each. Bake for
20–25 minutes or until the muffins are
well risen and golden. Remove from
the tin and cool slightly on a wire rack.

Drop Scones

Serve these scones while still warm, with butter and jam.

Makes 24

INGREDIENTS
225 g/8 oz/2 cups self-raising
   (self-rising) flour
50 g/2 oz/4 tbsp caster
   (superfine) sugar
50 g/2 oz/4 tbsp butter, melted
1 egg
300 ml/½ pint/1¼ cups milk
15 g/½ oz/1 tbsp hard white fat (shortening)

1 Mix the flour and sugar together in
a bowl. Add the melted butter and egg
with two-thirds of the milk. Mix to a
smooth batter – it should be thin
enough to have a level surface.

2 Heat a griddle or a heavy frying
pan and wipe it with a little hard
white fat. When it is hot, drop in
spoonfuls of the mixture. When
bubbles come to the surface of the
scones, flip them over to cook until
golden on the other side.

3 Remove the scones from the pan
and keep them warm, wrapped in a
dishtowel, while you cook the rest of
the mixture. Serve warm.

VARIATION: Add a little ground
cinnamon with the flour if you like
lightly spiced pancakes.

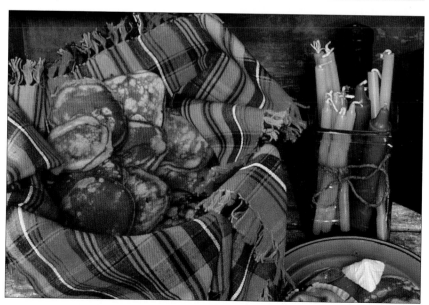

Cheese & Chive Scones

Feta cheese, used here instead of butter, gives these tangy savoury scones a lovely light texture and delicious flavour.

Makes 9

INGREDIENTS
115 g/4 oz/1 cup self-raising (self-rising) flour
150 g/5 oz/1 cup self-raising (self-rising) wholemeal (whole-wheat) flour
2.5 ml/½ tsp salt
75 g/3 oz feta cheese
15 ml/1 tbsp fresh chives
150 ml/¼ pint/⅔ cup milk, plus extra for glazing
1.5 ml/¼ tsp cayenne pepper

1 Preheat the oven to 200°C/400°F/ Gas 6. Sift the two different flours and the salt into a large mixing bowl, adding any bran that has been left over from the flour in the sieve (strainer).

2 Crumble the feta cheese and rub into the dry ingredients. Stir in the chives, then add the milk and mix to a soft dough.

3 Turn the dough out on to a floured surface and lightly knead until smooth. Roll out to a 2 cm/¾ in thickness and stamp out nine scones with a 6 cm/ 2½ in cookie cutter.

4 Transfer the scones to a non-stick baking sheet. Brush with a little milk, then sprinkle with a light dusting of cayenne pepper.

5 Bake the scones in the oven for 15 minutes, or until golden brown. Serve warm or cold.

316

Cheese Scones

These delicious scones make a good tea-time treat. They are best served fresh and still slightly warm.

Makes 12

INGREDIENTS
225 g/8 oz/2 cups plain (all-purpose) flour
12 ml/2½ tsp baking powder
2.5 ml/½ tsp dry mustard powder
2.5 ml/½ tsp salt
50 g/2 oz/4 tbsp butter, chilled
75 g/3 oz/¾ cup grated Cheddar cheese
150 ml/¼ pint/⅔ cup milk
1 egg, beaten

1 Preheat the oven to 230°C/450°F/ Gas 8. Sift the flour, baking powder, mustard powder and salt into a mixing bowl. Add the butter and rub it into the flour mixture until the mixture resembles breadcrumbs. Stir in 50 g/ 2 oz/½ cup of the cheese.

2 Make a well in the centre and add the milk and egg. Mix gently and then turn the dough out on to a lightly floured surface. Roll it out and cut it into triangles or squares.

3 Brush lightly with milk and sprinkle with the remaining cheese. Leave to rest for 15 minutes, then bake the scones for 15 minutes, or until risen.

Dill & Potato Scones

Potato scones are quite scrumptious and should be more widely made. Try this splendid combination and you are sure to be converted.

Makes 10

INGREDIENTS
225 g/8 oz/2 cups self-raising (self-rising) flour
40 g/1½ oz/3 tbsp butter, softened
pinch of salt
15 ml/1 tbsp finely chopped fresh dill
170 g/6 oz/scant 1 cup mashed potato, freshly made
30–45 ml/2–3 tbsp milk, as required

1 Preheat the oven to 230°C/450°F/Gas 8. Sift the flour into a bowl, and add the butter, salt and dill. Mix in the mashed potato and enough milk to make a soft, pliable dough.

2 Roll out the dough on a well-floured surface until it is fairly thin. Cut into neat rounds with a 7.5 cm/3 in cutter.

3 Bake the scones on a greased baking tray for 20–25 minutes, until risen and golden.

Brioche

Rich and buttery, yet light and airy, this wonderful loaf captures the essence of the classic French bread.

Makes 1 loaf

INGREDIENTS
350 g/12 oz/3 cups unbleached strong white
   bread flour
2.5 ml/½ tsp salt
15 g/½ oz fresh yeast
60 ml/4 tbsp lukewarm milk
3 eggs
175 g/6 oz/¾ cup butter, softened
25 g/1 oz/2 tbsp caster (superfine) sugar

FOR THE GLAZE
1 egg yolk
15 ml/1 tbsp milk

1 Sift the flour and salt into a large bowl and make a well in the centre. Stir together the yeast and milk. Add the yeast mixture to the well in the flour mixture with the eggs and mix together to form a soft dough.

2 Using your hand, beat the dough for 4–5 minutes until smooth and elastic. Cream the butter and sugar together. Gradually add the butter mixture to the dough in small amounts, making sure each amount is incorporated before adding more. Beat until smooth, shiny and elastic, then cover the bowl and leave in a warm place to rise for 1–2 hours.

3 Lightly knock back (punch down) the dough, then cover and place in the refrigerator for 8 hours or overnight.

4 Lightly grease a 1.6 litre/2¾ pint/ scant 7 cup brioche mould. Turn the dough out on to a lightly floured surface. Cut off almost a quarter, shape the rest into a ball and place in the mould. Shape the reserved dough into an elongated egg shape. Using two or three fingers, make a hole in the centre of the large ball of dough. Gently press the narrow end of the egg-shaped dough into the hole.

5 Mix together the egg yolk and milk for the glaze and brush a little over the brioche. Cover and leave in a warm place to rise for 1½–2 hours.

6 Meanwhile, preheat the oven to 230°C/450°F/Gas 8. Brush the brioche with the remaining glaze and bake for 10 minutes. Reduce the oven temperature to 190°C/375°F/Gas 5 and bake for a further 20–25 minutes, or until golden. Turn out on to a wire rack to cool.

Orange & Coriander Brioches

The warm, spicy flavour of coriander combines especially well with orange in these tempting little rolls.

Makes 12

INGREDIENTS
225 g/8 oz/2 cups strong white bread flour
10 ml/2 tsp easy-blend (rapid-rise)
   dried yeast
2.5 ml/½ tsp salt
15 ml/1 tbsp caster (superfine) sugar
10 ml/2 tsp coriander seeds,
   coarsely ground
grated rind of 1 orange
2 eggs, beaten
50 g/2 oz/4 tbsp unsalted (sweet)
   butter, melted
1 small (US medium) egg, beaten, to glaze
fine strips of orange rind,
   to decorate (optional)

1 Grease 12 individual brioche tins (pans). Sift the flour into a mixing bowl and stir in the yeast, salt, sugar, ground coriander seeds and orange rind.

2 Make a well in the centre of the mixture, pour in 30 ml/2 tbsp hand-hot water, the eggs and melted butter. Beat to form a soft dough.

3 Turn out the dough on to a lightly floured surface and knead it for 5 minutes until smooth and elastic. Return to the clean, lightly oiled bowl, cover with a damp dishtowel and leave in a warm place for 1 hour until doubled in bulk.

4 Turn on to a floured surface, knead again briefly and roll into a sausage. Cut into 12 pieces. Break off a quarter of each piece and set aside. Shape the larger pieces of dough into balls and place in the prepared tins.

5 With a floured wooden spoon, press a hole in each dough ball. Shape each small piece of dough into a little plug and press into the holes.

6 Place the tins on a baking sheet. Cover with a damp dishtowel and leave in a warm place until the dough rises almost to the top of the tins. Brush the brioches with beaten egg.

7 Preheat the oven to 220°C/425°F/ Gas 7. Bake the risen brioches for 15 minutes until golden brown. Scatter over a few fine strips of orange rind to decorate, if you like, and serve the brioches warm.

COOK'S TIP: These individual brioches look particularly attractive if they are made in special brioche tins (pans). However, they can also be made in bun tins or muffin tins.

Cheese and Courgette Cluster Bread

This unusual bread owes its moistness to grated courgettes, and its depth of flavour to freshly grated Parmesan.

Serves 8

INGREDIENTS

4 courgettes, coarsely grated
675 g/1½ lb/6 cups strong white bread flour
2 sachets easy-blend dried yeast
50 g/2 oz/⅔ cup freshly grated Parmesan
 cheese
30 ml/2 tbsp olive oil
milk, to glaze
poppy seeds or sesame seeds, to sprinkle
salt and ground black pepper

1 Put the grated courgettes into a colander and sprinkle with salt. Stand in a sink for about 20 minutes to drain the juices, then rinse thoroughly. Drain and pat dry with kitchen paper.

2 In a large bowl, mix the flour with the yeast, Parmesan and 2.5 ml/½ tsp salt. Add pepper to taste.

3 Stir in the oil and courgettes, then add enough hand-hot water to make a firm, but still soft dough. How much water you need depends on how wet the courgettes are, but start with about 45 ml/3 tbsp.

4 Gather the dough together with your hand, then turn it out on a lightly floured surface. Knead the dough for 5–10 minutes, or until it is smooth and elastic. Return to the bowl, cover with lightly oiled clear film and leave to rise in a warm place for about until doubled in bulk.

5 Punch down the dough and knead again. Divide it into eight pieces and roll into smooth balls.

6 Lightly grease a deep 23 cm/9 in cake tin. Fit the balls into the tin, placing one in the centre and the remainder around the outside.

7 Glaze the loaf with a little milk and sprinkle over poppy seeds or sesame seeds. Cover the tin lightly with oiled clear film and leave to rise in a warm place until the balls of dough have doubled in size.

8 Meanwhile, preheat the oven to 200°C/400°F/Gas 6. Bake the loaf for 35–45 minutes, until it is golden brown and sounds hollow when rapped on the base. Cool on a wire rack and eat as soon as possible.

VARIATION: Dry Jack could be used in place of Parmesan in this bread. Or try an aged Gouda or Pecorino.

Panettone

This classic bread can be found throughout Italy around Christmas. It is surprisingly light, even though it is rich with butter and dried fruit.

Makes 1 loaf

INGREDIENTS
400 g/14 oz/3½ cups unbleached strong
　　white bread flour
2.5 ml/½ tsp salt
15 g/½ oz fresh yeast
120 ml/4 fl oz/½ cup lukewarm milk
2 eggs
2 egg yolks
75 g/3 oz/6 tbsp caster (superfine) sugar
150 g/5 oz/⅔ cup butter, softened
115 g/4 oz/⅔ cup mixed chopped
　　(candied) peel
75 g/3 oz/½ cup raisins
melted butter, for brushing

1 Using a double layer of greaseproof paper, line and butter a 20 cm/8 in wide/15 cm/6 in deep cake tin (pan) or soufflé dish. Finish the paper 7.5 cm/3 in above the top of the tin.

2 Sift the flour and salt into a large bowl. Make a well in the centre. Cream the yeast with 60 ml/4 tbsp of the milk, then mix in the remainder.

3 Pour the yeast mixture into the centre of the flour, add the whole eggs and mix in sufficient flour to make a thick batter. Sprinkle a little of the remaining flour over the top and leave the batter to sponge, in a warm place, for 30 minutes.

4 Add the egg yolks and sugar and mix to a soft dough. Work in the softened butter, then turn out on to a lightly floured surface and knead for 5 minutes, until smooth and elastic. Place in a lightly oiled bowl, cover and leave to rise for 1½–2 hours.

5 Knock back (punch down) the dough and turn out on to a lightly floured surface. Gently knead in the peel and raisins. Shape into a ball and place in the prepared tin. Cover and leave to rise for about 1 hour.

6 Meanwhile, preheat the oven to 190°C/375°F/Gas 5. Brush the surface with melted butter, and cut a cross in the top using a sharp knife. Bake for 20 minutes, then reduce the oven temperature to 180°C/350°F/Gas 4. Brush the top with butter again and bake for a further 25–30 minutes, or until golden.

7 Allow the panettone to cool in the tin for 5–10 minutes, then turn it out on to a wire rack to cool.

COOK'S TIP: Once the dough has been enriched with butter, do not put to rise in too warm a place or the loaf will become greasy.

Greek Easter Bread

Traditionally decorated with red-dyed eggs, this bread is made by bakers and in homes throughout Greece at Easter.

Makes 1 loaf

INGREDIENTS
25 g/1 oz fresh yeast
15–30 ml/1–2 tbsp lukewarm water
120 ml/4 fl oz/½ cup lukewarm milk
675 g/1½ lb/6 cups strong white bread flour
2 eggs, beaten
2.5 ml/½ tsp caraway seeds
15 ml/1 tbsp caster (superfine) sugar
15 ml/1 tbsp brandy
50 g/2 oz/4 tbsp butter, melted
1 egg white, beaten
50 g/2 oz/½ cup split almonds

FOR THE EGGS
3 eggs
1.5 ml/¼ tsp bright red food
   colouring paste
15 ml/1 tbsp white wine vinegar
5 ml/1 tsp water
5 ml/1 tsp olive oil

1 First make the egg decoration. Place the eggs in a pan of water and bring to the boil. Allow to boil gently for 10 minutes.

2 Meanwhile, mix the red food colouring, vinegar, water and olive oil in a shallow bowl. Remove the eggs from the pan, place on a wire rack for a few seconds to dry, then roll in the colouring mixture. Return to the rack to cool and dry.

3 Crumble the yeast into a bowl. Mix with the water until softened. Add the milk and 115 g/4 oz/1 cup of the flour and mix to a creamy consistency. Cover and leave in a warm place for 1 hour.

4 Sift the remaining flour into a large bowl and make a well in the centre. Pour the yeast mixture into the well and draw in a little of the flour from the sides. Add the eggs, caraway seeds, sugar and brandy. Incorporate the remaining flour, until the mixture begins to form a dough.

5 Mix in the melted butter. Turn the dough on to a floured surface and knead for about 10 minutes, until smooth. Return to the bowl, cover and leave to rise for 3 hours.

6 Preheat the oven to 180°C/350°F/Gas 4. Knock back (punch down) the dough, turn on to a floured surface and knead for 2 minutes.

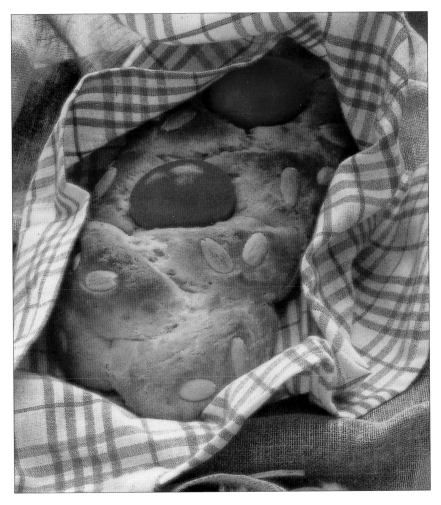

7 Divide the dough into three pieces and roll each piece into a long sausage shape. Make a braid and place the loaf on a greased baking sheet.

8 Tuck the ends under, brush with the egg white and decorate with the eggs and split almonds. Bake for about 1 hour. Cool on a wire rack.

Twelfth Night Bread

The traditional version of this Spanish bread contains a dried bean hidden inside – the lucky recipient is declared the king of the festival!

Makes 1 loaf

INGREDIENTS
450 g/1 lb/4 cups unbleached strong white
    bread flour
2.5 ml/½ tsp salt
25 g/1 oz fresh yeast
140 ml/scant ¼ pint/scant ⅔ cup mixed
    lukewarm milk and water
75 g/3 oz/6 tbsp butter
75 g/3 oz/6 tbsp caster (superfine) sugar
10 ml/2 tsp finely grated lemon rind
10 ml/2 tsp finely grated orange rind
2 eggs
15 ml/1 tbsp brandy
15 ml/1 tbsp orange flower water
dried bean (optional)
1 egg white, lightly beaten, for glazing

FOR THE DECORATION
a mixture of candied and glacé fruit slices
flaked (sliced) almonds

1 Lightly grease a large baking sheet. Sift the flour and salt into a large bowl. Make a well in the centre.

2 In a bowl, mix the yeast with the milk and water until the yeast has dissolved. Pour into the well and stir in enough of the flour to make a thick batter. Sprinkle a little of the remaining flour over the top of the batter and leave to sponge, in a warm place, for about 15 minutes, or until frothy.

3 Beat the butter and sugar together in a bowl until soft and creamy, then set aside.

4 Add the citrus rinds, eggs, brandy and orange flower water to the flour mixture and use a wooden spoon to mix to a sticky dough.

5 Using one hand, beat the mixture until it forms a fairly smooth dough. Gradually beat in the reserved butter mixture and beat for a few minutes until the dough is smooth and elastic. Cover and leave to rise for about 1½ hours.

6 Knock back (punch down) the dough and turn out on to a lightly floured surface. Gently knead for 2–3 minutes, incorporating the lucky bean, if using. Using a rolling pin, roll out the dough into a long strip measuring about 65 x 13 cm/26 x 5 in.

7 Roll up the dough from one long side like a Swiss roll (jelly roll) to make a long sausage shape. Place seam side down on the prepared baking sheet and seal the ends together. Cover and leave to rise for 1–1½ hours.

8 Meanwhile, preheat the oven to 180°C/350°F/Gas 4. Brush the dough ring with lightly beaten egg white and decorate with candied and glacé fruit slices, pushing them slightly into the dough. Sprinkle with almond flakes and bake for 30–35 minutes, or until risen and golden. Cool on a wire rack.

Malt Loaf

This is a rich and sticky loaf. If it lasts long enough to go stale, try toasting it for a delicious tea-time treat.

Makes 1 loaf

INGREDIENTS
150 ml/¼ pint/⅔ cup lukewarm milk
5 ml/1 tsp dried yeast
pinch of caster (superfine) sugar
350 g/12 oz/3 cups plain (all-purpose) flour
1.5 ml/¼ tsp salt
30 ml/2 tbsp light muscovado
    (brown) sugar
175 g/6 oz/generous 1 cup sultanas
    (golden raisins)
15 ml/1 tbsp sunflower oil
45 ml/3 tbsp malt extract

FOR THE GLAZE
30 ml/2 tbsp caster (superfine) sugar
30 ml/2 tbsp water

1 Pour the milk into a bowl. Sprinkle the yeast on top and add the sugar. Leave for 30 minutes, until frothy. Sift the flour and salt into a mixing bowl, stir in the muscovado sugar and sultanas, and make a well in the centre.

2 Add the yeast mixture together with the oil and the malt extract. Gradually incorporate the flour from the sides and mix to a soft dough, adding a little extra milk if necessary to achieve the right consistency.

3 Turn on to a floured surface and knead for about 5 minutes, until smooth and elastic. Grease a 450 g/ 1 lb loaf tin (pan).

4 Shape the dough and place it in the prepared tin. Cover and leave in a warm place to rise for 1–2 hours. Preheat the oven to 190°C/375°F/ Gas 5.

5 Bake the loaf for 30–35 minutes, until golden and ready. Meanwhile, prepare the glaze by dissolving the sugar in the water in a small pan. Bring to the boil, stirring, then lower the heat and simmer for 1 minute. Place the loaf on a wire rack and brush with the glaze while still hot. Leave the loaf to cool before serving.

VARIATION: To make buns, divide the dough into ten pieces, shape into rounds, leave to rise, then bake for about 15–20 minutes. Brush with the glaze while still hot.

Lardy Cake

This special rich fruit bread was originally made throughout many
counties of England for celebrating the harvest.

Serves 6

INGREDIENTS
450 g/1 lb/4 cups unbleached white bread
   flour
5 ml/1 tsp salt
15 g/½ oz/1 tbsp lard or white cooking fat
25 g/1 oz/2 tbsp caster (superfine) sugar
20 g/¾ oz fresh yeast
300 ml/½ pint/1¼ cups lukewarm water

FOR THE FILLING
75 g/3 oz/6 tbsp lard (shortening)
75 g/3 oz/6 tbsp soft light brown sugar
115 g/4 oz/½ cup currants, slightly warmed
75 g/3 oz/½ cup sultanas (golden raisins),
   slightly warmed
25 g/1 oz/3 tbsp mixed chopped (candied)
   peel
5 ml/1 tsp mixed (apple pie) spice

FOR THE GLAZE
10 ml/2 tsp sunflower oil
15–30 ml/1–2 tbsp caster (superfine) sugar

1 Grease a 25 x 20cm/10 x 8in
shallow roasting pan. Sift the flour and
salt into a large bowl and rub in the
lard, or white cooking fat. Stir in the
sugar and make a well in the centre.

2 In a bowl, cream the yeast with half
of the water, then blend in the
remainder. Add to the centre of the
flour and mix to a smooth dough.

3 Turn out on to a lightly floured
surface and knead for 10 minutes
until smooth and elastic. Place in a
lightly oiled bowl, cover with oiled
clear film (plastic wrap) and leave in
a warm place for 1 hour, or until
doubled in bulk.

4 Turn the dough out on to a lightly
floured surface and knock back (punch
down) until collapsed. Knead for 2–3
minutes. Roll into a rectangle about
5mm/¼in thick.

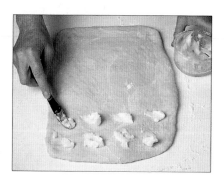

5 Using half the lard for the filling,
cover the top two-thirds of the dough
with flakes of lard. Sprinkle over half
the sugar, half the dried fruits and peel
and half the mixed spice. Fold the
bottom third up and the top third
down, sealing the edges with the
rolling pin.

6 Turn the dough by 90 degrees. Repeat the rolling and cover with the remaining lard or white cooking fat, fruit and peel and mixed spice. Fold, seal and turn as before. Roll out the dough to fit the prepared pan. Cover with lightly oiled clear film and leave to rise, in a warm place, for 30–45 minutes, or until doubled in size.

7 Meanwhile, preheat the oven to 200°C/400°F/Gas 6. Brush the top of the lardy cake with sunflower oil and sprinkle with caster sugar.

8 Score a criss-cross pattern on top using a sharp knife, then bake for 30–40 minutes until golden. Turn out on to a wire rack to cool slightly. Serve warm, cut into slices or squares.

Banana & Cardamom Bread

The combination of banana and cardamom is delicious in this soft-textured moist loaf. It is perfect for teatime, served with butter and jam.

Makes 1 loaf

INGREDIENTS
150 ml/¼ pint/⅔ cup warm water
5 ml/1 tsp dried yeast
pinch of sugar
10 cardamom pods
400 g/14 oz/3½ cups strong white
   bread flour
5 ml/1 tsp salt
30 ml/2 tbsp malt extract
2 ripe bananas, mashed
5 ml/1 tsp sesame seeds, to sprinkle

1 Put the water in a small bowl. Sprinkle the yeast on top, add the sugar and mix thoroughly. Leave for 10 minutes. Meanwhile, split the cardamom pods and remove the seeds. Chop the seeds finely.

2 Sift the flour and salt into a mixing bowl and make a well in the centre. Add the yeast mixture with the malt extract, chopped cardamom seeds and mashed bananas.

3 Gradually incorporate the flour and mix to a soft dough, adding a little extra water if necessary. Turn the dough on to a floured surface and knead for about 5 minutes, until smooth and elastic. Return to the clean bowl, cover and leave in a warm place to rise for about 2 hours.

4 Grease a baking sheet. Turn the dough on to a floured surface, knead briefly, then shape into a braid. Place the braid on the baking sheet, cover and leave to rise. Preheat the oven to 220°C/425°F/Gas 7.

5 Brush the braid lightly with water and sprinkle with the sesame seeds. Bake for 10 minutes, then lower the oven temperature to 200°C/400°F/Gas 6. Cook for 15 minutes more, or until the loaf is ready. Allow to cool on a wire rack.

Sultana & Walnut Bread

This bread is delicious with savoury or sweet toppings. Spread with butter or soft margarine and add salami, cheese, jam or honey.

Makes 1 loaf

INGREDIENTS
300 g/11 oz/2¾ cups strong white bread flour
2.5 ml/½ tsp salt
15 g/½ oz/1 tbsp butter
7.5 ml/1½ tsp easy-blend (rapid-rise)
    dried yeast
175 ml/6 fl oz/¾ cup lukewarm water
115 g/4 oz/scant 1 cup sultanas
    (golden raisins)
75 g/3 oz/½ cup walnuts, roughly chopped
melted butter, for brushing

1 Sift the flour and salt into a bowl, cut in the butter with a knife, then stir in the yeast.

2 Gradually add the lukewarm water, stirring with a spoon at first, then gathering the dough together with your hands.

3 Turn the dough out on to a floured surface. Knead for about 10 minutes, until smooth and elastic.

4 Knead the sultanas and walnuts into the dough until they are evenly distributed. Shape into an oval shape, place on a lightly oiled baking sheet, cover and leave in a warm place to rise for 1–2 hours. Preheat the oven to 220°C/425°F/Gas 7.

5 Uncover the loaf and bake for 10 minutes, then reduce the oven temperature to 190°C/375°F/Gas 5. Bake for a further 20–25 minutes.

6 Transfer the loaf to a wire rack, brush with the melted butter and cover with a dishtowel. Allow the loaf to cool before slicing.

Barm Brack

It used to be traditional to bake a wedding ring in this Irish Hallowe'en bread as a marriage charm.

Makes 1 loaf

INGREDIENTS

675 g/1½ lb/6 cups plain (all-purpose) flour
2.5 ml/½ tsp mixed (apple pie) spice
5 ml/1 tsp salt
1 sachet easy-blend (rapid-rise)
 dried yeast
50 g/2 oz/¼ cup caster (superfine) sugar
300 ml/½ pint/1¼ cups
 lukewarm milk
150 ml/¼ pint/⅔ cup
 lukewarm water
50 g/2 oz/4 tbsp butter, softened
225 g/8 oz/1⅓ cups sultanas (golden raisins)
50 g/2 oz/⅓ cup currants
50 g/2 oz/⅓ cup chopped mixed
 (candied) peel
milk, for glazing

1 Sift the plain flour, mixed spice and salt into a large bowl. Stir in the dried yeast and 15 ml/1 tbsp of the caster sugar. Make a well in the centre and pour in the lukewarm milk and water.

2 Mix well, gradually incorporating the dry ingredients to make a sticky dough. Place on a lightly floured board and knead the dough until smooth and elastic. Put into a clean bowl. Cover and leave to rise for about 1 hour.

3 Knead the dough lightly on a floured surface. Add the remaining ingredients, apart from the milk for glazing, and work them in. Return the dough to the bowl, cover and leave to rise for 30 minutes.

4 Grease a 23 cm/9 in round cake tin (pan). Pat the dough to a neat round and fit it in the tin. Cover and leave to rise for about 45 minutes.

5 Preheat the oven to 200°C/400°F/Gas 6. Brush the loaf lightly with milk and bake for 15 minutes. Cover the loaf with foil, reduce the oven temperature to 180°C/350°F/Gas 4 and bake for 45 minutes more, or until golden and ready. Cool on a wire rack.

Split Tin

As its name suggests, this popular and homely loaf is so called because of the distinctive centre split.

Makes 1 loaf

INGREDIENTS
500 g/1¼ lb/5 cups strong white bread flour,
    plus extra for dusting
10 ml/2 tsp salt
15 g/½ oz fresh yeast
300 ml/½ pint/1¼ cups lukewarm water
60 ml/4 tbsp lukewarm milk

1 Lightly grease a 900 g/2 lb loaf tin (pan). Sift the flour and salt into a bowl and make a well in the centre. Mix the yeast with the lukewarm water. Pour the yeast mixture into the well and mix in a little flour with your fingers. Gradually mix in more of the flour from around the edge of the bowl to form a thick, smooth batter.

2 Sprinkle a little more flour from around the edge of the bowl over the batter and leave in a warm place to sponge. Add the lukewarm milk and remaining flour; mix to a firm dough.

3 Knead on a lightly floured surface for about 10 minutes, until smooth and elastic. Place in a lightly oiled bowl, cover and leave in a warm place to rise for 1–1¼ hours.

4 Knock back (punch down) the dough and turn out on to a lightly floured surface. Shape it into a rectangle the length of the tin. Roll up lengthways, tuck the ends under and place seam side down in the tin. Cover and leave to rise for 20–30 minutes.

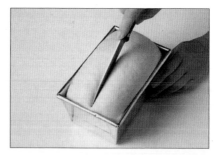

5 Using a sharp knife, make a deep slash along the length of the bread; dust with flour. Leave for 15 minutes.

6 Meanwhile, preheat the oven to 230°C/450°F/Gas 8. Bake for 15 minutes, then reduce the oven temperature to 200°C/400°F/Gas 6. Bake for 20–25 minutes more, or until the bread is golden and ready. Turn out on to a wire rack to cool.

COOK'S TIP: Another sure sign that the loaf is ready is that it will have shrunk slightly away from the sides of the tin (pan).

Country Bread

This traditional American loaf, made with a mixture of wholemeal and white flours, not only tastes delicious, but also looks wonderful.

Makes 2 loaves

INGREDIENTS
275 g/10 oz/2½ cups wholemeal
  (whole-wheat) flour, plus extra for dusting
275 g/10 oz/2½ cups plain (all-purpose) flour
115 g/4 oz/1 cup strong white
  bread flour
20 ml/4 tsp salt
50 g/2 oz/4 tbsp butter,
  at room temperature
475 ml/16 fl oz/2 cups lukewarm milk

FOR THE STARTER
1 sachet easy-blend (rapid-rise)
  dried yeast
250 ml/8 fl oz/1 cup lukewarm water
115 g/4 oz/1 cup plain (all-purpose) flour
1.5 ml/¼ tsp sugar

1 For the starter, stir together the yeast, water, flour and sugar. Cover and leave in a warm place for 2–3 hours or overnight in a cool place.

2 Place the flours, salt and butter in a food processor and process for 1–2 minutes, until just blended. Stir together the milk and starter, then slowly pour into the processor, with the motor running, until the mixture forms a dough. If necessary, add more water. Alternatively, mix the dough by hand. Transfer to a floured surface and knead until smooth and elastic.

3 Place in an ungreased bowl, cover and leave to rise for about 1½ hours.

4 Transfer to a floured surface and knead briefly. Return to the clean bowl and leave to rise for about 1½ hours.

5 Divide the dough in half. Cut off one-third of the dough from each half and shape into balls. Shape the larger remaining portion of each half into balls. Grease a baking sheet.

6 Top each large ball with a small one. Press the centre with the handle of a wooden spoon to secure. Slash the top, cover with a plastic bag and let rise.

7 Preheat the oven to 200°C/400°F/ Gas 6. Bake the dough, sprinkled with wholemeal flour, for 45–50 minutes, until browned. Cool on a rack.

Granary Cob

You can make this loaf plain, with a slash across the top for a Danish cob or with a cross cut in the top for a Coburg cob.

Makes 1 loaf

INGREDIENTS
450 g/1 lb/4 cups Granary (whole-wheat) flour
10 ml/2 tsp salt
15 g/½ oz fresh yeast
300 ml/½ pint/1¼ cups lukewarm water or milk and water mixed

FOR THE TOPPING
30 ml/2 tbsp water
2.5 ml/½ tsp salt
wheat flakes or cracked wheat

1 Lightly flour a baking sheet. Sift the flour and salt into a bowl and make a well in the centre. Place in a very low oven for 5 minutes to warm.

2 Mix the yeast with a little of the lukewarm water or milk mixture then blend in the rest. Add the yeast mixture to the centre of the warmed Granary flour and mix well to form a dough.

3 Turn the dough out on to a lightly floured surface and knead for about 10 minutes, until smooth and elastic. Place in a lightly oiled bowl, cover and leave in a warm place to rise for 1¼ hours.

4 Turn the dough out on to a lightly floured surface and knock back (punch down). Knead for 2–3 minutes, then roll into a ball. Place on the prepared baking sheet. Cover with an inverted bowl and leave to rise again for 30–45 minutes.

5 For the topping, mix the water and salt and brush over the bread. Sprinkle the surface with wheat flakes or cracked wheat. Preheat the oven to 230°C/450°F/Gas 8.

6 Bake the Granary loaf for 15 minutes, then reduce the oven temperature to 200°C/400°F/Gas 6 and bake for 20 minutes more, or until the loaf is ready. Leave to cool on a wire rack.

Jams, Jellies and Preserves

Strawberry Jam

Capture the essence of summer in a jar of home-made strawberry jam – a favourite with old and young alike.

Makes about 1.5 kg/3 lb

INGREDIENTS
1 kg/2¼ lb/8 cups small strawberries
900 g/2 lb/4½ cups
    granulated sugar
juice of 2 lemons
scones and clotted cream,
    to serve (optional)

1 Place the strawberries in layers in a large bowl, sprinkling each layer with sugar. Cover and leave overnight.

COOK'S TIPS: For best results, don't wash the strawberries. Instead, brush off any dirt, or wipe the strawberries with a damp cloth. If you have to wash any, pat them dry and then spread them out on a clean dishtowel to dry further. This jam can be stored in a cool, dark place for up to 1 year.

2 The next day, scrape the fruit and juice into a large, heavy pan. Add the lemon juice. Gradually bring to the boil over a low heat, stirring until the sugar has dissolved.

3 Boil steadily for 10–15 minutes, or until the jam reaches setting point. Cool for 10 minutes.

4 Pour the jam into warm sterilized jars, filling them right to the top. Cover and seal the jars while hot and label when cold. Serve the jam with scones and clotted cream, if you like.

Rhubarb & Ginger Mint Jam

Ginger mint is easily grown in the garden, and is just the thing to boost the flavour of rhubarb jam.

Makes about 2.75 kg/6 lb

INGREDIENTS
2 kg/4½ lb rhubarb, trimmed
250 ml/8 fl oz/1 cup water
juice of 1 lemon
5 cm/2 in piece fresh root
  ginger
1.5 kg/3 lb/6¾ cups sugar
115 g/4 oz/⅔ cup stem
  ginger, chopped
30–45 ml/2–3 tbsp very finely chopped
  ginger mint leaves

1 Cut the rhubarb into 2.5 cm/1 in pieces. Place the rhubarb, water and lemon juice in a large, heavy pan and bring to the boil.

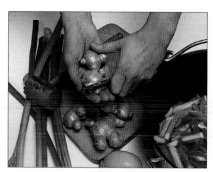

2 Peel and bruise the root ginger and add it to the pan. Simmer, stirring frequently, until the rhubarb is soft, then remove the ginger.

3 Add the sugar and stir until it has dissolved. Bring the mixture to the boil and boil rapidly for 10–15 minutes, or until setting point is reached. With a metal slotted spoon, remove any scum from the surface.

4 Add the stem ginger and ginger mint leaves. Pour into warm, sterilized jars, cover and seal while the jam is hot and label when cold.

VARIATION: If ginger mint is not available you can substitute garden or apple mint. Avoid peppermint or Moroccan mint as these are more suitable for making mint tea.

COOK'S TIP: The early, forced rhubarb has the finest flavour.

Melon & Star Anise Jam

Melon and ginger are classic companions. The addition of star anise imparts a wonderful aromatic flavour to the jam.

Makes 450 g/1 lb

INGREDIENTS
2 charentais or cantaloupe melons,
   peeled and seeded
450 g/1 lb/2¼ cups granulated sugar
2 star anise
4 pieces preserved stem ginger in syrup,
   drained and finely chopped
finely grated rind and juice of
   2 lemons

2 Pour the marinated melons and their juice into a large, heavy pan and add the star anise, chopped stem ginger, finely grated lemon rind and juice.

3 Bring to the boil over a medium heat, stirring to ensure that all the sugar has dissolved, then lower the heat. Simmer for 25 minutes, or until the melon has become transparent and the setting point has been reached. If preferred, remove the star anise, using a slotted spoon.

1 Dice the melons and layer with the granulated sugar in a large non-metallic bowl. Cover with clear film (plastic wrap) and leave overnight so the melons can release their juices.

4 Spoon the jam into warm, sterilized jars. Cover the fruit with liquid and seal while it is hot and label when cold. It will keep for several months in a cool, dark cupboard. Once a jar has been opened, the jam should be stored in the refrigerator and used within 2 weeks.

COOK'S TIP: The large amount of sugar is necessary for proper jelling. Use this jam in savoury dishes instead of honey to add a spicy, non-cloying sweetness.

Dried Apricot Jam

Make this jam when reserves look low in winter.

Makes about 2 kg/4½ lb

INGREDIENTS

675 g/1½ lb dried apricots
900 ml/1½ pints/3¾ cups apple juice made
   with concentrate
juice and rind of 2 lemons
675 g/1½ lb/3½ cups preserving sugar
50 g/2 oz/⅓ cup blanched almonds,
   coarsely chopped

1 Put the apricots in a large bowl
and add the apple juice. Set aside to
soak overnight.

2 Pour the apricots and juice into a
pan and add the lemon juice and rind.
Bring to the boil, lower the heat and
simmer for 15–20 minutes.

3 Meanwhile, warm the sugar in a
low oven. Add the warm sugar to the
apricots and bring back to the boil,
stirring constantly until the sugar has
completely dissolved. Boil until setting
point is reached.

4 Stir in the chopped almonds and set
aside for 15 minutes. Pour the apricot
jam into warm, sterilized jars. Cover
and seal while the jam is hot and label
when cold.

VARIATION: This recipe would
also work well using dried peaches
instead of the apricots.

Clementine Marmalade

Coriander seeds impart a warm and spicy flavour to this marmalade.

Makes about 2.75 kg/6 lb

INGREDIENTS
1.5 kg/3 lb clementines
6 lemons
30 ml/2 tbsp coriander seeds, roasted and
   roughly crushed
3 litres/5¼ pints/12 cups water
1.5 kg/3 lb/6¾ cups
   preserving sugar

1 Cut the clementines and lemons in half. Squeeze all the fruit and pour the juice into a large, heavy pan.

2 Scrape the pith from the citrus shells and tie it, with the pips (seeds) and half the coriander, in muslin (cheesecloth). Add the bag to the juice.

3 Slice the clementine and lemon peels into fine shreds and add them to the pan with the water.

4 Bring the water to the boil, lower the heat and simmer for 1½ hours or until the peel is very soft. Remove the muslin bag. Holding it over the pan, squeeze it between two saucers.

5 Add the sugar and the remaining coriander to the pan and stir over a low heat until dissolved. Boil rapidly until setting point is reached. Skim the surface, then leave to stand for 30 minutes, stirring occasionally. Pour into warm, sterilized jars, cover and seal while the marmalade is hot and label when cold.

Three-fruit Marmalade

This zesty marmalade is incomparably better than store-bought varieties.

Makes 2.75 kg/6 lb

INGREDIENTS
350 g/12 oz oranges
350 g/12 oz lemons
675 g/1½ lb grapefruit
2.5 litres/4½ pints/10 cups water
2.75 kg/6 lb/14 cups granulated sugar

3 Remove the fruit from the pan and cut it into quarters. Scrape out the pulp and add it to the pan with the cooking liquid.

1 Remove any labels from the oranges, lemons and grapefruit, then rinse and gently scrub the fruit with a vegetable brush.

2 Put all the fruit and water in a large, heavy pan. Ensure that the water covers the fruit. Bring to the boil then simmer, uncovered, for 2 hours. Leave in the pan until the fruit is cool enough to be handled.

VARIATION: You can adjust the amount of orange or lemon in this recipe, keeping the same total weight, to produce a sweeter or tarter flavour.

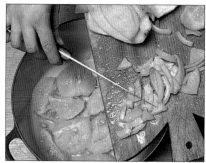

4 Cut the rinds into slivers and add to the pan. Add the sugar. Gently heat until the sugar has dissolved. Bring to the boil and cook until a setting point is reached. Leave to stand for 1 hour to allow the peel to settle. Pour into warm, sterilized jars, cover and seal while the marmalade is hot and label when cold.

Lemon & Lime Curd

Serve this creamy, tangy spread with toast or muffins, instead of jam, for a delightful change of flavour and texture.

Makes 900 g/2 lb

INGREDIENTS
115 g/4 oz/½ cup unsalted (sweet) butter
3 eggs
2 lemons and 2 limes
225 g/8 oz/generous 1 cup caster
  (superfine) sugar

1 Put the butter in a mixing bowl placed over a pan of simmering water, but not touching the surface.

3 Finely grate the rinds of the lemons and limes, then cut them in half and squeeze the juice. Add the lemon and lime rinds and juices to the eggs and butter, then add the sugar.

2 Lightly beat the eggs with a fork and add them to the butter.

4 Stir the mixture constantly until it thickens. Pour into small, warm sterilized jars. Cover and seal while the curd is hot and label when cold. The lemon and lime curd will keep unopened for up to a month. Once opened, keep in the refrigerator and consume within a week.

Bramble Jelly

This jelly has to be made with hand-picked wild blackberries for the best flavour. Include a few red, unripe berries for a good set.

Makes 900 g/2 lb

INGREDIENTS
900 g/2 lb/8 cups blackberries
300 ml/½ pint/1¼ cups water
juice of 1 lemon
about 900 g/2 lb/4½ cups caster
    (superfine) sugar
hot buttered toast or English muffins,
    to serve

1 Put the blackberries, water and lemon juice into a large, heavy pan. Cover the pan and cook over a gentle heat for 15–30 minutes, or until the blackberries are very soft.

2 Ladle into a jelly bag or a large sieve (strainer) lined with muslin (cheesecloth) and set over a large bowl. Leave to drip overnight to obtain the maximum amount of juice. Do not squeeze the bag as this will make the jelly cloudy.

3 Discard the fruit pulp. Measure the juice and allow 450 g/1 lb/2¼ cups sugar to every 600 ml/1 pint/2½ cups juice. Place the sugar and blackberry juice in a large, heavy pan and bring the mixture slowly to the boil, stirring constantly until the sugar has dissolved.

4 Boil rapidly until setting point is reached. This will take about 10 minutes. Cool for 10 minutes. Skim off any scum and pour the jelly into warm, sterilized jars. Cover and seal while the jelly is hot and label when cold. Serve the jelly with hot buttered toast or muffins.

VARIATION: Redcurrant jelly is made in the same way, but with less sugar. Reduce the quantity to 350 g/12 oz/1⅔ cups for every 600 ml/1 pint/2½ cups juice.

Crab Apple & Lavender Jelly

This delicate, clear jelly with its fragrance of summer looks even prettier with a sprig of fresh lavender suspended in the jar.

Makes about 900 g/2 lb

INGREDIENTS
900 g/2 lb/5 cups crab apples
1.75 litres/3 pints/7½ cups water
lavender stems
900 g/2 lb/4½ cups
    granulated sugar

3 Discard the crab apple pulp and measure the quantity of juice in the bowl. To each 600 ml/1 pint/2½ cups of juice add 450 g/1 lb/2¼ cups granulated sugar. Put the measured sugar and juice into a clean pan.

4 Heat the juice gently, stirring occasionally, until the sugar has dissolved. Bring to the boil and boil rapidly for about 8–10 minutes, until setting point has been reached. Remove the pan from the heat.

5 Skim the jelly with a slotted spoon. Ladle it into warm, sterilized jars. Dip the lavender stems quickly into boiling water, gently shake off the excess water, then insert a stem into each jar. Cover and seal while the jelly is hot and label the jars when cold.

1 Cut the unpeeled crab apples into chunks and place in a large, heavy pan with the water and 2 stems of lavender. Bring to the boil, cover and simmer very gently, stirring occasionally, for 1 hour, until the fruit is pulpy.

2 Pour the apple mixture into a large jelly bag or a sieve (strainer) lined with muslin (cheesecloth) and set over a large bowl. Leave to drain for several hours or overnight. Do not squeeze the bag or the jelly will become cloudy.

Crab Apple Jelly

Serve this jelly with scones or use it to glaze an apple tart.

Makes about 1 kg/2¼ lb from each 600 ml/1 pint/ 2½ cups liquid

INGREDIENTS
1 kg/2¼ lb/5⅔ cups crab apples
3 cloves
about 900 g/2 lb/4½ cups preserving sugar

1 Wash the apples and halve them, but do not peel or core. Place the apples and cloves in a large, heavy pan and cover with water. Bring to the boil, lower the heat and simmer until soft.

2 Ladle into a large jelly bag or a sieve (strainer) lined with muslin (cheesecloth) and set over a large bowl. Leave to drain.

3 Warm the sugar in a low oven (120°C/250°F/Gas ½) for 15 minutes. Measure the juice and discard the fruit. Allow 450 g/1 lb/2¼ cups sugar for each 600 ml/1 pint/2½ cups of juice.

4 Put the juice and sugar in a large, heavy pan. Heat gently, stirring until the sugar dissolves, then boil rapidly until setting point is reached. Pour into warm, sterilized jars, cover and seal while the jelly is still hot and label when cold.

Rosehip & Apple Jelly

You can use windfall apples and rosehips from the hedgerows.

Makes about 1 kg/2¼ lb from each 600 ml/1 pint/ 2½ cups liquid

INGREDIENTS
1 kg/2¼ lb cooking apples, peeled, trimmed and quartered
450 g/1 lb firm, ripe rosehips
preserving sugar

1 Put the apples in a large, heavy pan with just enough water to cover, plus 300 ml/½ pint/1¼ cups extra. Bring to the boil and cook the apples until they are a pulp. Coarsely chop the rosehips in a food processor. Add them to the pan and simmer for 10 minutes.

2 Leave to stand for 10 minutes, then ladle into a jelly bag or sieve (strainer) lined with muslin (cheesecloth) and set over a bowl. Leave to drain overnight.

3 Measure the juice and discard the fruit. Allow 400 g/14 oz/2 cups sugar for each 600 ml/1 pint/2½ cups of liquid. Warm the sugar in a low oven. Bring the juice to the boil in a large, heavy pan and add the sugar. Stir until it has dissolved, then boil until setting point is reached. Pour into warm, sterilized jars, cover and seal while the jelly is still hot and label when cold.

Rose Petal Jelly

This subtle jelly is ideal for traditional afternoon teas with thinly sliced bread and butter – it adds a real summer flavour.

Makes about 900 g/2 lb

INGREDIENTS
600 ml/1 pint/2½ cups red or
    pink roses
450 ml/¾ pint/scant 2 cups water
700 g/1 lb 9 oz/3½ cups caster
    (superfine) sugar
100 ml/3½ fl oz/scant ½ cup white
    grape juice
100 ml/3½ fl oz/scant ½ cup red
    grape juice
50 g/2 oz packet powdered
    fruit pectin
30 ml/2 tbsp rosewater

1 Carefully pull the rose petals away from the flower and trim them at the base to remove the white tips. Place the petals, water and about one-eighth of the sugar in a pan and bring to the boil. Reduce the heat and simmer for 5 minutes. Remove from the heat and leave to stand overnight for the rose fragrance to infuse.

2 Strain the flowers from the syrup, and put the syrup in a large, heavy pan. Add the grape juices and pectin. Boil hard for 1 minute.

3 Add the remaining sugar and stir well. Boil the mixture hard for 1 minute more. Remove from the heat. Test for setting point – it should make a soft jelly, not a thick jam.

4 Finally, add the rosewater. Ladle the jelly into warm, sterilized jars, cover and seal while the jelly is hot and label when cold.

COOK'S TIP: Powdered pectin is needed here because the jelly does not include fruit which contains its own pectin.

Jellies should be bright and clear and not too firmly set.

Mint & Apple Jelly

Makes 4 small jars

INGREDIENTS
1.5 kg/3 lb cooking apples
150 ml/¼ pint/⅔ cup cider vinegar
750 ml/1¼ pints/3 cups water
500–675 g/1¼–1½ lb/3–3½ cups
    granulated sugar
60 ml/4 tbsp chopped fresh mint
few drops green food colouring (optional)

1 Roughly chop the apples, including cores and skin, and put into a large, heavy pan. Add the vinegar and water and bring to the boil. Reduce the heat and simmer for 30 minutes, or until the apples are pulpy.

2 Ladle the apple mixture into a jelly bag or sieve (strainer) lined with muslin (cheesecloth) and set over a bowl. Drain for several hours.

3 Measure the juice and pour back into the pan. For each 600 ml/1 pint/ 2½ cups of juice, add 450 g/1 lb/ 2¼ cups sugar. Boil until the sugar has completely dissolved.

4 Boil rapidly for 10–15 minutes, or until setting point is reached. Skim with a slotted spoon. Stir in the mint and food colouring, if liked. Ladle into warm, sterilized jars, cover and seal while hot.

Apple & Strawberry Jelly

This delicious jelly can be served with scones or home-made bread.

Makes 5 medium-sized jars

INGREDIENTS
900 g/2 lb cooking apples
1.2 litres/2 pints/5 cups water
900 g/2 lb strawberries
1 kg/2¼ lb/generous 5 cups
    granulated sugar
5 stems rosemary

1 Chop the apples, including cores and skin, and put in a large heavy pan with the water. Bring to the boil and simmer for 15 minutes. Thickly slice the strawberries, add them to the pan, bring back to the boil and simmer for 15 minutes.

2 Ladle the fruit mixture into a large jelly bag or a sieve (strainer) lined with muslin (cheesecloth) and set over a large bowl. Leave to drain for several hours or overnight.

3 Measure the juice and add 450 g/1 lb/2¼ cups sugar to every 600 ml/1 pint/2½ cups juice. Dissolve the sugar slowly then boil rapidly until setting point is reached.

4 Skim the jelly with a slotted spoon. Ladle it into warm, sterilized jars and leave to stand for 10 minutes. Add a sprig of rosemary to each jar, cover and seal. Label the jars when cold.

Red Pepper & Rosemary Jelly

This wonderful amber-coloured jelly may be made with either red or yellow peppers and flavoured with any full-flavoured herbs.

Makes 1.75 kg/4 lb

INGREDIENTS
450 g/1 lb/8 tomatoes, quartered
4 red (bell) peppers, seeded and chopped
2 red chillies, seeded and chopped
rosemary sprigs, blanched in boiling water
300 ml/½ pint/1¼ cups water
300 ml/½ pint/1¼ cups red wine vinegar
2.5 ml/½ tsp salt
900 g/2 lb/4½ cups preserving sugar
250 ml/8 fl oz/1 cup liquid pectin

3 Place the juice in a clean pan with the vinegar, salt and sugar. Heat gently, stirring occasionally, until the sugar has dissolved. Boil rapidly for 3 minutes.

4 Remove the pan from the heat and stir in the liquid pectin. Skim the surface with a piece of kitchen paper to remove any foam.

1 Place the tomatoes, peppers, chillies, a few rosemary sprigs and the water into a large, heavy pan and bring to the boil. Cover and simmer for 1 hour, or until the peppers are tender and pulpy.

2 Ladle the mixture into a large jelly bag or a sieve (strainer) lined with muslin (cheesecloth) and set over a large bowl. Leave to drain for several hours or, preferably, overnight.

5 Pour the liquid into warm, sterilized jars and add a sprig of rosemary to each jar. Cover and seal while hot and label when cold.

Fruits in Liqueur

Choose from apricots, clementines, kumquats, physalis, cherries, strawberries, raspberries, peaches, plums, star fruit or seedless grapes and team them with rum, brandy, kirsch or Cointreau.

Makes 450 g/1 lb

INGREDIENTS
450 g/1 lb/3 cups fresh fruit
225 g/8 oz/generous 1 cup
  granulated sugar
300 ml/½ pint/1¼ cups water
150 ml/¼ pint/⅔ cup liqueur or spirit

1 Wash the fruit. Halve and stone (pit) apricots, plums or peaches. Slice star fruit (carambola), remove the husk from physalis, hull strawberries or raspberries, and prick kumquats, cherries or grapes all over with a cocktail stick (toothpick). Pare the rind from clementines using a sharp knife, taking care not to include any white pith.

2 Place 115 g/4 oz/scant ½ cup of the sugar and the water into a pan. Heat gently, stirring occasionally, until the sugar has dissolved. Bring to the boil.

3 Add the fruit and simmer gently for 1–2 minutes, until the fruit is just tender, but the skins are intact and the fruits are whole.

4 Carefully remove the fruit using a slotted spoon and arrange neatly in warm, sterilized jars. Add the remaining sugar to the syrup in the pan and stir until dissolved.

5 Boil the syrup rapidly until it reaches 107°C/225°F or the thread stage. Test by pressing a small amount of syrup between 2 teaspoons; when they are pulled apart, a thread should form. Allow to cool.

6 Measure the cooled syrup, then add an equal quantity of liqueur or spirit. Mix until blended. Pour over the fruit until covered. Seal each jar and keep for up to 4 months.

Fruit Preserves

The time to make these luxurious preserves is in high summer when the fruit is at its cheapest and most flavoursome. They are delicious served with cream or ice cream.

Brandied Peaches

Makes 1.75 kg/4 lb peaches, plus syrup

INGREDIENTS
1.75 kg/4 lb/10¼ cups granulated sugar
600 ml/1 pint/2½ cups water
2 cinnamon sticks, broken
15 ml/1 tbsp cloves
1.75 kg/4 lb ripe but firm peaches, scalded and peeled
400 ml/14 fl oz/1⅔ cups brandy

1 Dissolve the sugar in the water in a pan over a gentle heat. Tie the cinnamon sticks and cloves in a piece of muslin (cheesecloth) and add them to the sugar water. Bring to the boil.

2 Add the peaches, a few at a time, and simmer each batch for about 5 minutes, until just tender. Drain the cooked peaches, pouring the syrup back into the pan. When all the peaches are cooked, boil the syrup until it has thickened slightly. Cool for 10 minutes.

3 Stir the brandy into the syrup. Pack the peaches into hot, sterilized bottles, cover with the syrup and seal.

Cherries in Eau-de-vie

Makes 450 g/1 lb cherries, plus syrup

INGREDIENTS
450 g/1 lb/2⅔ cups ripe cherries
8 blanched almonds
90 ml/6 tbsp granulated sugar
550 ml/18 fl oz/2½ cups eau-de-vie

1 Wash and pit the cherries and then pack them, together with the blanched almonds, into a sterilized, wide-necked bottle.

2 Spoon the sugar over the cherries and almonds, then add the eau-de-vie so that the cherries are just covered. Seal the top securely.

3 Store in a cool, dark place for 1 month before using the cherries, shaking the bottle from time to time to help dissolve the sugar.

COOK'S TIP: Whole, preserved cherries can also be dipped in melted chocolate.

Poached Spiced Plums in Brandy

Makes 900 g/2 lb

INGREDIENTS
600 ml/1 pint/2½ cups brandy
rind of 1 lemon, peeled in a long strip
350 g/12 oz/1⅔ cups caster (superfine) sugar
1 cinnamon stick
900 g/2 lb fresh plums

1 Put the brandy, lemon rind, sugar and cinnamon stick in a large pan and heat gently to dissolve the sugar. Add the plums and poach for about 15 minutes, or until soft. Remove with a slotted spoon.

2 Reduce the syrup by a third by rapid boiling. Strain it over the plums. Bottle the plums in large sterilized jars. Seal tightly and store for up to 6 months in a cool, dark place.

COOK'S TIP: This recipe would also work well with golden plums or damsons. For an extra fruity flavour, you could use plum brandy, quetsch or prunella, and mirabelle would be ideal for golden plums.

Above: Poached Spiced Plums in Brandy

Raspberry Preserve

The wonderfully fresh flavour of this fruit preserve turns a home-made scone or teabread into a delicious treat.

Makes 900 g/2 lb

INGREDIENTS
675 g/1½ lb/4 cups raspberries
900 g/2 lb/4½ cups caster
   (superfine) sugar
30 ml/2 tbsp lemon juice
120 ml/4 fl oz/½ cup
   liquid pectin

1 Place the raspberries in a large bowl and lightly crush with a wooden spoon. Stir in the caster sugar. Leave for 1 hour at room temperature, stirring occasionally.

2 Add the lemon juice and pectin to the raspberries and stir until thoroughly blended.

3 Spoon the raspberry mixture into sterilized jars, leaving a 1 cm/½ in space at the top if the jam is to be frozen. Cover the surface of each with a baking parchment disc and seal with a lid or cellophane paper and a rubber band. Do not use a screw-topped lid if the jam is to be frozen. Label and freeze for up to 6 months, or refrigerate for up to 4 weeks.

Traditional Mincemeat

Mince pies are an essential part of the traditional Christmas fare, enjoyed in considerable quantities throughout the holiday.

Makes about 1.75 g/4 lb

INGREDIENTS
450 g/1 lb cooking apples
225 g/8 oz/1½ cups candied citrus peel
225 g/8 oz/1 cup currants
225 g/8 oz/1⅓ cups sultanas (golden raisins)
450 g/1 lb/3¼ cups seedless raisins
115 g/4 oz/⅔ cup blanched almonds, chopped
225 g/8 oz/1⅔ cup suet (US chilled, grated
   shortenings) or vegetarian suet
225 g/8 oz/1 cup soft dark brown sugar
5 ml/1 tsp ground cinnamon
5 ml/1 tsp ground allspice
5 ml/1 tsp ground ginger
2.5 ml/½ tsp grated nutmeg
grated rind and juice of 2 oranges
grated rind and juice of 2 lemons
about 150 ml/¼ pint/⅔ cup brandy or port

1 Peel, core and chop the cooking apples. Chop the candied citrus peel.

2 Place all the ingredients, except the brandy or port, in a large mixing bowl. Stir well.

3 Cover the bowl with a cloth and set aside in a cool place overnight for the fruit to swell.

4 The following day, stir in enough brandy or port to make a mixture moist enough to drop from a spoon.

5 Spoon the mixture into sterilized jars and cover and store in a cool, dry place.

Candied Citrus Slices

To preserve the individual flavour of each citrus fruit they should all be candied separately.

Makes about 675 g/1½ lb

INGREDIENTS
5 large oranges or 10 lemons
    or 10 limes
675 g/1½ lb/3½ cups granulated sugar,
    plus extra for sprinkling
250 ml/8 fl oz/1 cup cold water

1 Halve the fruit, squeeze out the juice and discard the flesh, but retain the pith.

2 Cut the peel into strips about 1 cm/½ in wide and place them in a pan. Cover with boiling water and simmer for 5 minutes. Drain and then repeat this process 4 times, using fresh boiling water each time, to remove the peel's bitterness.

3 Put the sugar in a heavy pan and pour in the cold water. Heat gently to dissolve the sugar. Add the peel, partially cover and simmer over a low heat for 30–40 minutes, until soft. Leave to cool completely, then sprinkle with sugar to thoroughly cover the peel. Store the candied peel in an airtight container for up to 1 year.

Right: Candied Citrus Slices

Candied Ginger

You can use candied ginger in your cakes and cookies or simply nibble a piece as a treat.

Makes about 675 g/1½ lb

INGREDIENTS
350 g/12 oz fresh root ginger
225 g/8 oz/generous 1 cup granulated sugar
120 ml/4 fl oz/½ cup water
caster (superfine) sugar, for coating

1 Place the ginger in a pan and cover with water. Bring to the boil and simmer for 15 minutes. Drain and leave to cool. Peel the ginger and cut it into 5 mm/¼ in slices.

2 Place the sugar and water in a heavy pan. Heat gently until the sugar has dissolved, then simmer without stirring, for 15 minutes or until the mixture is syrupy.

3 Add the ginger and cook over a low heat, shaking the pan occasionally until the syrup has been absorbed. Remove the ginger slices from the pan and place them on a wire rack to cool.

4 Coat the slices with caster sugar and spread them out on baking parchment for 2–3 days, until the sugar has crystallized. Stored in an airtight jar, they will keep indefinitely.

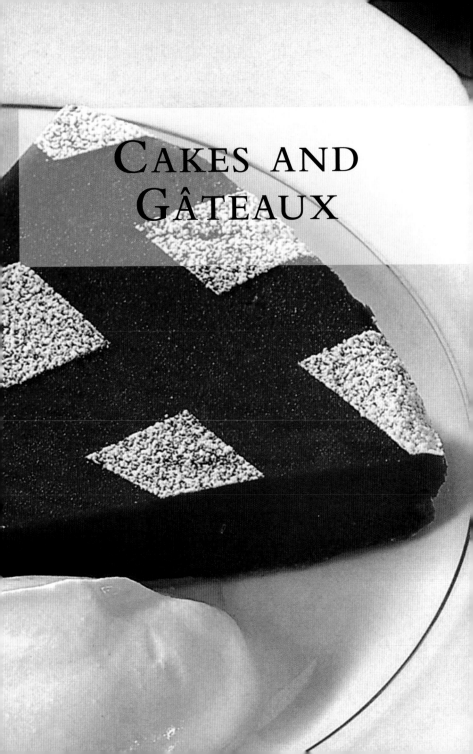

CAKES AND GÂTEAUX

One-stage Victoria Sandwich

This melt-in-the-mouth sponge is easy and quick to make.

Serves 6–8

INGREDIENTS
175 g/6 oz/1½ cups self-raising
  (self-rising) flour
pinch of salt
175 g/6 oz/¾ cup butter, softened
175 g/6 oz/¾ cup caster (superfine) sugar
3 eggs

TO SERVE
60–90 ml/4–6 tbsp raspberry jam
icing (confectioners') sugar

1 Preheat the oven to 180°C/350°F/
Gas 4. Grease two deep 18 cm/7 in
cake tins (pans), line the bases with
baking parchment and lightly grease
the paper itself.

2 Place the ingredients in a mixing
bowl and whisk together using a
hand-held whisk. Divide the mixture
between the prepared tins and smooth
the surfaces.

3 Bake in the centre of the oven for
25–30 minutes, or until a skewer
inserted into the centre of the cakes
comes out clean. Turn out on to a
wire rack, peel off the lining paper and
leave to cool completely.

4 Place one of the cakes on a serving
plate and spread with the raspberry
jam. Place the other cake
on top, then dredge with icing
(confectioners') sugar, to serve. Use a
stencil to make a pattern, if liked.

Honey Spice Cake

Use a strongly flavoured honey, such as chestnut honey, for this cake.

Serves 8–10

INGREDIENTS
150 g/5 oz/⅔ cup butter
115 g/4 oz/½ cup soft light brown sugar
175 g/6 oz/¾ cup clear honey
15 ml/1 tbsp water
200 g/7 oz/1¾ cups self-raising (self-rising) flour, sifted
2.5 ml/½ tsp ground ginger
2.5 ml/½ tsp ground cinnamon
1.5 ml/¼ tsp caraway seeds
1.5 ml/¼ tsp ground cloves
2 eggs, beaten
350 g/12 oz/3 cups icing (confectioners') sugar, sifted
crushed sugar, to decorate

1 Preheat the oven to 180°C/350°F/Gas 4. Grease a 900 ml/1½ pint/3¾ cup fluted mould.

2 Melt the butter in a pan with the sugar, honey and water. Cool.

3 Mix the flour, ginger, cinnamon, caraway seeds and ground cloves in a bowl. Pour in the honey mixture and the eggs and beat well. Pour the batter into the tin and bake for 45 minutes, until a skewer inserted into the centre comes out clean. Cool in the tin for 2 minutes, then remove to a wire rack.

4 Mix the icing sugar with warm water to make the icing. Spoon over the cake. Decorate with crushed sugar.

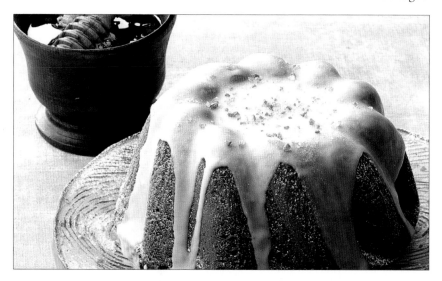

Crunchy-topped Madeira Cake

Traditionally served with a glass of Madeira wine in Victorian England, this light sponge also makes a perfect teatime treat.

Serves 8–10

INGREDIENTS
200 g/7 oz/scant 1 cup butter, softened
finely grated rind of 1 lemon
150 g/5 oz/⅔ cup caster (superfine) sugar
3 eggs
75 g/3 oz/⅔ cup plain (all-purpose) flour
150 g/5 oz/1¼ cups self-raising
   (self-rising) flour

FOR THE TOPPING
45 ml/3 tbsp clear honey
115 g/4 oz/¾ cup chopped mixed (candied)
   peel
50 g/2 oz/½ cup flaked (sliced) almonds

1 Preheat the oven to 180°C/350°F/ Gas 4. Grease and line a 450 g/1 lb loaf tin (pan) and grease the paper.

2 Beat the butter, lemon rind and sugar in a bowl until light and fluffy. Beat in the eggs, one at a time.

3 Sift together the flours, then stir into the egg mixture. Transfer the cake mixture to the prepared tin and smooth the surface.

4 Bake in the centre of the oven for 45–50 minutes, or until a skewer inserted into the centre of the cake comes out clean. Leave the cake in the tin for about 5 minutes. Turn out on to a wire rack, peel off the lining paper and leave to cool completely.

5 To make the topping, place the honey, mixed peel and almonds in a small pan and heat gently until the honey melts.

6 Remove from the heat and stir briefly to coat the peel and almonds, then spread over the cake. Allow to cool completely before serving.

Carrot Cake

This deliciously sweet and light-textured cake – which doesn't taste of carrots – is covered with an unusual frosting made with soft cheese.

Makes a 20 cm/8 in round cake

INGREDIENTS
250 ml/8 fl oz/1 cup corn oil
175 g/6 oz/scant 1 cup sugar
3 eggs
175 g/6 oz/1½ cups plain (all-purpose) flour
7.5 ml/1½ tsp baking powder
7.5 ml/1½ tsp bicarbonate of soda (baking soda)
3 ml/¾ tsp salt
7.5 ml/1½ tsp ground cinnamon
a pinch of freshly grated nutmeg
1.5 ml/¼ tsp ground ginger
115 g/4 oz/1 cup chopped walnuts
225 g/8 oz (2 large) carrots, finely grated
5 ml/1 tsp vanilla extract
30 ml/2 tbsp sour cream

FOR THE FROSTING
175 g/6 oz/¾ cup full-fat soft cheese
25 g/1 oz/2 tbsp butter, softened
225 g/8 oz/2 cups icing (confectioners') sugar, sifted
8 tiny carrots made from orange and green coloured marzipan, to decorate

1 Preheat the oven to 180°C/350°F/ Gas 4. Grease two 20 cm/8 in loose-based round cake tins (pans) and line them with baking parchment.

2 Put the corn oil and sugar into a bowl and beat well. Add the eggs, one at a time, and beat them very thoroughly into the mixture.

3 Sift the flour, baking powder, bicarbonate of soda, salt, cinnamon, nutmeg and ginger into the bowl and beat well. Fold in the walnuts and carrots and stir in the vanilla extract and sour cream.

4 Divide the mixture between the prepared tins and bake in the centre of the oven for about 1 hour 5 minutes, or until a skewer inserted into the centre of the cake comes out clean.

5 Leave the cake in the tins for 5 minutes then turn out to cool on a wire rack. For the frosting mix the soft cheese, butter and icing sugar together in a bowl. Beat until smooth.

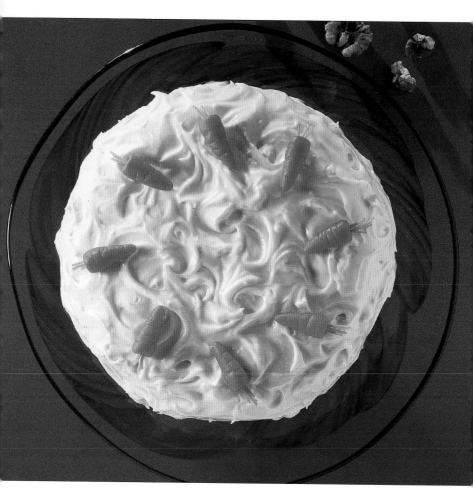

6 Sandwich the cooled cakes together with a little of the frosting. Spread the remaining frosting over the top of the cake and down the sides, making a swirling pattern with a round-bladed knife. Just before you are ready to serve the cake, decorate the top with the orange and green marzipan carrots, arranged in an attractive pattern.

Passion Cake

So called because this is a cake associated with Passion Sunday. The carrot and banana give the cake a rich, moist texture.

Serves 6–8

INGREDIENTS

200 g/7 oz/1¾ cups self-raising (self-rising) flour
10 ml/2 tsp baking powder
5 ml/1 tsp cinnamon
2.5 ml/½ tsp freshly grated nutmeg
150 g/5 oz/⅔ cup butter, softened, or sunflower margarine
150 g/5 oz/⅔ cup soft brown sugar
grated rind of 1 lemon
2 eggs, beaten
2 carrots, coarsely grated
1 ripe banana, mashed
115 g/4 oz/¾ cup raisins
50 g/2 oz/½ cup chopped walnuts or pecans
30 ml/2 tbsp milk
6–8 walnuts, halved, to decorate
coffee crystal sugar, to sprinkle

FOR THE FROSTING

200 g/7 oz/scant 1 cup cream cheese, softened
40 g/1½ oz/⅓ cup icing (confectioners') sugar
juice of 1 lemon
grated rind of 1 orange

1 Line and grease a deep 20 cm/8 in round cake tin (pan). Preheat the oven to 180°C/350°F/Gas 4. Sift the flour, baking powder, cinnamon and freshly grated nutmeg together into a large mixing bowl.

2 Using an electric mixer, cream the butter or margarine and sugar with the lemon rind until it is light and fluffy, then beat in the eggs. Fold in the flour mixture, then the carrots, banana, raisins, nuts and milk.

3 Spoon the mixture into the prepared tin, level the top and bake for about 1 hour, until it has risen and the top is springy to touch. Turn the tin upside down and allow the cake to cool in the tin for 30 minutes. Transfer the cake to a wire rack.

4 When cold, split the cake in half. Cream the cheese with the icing sugar, lemon juice and orange rind, then sandwich the two halves together with half the frosting.

5 Spread the rest of the frosting on top of the cake, swirling it attractively with a knife. Decorate the top with the walnut halves and sprinkle with coffee crystal sugar.

Dundee Cake

This traditional rich fruit cake is topped with a mixture of nuts and glacé cherries and tastes every bit as good as it looks.

Serves 8–10

INGREDIENTS
350 g/12 oz/3 cups plain wholemeal (whole-wheat) flour
5 ml/1 tsp mixed (apple pie) spice
175 g/6 oz/¾ cup unsalted (sweet) butter
175 g/6 oz/¾ cup dark muscovado (molasses) sugar
175 g/6 oz/1 cup sultanas (golden raisins)
175 g/6 oz/¾ cup currants
175 g/6 oz/generous 1 cup raisins
75 g/3 oz/½ cup chopped mixed (candied) peel
150 g/5 oz/⅔ cup glacé (candied) cherries, halved
finely grated zest of 1 orange
30 ml/2 tbsp ground almonds
25 g/1 oz/¼ cup blanched almonds, chopped
120 ml/4 fl oz/½ cup milk
75 ml/5 tbsp sunflower oil
30 ml/2 tbsp malt vinegar
5 ml/1 tsp bicarbonate of soda (baking soda)

TO DECORATE
mixed nuts, such as pistachios, pecans and macadamias; glacé (candied) cherries and angelica
60 ml/4 tbsp clear honey, warmed

1 Preheat the oven to 150°C/300°F/ Gas 2. Grease a deep 20 cm/8 in square loose-based cake tin (pan), line with a double thickness of baking parchment and grease the paper.

2 Sift the flour and mixed spice into a large mixing bowl, adding the bran left in the sieve (strainer). Rub the butter into the flour until it resembles fine breadcrumbs. Stir in the sugar, dried fruits, peel, cherries, zest and almonds.

3 Warm 50 ml/2 fl oz/¼ cup of the milk in a pan, then add the sunflower oil and vinegar. Dissolve the bicarbonate of soda in the rest of the milk, then combine the two mixtures and stir into the dry ingredients.

4 Spoon the mixture into the tin and smooth the surface. Bake for about 2½ hours, or until a skewer inserted into the centre comes out clean. Leave in the tin for 5 minutes, then turn on to a wire rack, peel off the paper and leave to cool.

5 Place the mixed nuts, glacé cherries and angelica on top of the cake, then brush with the warmed honey.

Lemon Coconut Layer Cake

The tangy citrus flavour of lemon perfectly counterbalances the sweetness of the coconut in this rich cake.

Serves 8–10

INGREDIENTS
7 eggs
350 g/12 oz/scant 1¾ cups caster (superfine) sugar
15 ml/1 tbsp grated orange rind
grated rind of 2 lemons
juice of 1 lemon
65 g/2½ oz/¾ cup desiccated (dry unsweetened), coconut
75 g/6 oz/1½ cups plain (all-purpose) flour, sifted with 1.5 ml/¼ tsp salt
15 ml/1 tbsp cornflour (cornstarch)
120 ml/4 fl oz/½ cup water
40 g/1½ oz/3 tbsp butter

FOR THE FROSTING
75 g/3 oz/6 tbsp unsalted (sweet) butter
175 g/6 oz/1½ cups icing (confectioners') sugar
grated rind of 1½ lemon
30 ml/2 tbsp lemon juice
200 g/7 oz/2½ cups desiccated (dry unsweetened) coconut

1 Preheat the oven to 180°C/350°F/ Gas 4. Line and grease three round 20 cm/8 in cake tins (pans) with a layer of baking parchment.

2 Place 6 of the eggs in a bowl set over hot water and beat until frothy. Beat in 225 g/8 oz/1 cup of the sugar until the mixture has doubled in volume.

3 Remove from the heat. Fold in the orange rind, half the lemon rind, 15 ml/1 tbsp of the lemon juice and the coconut. Sift over the flour mixture and gently fold in until combined.

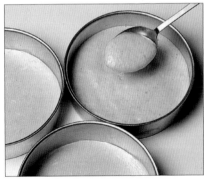

4 Divide the mixture evenly between the three prepared cake tins. Bake for 20–25 minutes until the cakes start to pull away from the sides of the tins. Leave the cakes in the tins for 5 minutes, then transfer them to a wire rack to cool.

5 For the lemon custard, blend the cornflour with water. Whisk in the remaining egg. Mix the remaining ingredients in a pan and bring to the boil. Add the cornflour and return to the boil. Whisk until thick. Remove and cover with clear film (plastic wrap).

6 For the frosting, cream the butter and icing sugar. Stir in the lemon rind and enough lemon juice to obtain a spreadable consistency. Sandwich the cake layers with the lemon custard. Spread the frosting over the top and sides. Cover with the coconut.

Apple Cake

Try this moist cake hot or cold.

Serves 8–10

INGREDIENTS
250 g/9 oz/2¼ cups self-raising (self-rising)
    flour
10 ml/2 tsp baking powder
5 ml/1 tsp ground cinnamon
130 g/4½ oz/generous ½ cup caster
    (superfine) sugar
50 g/2 oz/¼ cup butter, melted
2 eggs, beaten
150 ml/¼ pint/⅔ cup milk

FOR THE TOPPING
2 eating apples, peeled, cored and sliced
15 g/½ oz/1 tbsp butter, melted
60 ml/4 tbsp demerara (raw) sugar
1.5 ml/¼ tsp ground cinnamon

1 Preheat the oven to 200°C/400°F/
Gas 6. Grease and line a 20 cm/8 in
cake tin (pan). Sift the flour, baking
powder and cinnamon into a bowl.
Add the sugar. Whisk the butter, eggs
and milk, then stir these in too.

2 Pour the mixture into the tin, make
a shallow hollow around the edge, and
lay the apples around it. Brush with
the butter, then sprinkle with
demerara sugar and cinnamon.

3 Bake for 45–50 minutes, or until
a skewer inserted into the centre
comes out clean. Serve immediately or
cool on a wire rack.

Pear Cake

Polenta gives this a nutty flavour.

Serves 10

INGREDIENTS
175 g/6 oz/¾ cup golden caster
    (superfine) sugar
4 ripe pears, peeled, cored and sliced
juice of ½ lemon
30 ml/2 tbsp clear honey
3 eggs
seeds from 1 vanilla pod (bean)
120 ml/4 fl oz/½ cup sunflower oil
115 g/4 oz/1 cup self-raising
    (self-rising) flour
50 g/2 oz/½ cup instant polenta

1 Preheat the oven to 180°C/350°F/
Gas 4. Grease and line a 21 cm/
8½ in cake tin (pan). Sprinkle 30 ml/
2 tbsp sugar over the base of the tin.
Toss the pear slices in the lemon juice.
Arrange them on the base of the cake
tin. Drizzle the honey over the pears.

2 Beat together the eggs, vanilla pod
seeds and the remaining sugar in a
bowl until thick. Gradually beat in the
oil. Sift together the flour and polenta
and fold into the egg mixture.

3 Pour the mixture into the tin. Bake
for about 50 minutes, or until a skewer
inserted into the centre comes out
clean. Cool for 10 minutes, then peel
off the lining paper and slice.

Right: Apple Cake (top); Pear Cake

Greek Yogurt & Fig Cake

Baked fresh figs, thickly sliced, make a delectable base for a feather–light sponge. Firm figs work best for this recipe.

Serves 6–8

INGREDIENTS
6 firm fresh figs, thickly sliced
45 ml/3 tbsp clear honey, plus extra
    for glazing cooked figs
200 g/7 oz/scant 1 cup butter, softened
175 g/6 oz/scant 1 cup caster
    (superfine) sugar
grated rind of 1 lemon
grated rind of 1 orange
4 eggs, separated
225 g/8 oz/2 cups plain (all-purpose) flour
5 ml/1 tsp baking powder
5 ml/1 tsp bicarbonate of soda (baking soda)
250 ml/8 fl oz/1 cup Greek (US strained
    plain) yogurt

1 Preheat the oven to 180°C/350°F/ Gas 4. Grease a 23 cm/9 in cake tin (pan) and line the base with non-stick baking parchment. Arrange the figs over the base of the tin and drizzle the honey over the top.

2 Cream the butter and caster sugar with the lemon and orange rinds until the mixture is pale and fluffy, then gradually beat in the egg yolks.

3 Sift the dry ingredients together. Add a little to the creamed mixture, beat well, then beat in a spoonful of yogurt. Repeat this process until all the dry ingredients and yogurt have been incorporated.

4 Whisk the egg whites until they form stiff peaks. Stir half the whites into the cake mixture to slacken it, then fold in the rest. Pour the mixture over the figs in the tin, then bake for 1¼ hours, or until a skewer inserted into the centre comes out clean.

5 Turn the cake out on to a wire rack, peel off the lining paper and cool. Drizzle the figs with extra honey before serving.

Upside-down Pear & Ginger Cake

A light, spicy sponge topped with glossy, baked fruit and ginger. This is also good served as a warm pudding, with cream or custard.

Serves 6–8

INGREDIENTS

900 g/2 lb can pear halves, drained
120 ml/8 tbsp finely chopped preserved
  stem ginger
120 ml/8 tbsp ginger syrup from the jar
175 g/6 oz/1½ cups self-raising
  (self-rising) flour
2.5 ml/½ tsp baking powder
5 ml/1 tsp ground ginger
175 g/6 oz/¾ cup soft brown sugar
175 g/6 oz/¾ cup butter, softened
3 eggs, lightly beaten

1 Preheat the oven to 180°C/350°F/ Gas 4. Grease and line a deep 20 cm/ 8 in cake tin (pan).

2 Fill the hollow in each pear with half the chopped ginger. Arrange the pears, flat sides down, over the base of the cake tin, then spoon half the ginger syrup over the top.

3 Sift the flour, baking powder and ground ginger into a mixing bowl. Stir in the soft brown sugar and butter, then add the lightly beaten eggs and beat together for 1–2 minutes until the mixture is creamy.

4 Carefully spoon the mixture into the tin, spreading it out evenly so that all the pears are covered, and smooth the surface.

5 Bake for about 50 minutes, or until a skewer inserted into the centre comes out clean. Leave the cake to cool in the tin for about 5 minutes.

6 Turn out on to a wire rack, peel off the lining paper and leave to cool completely. Add the reserved chopped ginger to the pear halves on top of the cake and drizzle over the remaining ginger syrup.

Rich Chocolate Cake

This dark, fudgy cake is easy to make, stores well and is a chocolate lover's dream come true.

Serves 14–16

INGREDIENTS
250 g/9 oz plain (semisweet) chocolate, broken or chopped
225 g/8 oz/1 cup unsalted (sweet) butter, cut into pieces
5 eggs
90 g/3½ oz/½ cup caster (superfine) sugar, plus 15 ml/1 tbsp and extra for sprinkling
15 ml/1 tbsp unsweetened cocoa powder
10 ml/2 tsp vanilla extract
unsweetened cocoa powder, for dusting
chocolate shavings, to decorate

1 Preheat the oven to 160°C/325°F/Gas 3. Lightly butter a 23 cm/9 in springform tin (pan) and line the base with non-stick baking parchment. Butter the parchment and sprinkle with a little sugar, then shake out the excess. Wrap a double thickness of foil around the outside of the base and sides of the tin.

2 Melt the chocolate and butter in a pan over a low heat, stirring frequently, until smooth, then remove from the heat.

3 Beat the eggs and the 90 g/3½ oz/½ cup of the sugar with an electric mixer for 1 minute.

4 Beat the cocoa and the remaining sugar into the egg mixture until well blended. Beat in the vanilla extract, then gradually beat in the melted chocolate until well blended. Pour the mixture into the prepared tin and tap gently to allow any air bubbles to rise to the surface.

5 Place the cake tin in a roasting pan and carefully pour in boiling water to come 2 cm/¾ in up the sides of the wrapped tin. Bake for 45–50 minutes, until the edge of the cake is set and the centre still soft.

6 Lift the tin out of the water and remove the foil wrapping. Place the cake, still in its tin, on a wire rack, remove the sides of the tin and leave it to cool completely (it will sink a little in the centre).

7 Invert the cake on to the wire rack. Remove the base of the tin and the paper. Dust the cake liberally with cocoa powder and arrange the chocolate shavings around the edge. Slide the cake on to a serving plate.

Summer Shortcake

A summertime treat. Don't add the cream and strawberries until just before serving, or the shortcakes will go soft.

Serves 8

INGREDIENTS
225 g/8 oz/2 cups plain (all-purpose) flour
15 ml/1 tbsp baking powder
2.5 ml/½ tsp salt
50 g/2 oz/4 tbsp caster (superfine) sugar
50 g/2 oz/4 tbsp butter, softened
150 ml/¼ pint/⅔ cup milk
300 ml/½ pint/1¼ cups double (heavy) cream
450 g/1 lb/4 cups fresh strawberries,
    halved and hulled

1 Preheat the oven to 220°C/425°F/ Gas 7. Grease a baking sheet, and line the base with baking parchment.

2 Sift the flour, baking powder and salt into a large mixing bowl. Stir in the sugar, cut in the butter and toss into the flour mixture with your fingers until it resembles coarse breadcrumbs. Stir in just enough milk to make a soft dough.

3 Turn out the dough on to a lightly floured work surface and, using your fingers, pat into a 30 x 15 cm/ 12 x 6 in rectangle. Using a template, cut out two 15 cm/6 in rounds, indent one dividing into eight portions, and place both on the baking sheet.

4 Bake in the centre of the oven for 10–15 minutes, or until slightly risen and golden. Leave on the baking sheet for about 5 minutes, then transfer to a wire rack, peel off the paper and let cool completely.

5 Place the cream in a mixing bowl and whip with an electric mixer until it holds soft peaks. Place the unmarked shortcake on a serving plate and spread or pipe with half the cream. Top with two-thirds of the strawberries, then the other shortcake. Decorate with the remaining cream and strawberries and serve chilled.

Frosted Chocolate Fudge Cake

Rich and dreamy, with an irresistible chocolate fudgy frosting, this cake couldn't be easier to make, or more wonderful to eat!

Serves 6–8

INGREDIENTS

115 g/4 oz plain (semisweet) chocolate, broken into squares
175 g/6 oz/¾ cup unsalted (sweet) butter or margarine, softened
200 g/7 oz/scant 1 cup light muscovado (brown) sugar
5 ml/1 tsp vanilla extract
3 eggs, beaten
150 ml/¼ pint/⅔ cup Greek (US strained plain) yogurt
150 g/5 oz/1¼ cups self-raising (self-rising) flour
chocolate curls, to decorate

FOR THE FROSTING

115 g/4 oz dark (bittersweet) chocolate
50 g/2 oz/4 tbsp unsalted (sweet) butter
350 g/12 oz/3 cups icing (confectioners') sugar
90 ml/6 tbsp Greek (US strained plain) yogurt

1 Preheat the oven to 190°C/375°F/ Gas 5. Grease two 20 cm/8 in round sandwich cake tins (pans) and line the base of each with a piece of non-stick baking parchment.

2 Break the plain chocolate into squares and place in a heatproof bowl over a pan of hot water.

3 In a mixing bowl, cream the butter or margarine with the sugar until light and fluffy. Beat in the vanilla extract, then gradually add the beaten eggs, beating well after each addition.

4 Stir in the melted chocolate and yogurt evenly. Fold in the flour using a metal spoon.

5 Divide the mixture between the tins. Bake for 25–30 minutes, or until firm to the touch. Turn out and cool on a wire rack.

6 Make the frosting. Melt the chocolate and butter in a pan over a low heat. Remove the pan from the heat and stir in the icing sugar and yogurt. Stir the mixture with a rubber spatula until it is smooth, then beat until the frosting begins to cool and thicken slightly. Use about a third of the mixture to sandwich the cooled cakes together.

7 Working quickly, spread the remaining frosting over the top. Decorate the cake with chocolate curls before serving.

COOK'S TIP: If the frosting begins to set too quickly, heat it gently to soften, and beat in a little extra yogurt if necessary.

Chocolate Layer Cake

The cake layers can be made ahead, wrapped and frozen for future use. Always thaw cakes completely before icing.

Serves 10–12

INGREDIENTS
unsweetened cocoa powder for dusting
225 g/8 oz can cooked whole beetroot, drained and juice reserved
115 g/4 oz/½ cup unsalted (sweet) butter, softened
500 g/1¼ lb/2½ cups (packed) soft light brown sugar
3 eggs
15 ml/1 tbsp vanilla extract
75 g/3 oz unsweetened chocolate, melted
275 g/10 oz/2½ cups plain (all-purpose) flour
10 ml/2 tsp baking powder
2.5 ml/½ tsp salt
120 ml/4 fl oz/½ cup buttermilk
chocolate curls (optional)

FOR THE GANACHE FROSTING
475 ml/16 fl oz/2 cups whipping or double (heavy) cream
500 g/1¼ lb fine quality plain (semisweet) chocolate, chopped
15 ml/1 tbsp vanilla extract

1 Preheat the oven to 180°C/350°F/ Gas 4. Grease two 23 cm/9 in cake tins and dust the base and sides with cocoa. Grate the beetroot and add it to the juice. With an electric mixer, beat the butter, brown sugar, eggs and vanilla for 3–5 minutes, until pale and fluffy. Reduce the speed and beat in the chocolate.

2 Sift the flour, baking powder and salt into a bowl. On a low speed, alternately beat in the flour mixture (in quarters) and the buttermilk (in thirds).

3 Add the beetroot mixture and beat for 1 minute. Divide between the tins and bake for 30–35 minutes, or until a cake tester inserted in the centre comes out clean. Cool for 10 minutes, unmould and cool completely.

4 To make the frosting, heat the cream in a heavy pan over a medium heat until it just begins to boil, stirring occasionally.

5 Off the heat, add the chocolate, stirring constantly until melted and smooth. Stir in the vanilla. Strain into a bowl and chill, stirring every 10 minutes, for about 1 hour, until spreadable.

6 Assemble the cake. Place one layer on a serving plate and spread with one-third of the ganache. Place the second layer over and spread the remaining ganache over the top and sides of the cake. If using, top with the chocolate curls. Allow the ganache to set for 20–30 minutes, then chill in the refrigerator before serving.

Simple Chocolate Cake

An easy, everyday chocolate cake which is delicious simply filled with chocolate buttercream.

Serves 6–8

INGREDIENTS
115 g/4 oz plain (semisweet) chocolate
45 ml/3 tbsp milk
150 g/5 oz/⅔ cup unsalted (sweet) butter or
    margarine, softened
150 g/5 oz/scant 1 cup light muscovado
    (brown) sugar
3 eggs
200 g/7 oz/1¾ cups self-raising (self-rising) flour
15 ml/1 tbsp cocoa powder (unsweetened)
icing (confectioners') sugar and cocoa
    powder, for dusting

FOR THE CHOCOLATE BUTTERCREAM
75 g/3 oz/6 tbsp unsalted (sweet) butter or
    margarine, softened
175 g/6 oz/1½ cups icing (confectioners') sugar
15 ml/1 tbsp cocoa powder (unsweetened)
2.5 ml/½ tsp vanilla essence (extract)

1 Preheat the oven to 180°C/350°F/ Gas 4. Grease two 18 cm/7 in round cake tins (pans) and line the base of each with baking parchment. Melt the chocolate with the milk in a heatproof bowl set over a pan of barely simmering water.

2 Cream the butter or margarine with the sugar until pale and fluffy. Add the eggs one at a time, beating well after each. Stir in the chocolate mixture until well combined.

3 Sift the flour and cocoa over the mixture and fold in with a metal spoon until evenly mixed. Scrape into the prepared tins, smooth level and bake for 35–40 minutes, or until well risen and firm. Turn out on wire racks to cool.

4 To make the chocolate buttercream, place all the ingredients in a large bowl. Beat well to a smooth, spreadable consistency.

5 Sandwich the cake layers together with the buttercream. Dust with a mixture of icing sugar and cocoa just before serving.

COOK'S TIP: For a richer finish, make a double quantity of buttercream and spread or pipe over the top of the cake as well as using for the filling.

Marbled Chocolate & Peanut Butter Cake

This cake cannot be tested with a cake tester because the peanut butter remains soft in the centre. Rely on the fingertip method: when it is done, the cake should spring back when touched.

Serves 12–14

INGREDIENTS
225 g/8 oz/1 cup unsalted (sweet) butter, softened
225 g/8 oz/1 cup smooth or crunchy peanut butter
200 g/7 oz/1 cup granulated sugar
225 g/8 oz/1 cup (packed) soft light brown sugar
5 eggs
275 g/10 oz/2½ cups plain (all-purpose) flour
10 ml/2 tsp baking powder
2.5 ml/½ tsp salt
120 ml/4 fl oz/½ cup milk
115 g/4 oz plain (semisweet) chocolate, melted
50 g/2 oz/⅓ cup chocolate chips

FOR THE GLAZE
25 g/1 oz/2 tbsp butter, cut up
25 g/1 oz/2 tbsp smooth peanut butter
45 ml/3 tbsp golden (light corn) syrup
5 ml/1 tsp vanilla extract
175 g/6 oz plain (semisweet) chocolate, broken into pieces
15 ml/1 tbsp water

1 Preheat the oven to 180°C/350°F/ Gas 4. Generously grease and flour a 3 litre/5 pint/12 cup tube or ring mould.

2 Put the butter, peanut butter and sugars into a large mixing bowl. Beat with an electric mixer, scraping the side of the bowl occasionally, for about 3–5 minutes, until light and creamy. Add the eggs, one at a time, beating well after each addition.

3 Stir the flour, baking powder and salt together in a bowl. Add to the butter mixture alternately with the milk until just blended.

4 Pour half the batter into another bowl. Stir the melted chocolate into one half of the batter until well blended. Stir the chocolate chips into the other half of the batter.

5 Using a large spoon, drop alternate spoonfuls of each batter into the mould. Pull a knife through to create a marbled effect; do not let the knife touch the sides or over-mix. Bake for 50–60 minutes. Cool in the mould on a wire rack for 10 minutes, then unmould on to the rack.

6 Prepare the glaze. Combine all the ingredients in a small pan. Melt over a low heat, stirring continuously, until well blended and smooth. Cool for 5 minutes. When slightly thickened, drizzle the glaze over the cooled cake, allowing it to run down the sides.

Chocolate Ginger Crunch Cake

Ginger adds a flicker of fire to this delectable uncooked cake. Keep one in the refrigerator for midnight feasts and other late-night treats.

Serves 6

INGREDIENTS
150 g/5 oz plain (semisweet) chocolate
50 g/2 oz/4 tbsp unsalted (sweet) butter
115 g/4 oz ginger nut biscuits (gingersnaps)
4 pieces preserved stem ginger
30 ml/2 tbsp stem ginger syrup
45 ml/3 tbsp desiccated (dry unsweetened shredded) coconut

TO DECORATE
25 g/1 oz milk chocolate
pieces of crystallized ginger

1 Grease a 15 cm/6 in flan (quiche) ring; place it on a baking sheet lined with baking parchment. Melt the plain chocolate with the butter in a heatproof bowl over barely simmering water. Remove from the heat.

2 Crush the ginger nut biscuits into small pieces (see Cook's Tip), and place them in a bowl.

3 Chop the stem ginger fairly finely and mix with the crushed ginger nut biscuits. Stir the biscuit mixture, ginger syrup and desiccated coconut into the melted chocolate and butter, mixing well until evenly combined.

4 Scrape the mixture into the prepared flan ring and press down firmly and evenly. Chill in the refrigerator until set.

5 Remove the flan ring and slide the cake on to a plate. Melt the milk chocolate, drizzle it over the top of the cake and decorate with the pieces of crystallized ginger.

COOK'S TIP: Do not crumb the biscuits as you need crunchy pieces for texture. Put in a strong plastic bag and crush them with a rolling pin, or chop them in a food processor, using the pulse setting.

Bitter Marmalade Chocolate Loaf

Do not be alarmed by the amount of cream in this recipe – it is naughty but necessary, and replaces butter to make a moist dark cake, topped with a bitter-sweet sticky marmalade topping.

Serves 8

INGREDIENTS
3 eggs
200 g/7 oz/1 cup caster
   (superfine) sugar
175 ml/6 fl oz/¾ cup sour cream
115 g/4 oz plain (semisweet)
   chocolate, melted
200 g/7 oz/1¾ cups self-raising
   (self-rising) flour

FOR THE FILLING AND GLAZE
175 g/6 oz/⅔ cup bitter orange
   marmalade
115 g/4 oz plain (semisweet)
   chocolate, melted
60 ml/4 tbsp sour cream
shredded orange rind,
   to decorate (optional)

1 Preheat the oven to 180°C/350°F/ Gas 4. Lightly grease a 900 g/2 lb loaf tin (pan) and line it with baking parchment.

2 Combine the eggs and sugar in a bowl. Using a hand-held electric mixer, whisk the mixture until it is thick and creamy, then stir in the sour cream and melted chocolate. Fold in the self-raising flour evenly.

3 Scrape the mixture into the prepared tin and bake for about 1 hour, or until well risen and firm to the touch. Cool for a few minutes in the tin, then turn out on to a wire rack and leave to cool completely.

4 Make the filling. Spoon two-thirds of the marmalade into a small pan and melt over a low heat. Stir the melted chocolate into the marmalade with the sour cream.

5 Slice the cake across into three layers and sandwich back together with about half the marmalade filling. Spread the rest over the top of the cake and leave to set. Spoon the remaining marmalade over the cake and decorate with shredded orange rind, if using.

COOK'S TIP: If you do not particularly like marmalade, use apricot jam instead.

French Chocolate Cake

This very dense chocolate cake can be made up to 3 days before serving, but decorate with icing sugar on the day it is to be served.

Serves 10

INGREDIENTS
250 g/9 oz dark (bitters·· chocolate, chopped
225 g/8 oz/1 cup unsalted (sweet) butter,
    cut into pieces
90 g/3½ oz/½ cup sugar
30 ml/2 tbsp brandy or orange liqueur
5 eggs
15 ml/1 tbsp plain (all-purpose) flour
icing (confectioners') sugar, for dusting
whipped or sour cream, to serve

1 Preheat the oven to 180°C/350°F/ Gas 4. Generously grease a 23 x 5 cm/ 9 x 2 in springform tin (pan). Line the base with baking parchment and grease the paper. Wrap the base and sides in foil to keep water out.

2 Melt the chocolate, butter and sugar in a pan over a low heat, stirring frequently, until smooth. Cool slightly. Stir in the brandy or liqueur. Using an electric mixer, beat the eggs for about 1 minute. Beat in the flour, then slowly beat in the chocolate mixture until well blended. Pour into the tin.

3 Place the tin in a large roasting tin (pan) and pour boiling water into the roasting tin to a depth of 2 cm/¾ in. Bake for 25–30 minutes, until the edge of the cake is set, but the centre is still soft to the touch. Remove the tin from the water bath and remove the foil. Cool on a wire rack completely (the cake will sink in the centre and may crack).

4 Carefully run a knife around the edge of the cake. Remove the side of the springform tin and turn the cake on to a wire rack. Remove the springform tin base and the paper, so the bottom of the cake is now the top.

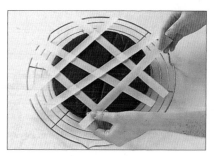

5 Cut 6–8 strips of baking parchment 2.5 cm/1 in wide and place randomly over the cake or make a lattice-style pattern if you prefer. Dust the cake with icing sugar; then carefully remove the paper. Slide the cake on to a serving plate and serve with cream.

Black Forest Gâteau

A rich, melt-in-the-mouth, layered gâteau that is ideal for serving as a sumptuous teatime treat.

Serves 10–12

INGREDIENTS
5 eggs
175 g/6 oz/scant 1 cup caster
    (superfine) sugar
50 g/2 oz/½ cup plain (all-purpose) flour
50 g/2 oz/½ cup unsweetened cocoa powder
75 g/3 oz/6 tbsp butter, melted

FOR THE FILLING
75–90 ml/5–6 tbsp kirsch
600 ml/1 pint/2½ cups double (heavy) cream
425 g/15 oz can black cherries, drained,
    pitted and chopped

TO DECORATE
chocolate curls
15–20 fresh cherries, preferably with stems
icing (confectioners') sugar

1 Preheat the oven to 180°C/350°F/ Gas 4. Base-line and grease two deep 20 cm/8 in round cake tins (pans).

2 Beat together the eggs and sugar for 10 minutes. Sift over the flour and cocoa, and fold in gently. Trickle in the melted butter and fold in gently.

3 Transfer to the cake tins. Bake for 30 minutes, or until springy. Leave in the tins for 5 minutes, then turn out on to a wire rack, peel off the paper and leave to cool.

4 Cut each cake in half horizontally and sprinkle each half with a quarter of the kirsch.

5 Whip the cream until softly peaking. Combine two-thirds of the cream with the chopped cherries. Place a layer of cake on a serving plate and spread with one-third of the filling. Repeat twice, and top with a layer of cake. Use the reserved cream to cover the top and sides.

6 Decorate the gâteau with chocolate curls and fresh cherries and dredge with icing sugar.

Tia Maria Gâteau

Whipped cream and Tía Maria make a mouth-watering filling for this light chocolate and walnut cake.

Serves 6–8

INGREDIENTS
150 g/5 oz/1¼ cups self-raising
   (self-rising) flour
25 g/1 oz/¼ cup unsweetened cocoa powder
7.5 ml/1½ tsp baking powder
3 eggs, beaten
175 g/6 oz/¾ cup butter, softened
175 g/6 oz/1 cup caster (superfine) sugar
50 g/2 oz/½ cup chopped walnuts
walnut brittle, to decorate

FOR THE FILLING AND COATING
600 ml/1 pint/2½ cups double (heavy) cream
45 ml/3 tbsp Tía Maria
50 g/2 oz/⅔ cup desiccated (dry unsweetened
   shredded) coconut, toasted

1 Preheat the oven to 160°C/325°F/ Gas 3. Grease and base-line two 18 cm/7 in sandwich tins (pans). Sift the flour, cocoa and baking powder into a large bowl.

2 Add the eggs, butter, sugar and walnuts and mix together. Divide between the cake tins, level the surface and bake for 35–40 minutes, until risen. Turn out and leave to cool.

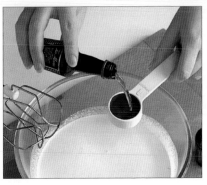

3 For the filling add the Tía Maria to the cream and whisk until the mixture forms soft peaks.

4 Slice each cake horizontally in half to give four layers. Sandwich the layers together with some of the flavoured whipped cream.

COOK'S TIP: To make walnut brittle, melt 75 g/3 oz/6 tbsp caster (superfine) sugar in a pan. Stir in 50 g/2 oz/½ cup broken walnuts. Turn the mixture on to non-stick baking parchment and leave to set. Break the brittle into pieces with a rolling pin.

5 Coat the sides of the cake with cream, saving some for the top. Spread out the toasted coconut on a sheet of non-stick baking parchment. Then, holding the top and bottom of the cake, roll the sides in the coconut until evenly coated. Put the cake on a serving plate, spread more of the cream on top and pipe the remainder around the outside rim. Decorate inside the rim with walnut brittle.

White Chocolate Cappuccino Gâteau

Luscious, lavish and laced with liqueur, this magnificent gâteau is strictly for adults only!

Serves 8

INGREDIENTS
4 eggs
115 g/4 oz/generous ½ cup caster
   (superfine) sugar
15 ml/1 tbsp strong black coffee
2.5 ml/½ tsp vanilla extract
115 g/4 oz/1 cup plain (all-purpose)
   flour
75 g/3 oz white chocolate,coarsely grated

FOR THE FILLING
120 ml/4 fl oz/½ cup double
   (heavy) cream
15 ml/1 tbsp coffee liqueur

FOR THE FROSTING AND TOPPINGS
175 g/6 oz white chocolate broken
   into squares
75 g/3 oz/6 tbsp unsalted (sweet) butter
115 g/4 oz/1 cup icing
   (confectioners') sugar
90 ml/6 tbsp double (heavy) cream
15 ml/1 tbsp coffee liqueur
white chocolate curls
unsweetened cocoa powder, for dusting

1 Preheat the oven to 180°C/350°F/ Gas 4. Grease two deep 19 cm/7½ in round sandwich cake tins (pans) and line the base of each with non-stick baking parchment.

2 Whisk together the eggs, caster sugar, black coffee and vanilla extract in a bowl set over a pan of hot water, until the mixture is pale and thick enough to hold its shape when the whisk is lifted.

3 Sift half the flour over the mixture; fold in gently and evenly. Carefully fold in the remaining flour with the grated white chocolate.

4 Divide the mixture between the prepared tins and smooth. Bake for 20–25 minutes, until firm and golden brown, then turn out on wire racks and leave to cool completely.

5 Make the filling. Whip the cream with the coffee liqueur in a bowl until it holds its shape. Spread over one of the cakes, then place the second layer on top.

6 To make the frosting, melt the chocolate with the butter in a bowl set over hot water. Remove from the heat and beat in the icing sugar.

7 Whip the double cream until it just holds its shape, then beat into the chocolate mixture.

8 Allow the frosting to cool, stirring occasionally, until it begins to hold its shape. Stir the coffee liqueur into the frosting. Spread over the top and sides of the cake, swirling with a palette knife or metal spatula. Decorate the cake with curls of white chocolate and dust the top with cocoa powder.

425

Raspberry Meringue Gâteau

This rich meringue gâteau makes the most of wonderful fresh raspberries when they are in season.

Serves 6

INGREDIENTS
4 egg whites
225 g/8 oz/generous 1 cup caster
  (superfine) sugar
few drops vanilla extract
5 ml/1 tsp distilled malt vinegar
115 g/4 oz/1 cup roasted and chopped
  hazelnuts, ground
300 ml/½ pint/1¼ cups double
  (heavy) cream
350 g/12 oz/2 cups raspberries
icing (confectioners') sugar, for dusting
mint sprigs, to decorate

FOR THE SAUCE
225 g/8 oz/1⅓ cups raspberries
45–60 ml/3–4 tbsp icing (confectioners')
  sugar, sifted
15 ml/1 tbsp orange liqueur

1 Preheat the oven to 180°C/350°F/ Gas 4. Grease and base-line two 20 cm/8 in sandwich tins (pans).

2 Whisk the egg whites until they hold stiff peaks, then whisk in the caster sugar a tablespoon at a time, whisking well after each addition.

3 Continue whisking the meringue mixture for 1–2 minutes, until very stiff, then fold in the vanilla extract, vinegar and ground hazelnuts.

4 Divide the mixture between the sandwich tins and spread level. Bake for 50–60 minutes, until crisp. Remove from the tins and leave to cool on a wire rack.

5 To make the sauce, process the raspberries with the icing sugar and liqueur in a blender or food processor, then press the purée through a fine sieve (strainer) to remove any pips (seeds). Chill until ready to serve.

6 Whip the cream until it forms soft peaks, then fold in the raspberries. Sandwich the meringue rounds together with the raspberry cream.

7 Dust the top of the gâteau with icing sugar. Decorate with mint sprigs and serve with the raspberry sauce.

Apricot Brandy-snap Roulade

A magnificent combination of soft and crisp textures, this cake looks impressive and is easy to prepare.

Serves 6–8

INGREDIENTS
4 eggs, separated
7.5 ml/1½ tsp fresh orange juice
115 g/4 oz/½ cup caster (superfine) sugar
175 g/6 oz/1½ cups ground almonds
4 brandy-snaps, crushed, to decorate

FOR THE FILLING
150 g/5 oz canned apricots, drained
300 ml/½ pint/1¼ cups double (heavy) cream
25 g/1 oz/4 tbsp icing (confectioners') sugar

1 Preheat the oven to 190°C/375°F/ Gas 5. Grease a 33 x 23 cm/13 x 9 in Swiss roll tin (jelly roll pan), line the base of the tin with baking parchment and grease the paper.

2 Beat the egg yolks, orange juice and sugar with an electric mixer for about 10 minutes, until thick and pale. Fold in the ground almonds.

3 Whisk the egg whites until they hold stiff peaks. Fold them into the almond mixture, then transfer to the tin and smooth the surface.

4 Bake for about 20 minutes, or until a skewer inserted into the centre of the cake comes out clean. Leave the cake to cool in the tin, covered with a clean, just-damp cloth.

5 To make the filling, process the drained apricots in a blender or food processor until they reach a smooth consistency. Whip the cream and icing sugar until the cream holds soft peaks. Fold the apricot purée into the cream and icing sugar mixture.

6 Spread out the crushed brandy-snaps on a sheet of baking parchment. Spread about one-third of the cream mixture over the cooled cake, then invert it on to the layer of crushed brandy-snaps. Peel away the lining paper from the cake.

7 Cover the cake with the remaining cream mixture, then, using the baking parchment as a guide, roll up the roulade from a short end. Transfer to a serving dish with the join underneath, sticking on any extra pieces of crushed brandy-snaps.

Apricot & Orange Roulade

This elegant dessert is very good served with a spoonful of low fat, thick natural yogurt or low fat crème fraîche.

Serves 6

INGREDIENTS

FOR THE ROULADE
4 egg whites
115 g/4 oz/½ cup golden caster (superfine) sugar
50 g/2 oz/½ cup plain (all-purpose) flour
finely grated rind of 1 small orange
45 ml/3 tbsp orange juice

FOR THE FILLING
115 g/4 oz/½ cup ready-to-eat dried apricots
150 ml/¼ pint/⅔ cup orange juice

TO DECORATE
10 ml/2 tsp icing (confectioners') sugar
shreds of orange rind

1 Preheat the oven to 200°C/400°F/Gas 6. Grease a 23 x 33 cm/9 x 13 in Swiss roll tin (jelly roll pan) and line it with baking parchment. Grease the paper.

2 To make the roulade, place the egg whites in a large bowl and whisk until they form soft peaks. Gradually add the sugar, whisking hard between each addition. Fold in the flour, orange rind and juice. Spoon the mixture into the prepared tin and spread it evenly.

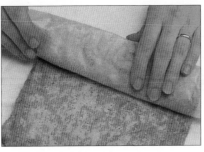

3 Bake for 15–18 minutes until golden. Turn out on to a sheet of baking parchment and roll it up from one short side. Leave to cool.

4 Roughly chop the apricots, place them in a pan with the orange juice and heat gently. Cover the pan and simmer until most of the liquid has been absorbed. Blend the apricots in a food processor to make a purée.

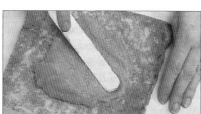

5 Unroll the roulade and spread with the apricot mixture. Roll up, arrange strips of paper diagonally across the roll, sprinkle lightly with lines of icing sugar, then remove the paper strips. Scatter the roulade with orange rind to serve.

Chocolate Roulade

A ravishing roulade topped with curls of fresh coconut, perfect for that special anniversary.

Serves 8

INGREDIENTS
150 g/5 oz/¾ cup caster (superfine) sugar
5 eggs, separated
50 g/2 oz/½ cup unsweetened cocoa powder
coarsely grated curls of fresh coconut, and chocolate curls, to decorate

FOR THE FILLING
300 ml/½ pint/1¼ cups double (heavy) cream
45 ml/3 tbsp whisky
50 g/2 oz solid creamed coconut, finely grated, or desiccated (dry unsweetened shredded) coconut
25 g/1 oz/2 tbsp caster (superfine) sugar

1 Preheat the oven to 180°C/350°F/Gas 4. Grease and line a 33 x 23 cm/13 x 9 in Swiss roll tin (jelly roll pan). Dust a large sheet of baking parchment with 30 ml/2 tbsp of the sugar.

2 Place the egg yolks in a bowl. Add the remaining sugar and whisk with a hand-held electric mixer until it leaves a trail. Sift the cocoa over, then fold in carefully.

3 Whisk the egg whites in a clean, grease-free bowl until they form soft peaks. Fold about 15 ml/1 tbsp of the whites into the chocolate mixture to lighten it, then fold in the remaining whites evenly.

4 Scrape the mixture into the prepared tin, taking it right into the corners. Smooth the surface with a palette knife or metal spatula, then bake for 20–25 minutes, or until well risen and springy to the touch.

5 Turn the cooked roulade out on to the sugar-dusted paper and carefully peel off the lining paper. Cover with a damp, clean dishtowel and leave to cool.

6 Make the filling. Whisk the cream with the whisky in a bowl until the mixture just holds its shape, then stir in the grated creamed coconut, or desiccated coconut, with the sugar.

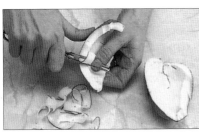

7 Uncover the sponge and spread about three-quarters of the cream mixture to the edges. Roll up carefully from a long side. Transfer to a plate, pipe or spoon the remaining cream mixture on top, then make the coconut curls and place on top with the chocolate curls.

Kiwi Fruit Roulade

This sophisticated dessert just melts in the mouth and would make the perfect end to a formal dinner party.

Serves 6

INGREDIENTS
12–16 young geranium leaves
5 eggs, separated
275 g/10 oz/2¼ cups caster (superfine) sugar
30 ml/2 tbsp icing (confectioners') sugar,
  plus extra for dusting
a few drops of rose water
300 ml/½ pint/1¼ cups double (heavy) cream
2 kiwi fruit
10–15 fresh or crystallized geranium petals

1 Preheat the oven to 180°C/350°F/ Gas 4. Line a 20 x 28 cm/8 x 11 in baking tray with baking parchment and lay the geranium leaves all over it.

2 Beat together the egg yolks and caster sugar until the mixture is light and fluffy.

3 In a separate bowl, whisk the egg whites until they are stiff and then fold into the egg yolk and sugar mixture until it is smooth.

4 Pour the mixture on top of the geranium leaves on the baking tray and bake for about 10 minutes, until just set. Remove from the oven and leave to cool.

5 Turn the roulade out on to a clean piece of baking parchment dusted with 30 ml/2 tbsp icing sugar. Carefully remove the geranium leaves.

6 Add a few drops of rose water to the cream and then whip until soft peaks form.

7 Spread the whipped cream over the roulade. Peel and thinly slice the kiwi fruit and distribute the slices over the surface of the cream.

8 Roll up the roulade, holding the short edges. Dust with icing sugar and arrange the petals on top.

Cinnamon Apple Gâteau

Make this lovely cake for an autumn celebration or dinner party dessert.

Serves 8

INGREDIENTS
3 eggs
115 g/4 oz/½ cup caster (superfine) sugar
75 g/3 oz/⅔ cup plain (all-purpose) flour
5 ml/1 tsp ground cinnamon

FOR THE FILLING AND TOPPING
4 large eating apples
60 ml/4 tbsp clear honey
15 ml/1 tbsp water
75 g/3 oz/½ cup sultanas (golden raisins)
2.5 ml/½ tsp ground cinnamon
350 g/12 oz/1½ cups low fat soft cheese
60 ml/4 tbsp low fat fromage frais or ricotta
10 ml/2 tsp lemon juice
mint sprigs, to decorate

FOR THE APRICOT GLAZE
45 ml/3 tbsp apricot jam
dash of lemon juice

1 Preheat the oven to 190°C/375°F/ Gas 5. Grease and line a 23 cm/9 in round cake tin (pan). Place the eggs and sugar in a bowl and beat with a hand-held electric whisk until the mixture has the texture of mousse. When the whisk is lifted, a trail should remain on the surface of the mixture for at least 15 seconds.

2 Sift the flour and cinnamon over the egg mixture and carefully fold in with a large spoon.

3 Pour into the prepared tin and bake for 25–30 minutes or until the cake springs back when lightly pressed. Turn the cake out on to a wire rack, remove the paper and leave it to cool.

4 To make the filling, peel, core and slice three of the apples and put them in a pan. Add 30 ml/2 tbsp of the honey and the water. Bring to the boil, cover and cook over a low heat for about 10 minutes, or until the apples have softened. Add the sultanas and cinnamon, stir well, replace the lid and leave to cool.

5 Put the soft cheese in a bowl with the remaining honey, the fromage frais or ricotta and half the lemon juice. Beat until the mixture is smooth. Cut the cake in half horizontally, place the bottom half on a board and drizzle over any liquid from the apples. Spread with two-thirds of the cheese mixture, then top with the apple filling. Fit the top of the cake in place.

6 To make the apricot glaze, heat the jam with the lemon juice over a low heat until it is runny. Press through a strainer and return to the pan to keep warm over low heat.

7 Swirl the remaining cheese mixture over the top of the cake. Slice the remaining apple, sprinkle with lemon juice and use to decorate the edge.

8 Brush the slices of apple with apricot glaze and place mint sprigs on top to decorate.

Pineapple & Kirsch Gâteau

A dramatic effect is created when this cake, with its kirsch-flavoured creamy filling, is sliced to reveal the striped pattern inside.

Serves 10–12

INGREDIENTS
175 g/6 oz/¾ cup butter
115 g/4 oz/½ cup caster (superfine) sugar, plus extra for sprinkling
2 eggs, lightly beaten
115 g/4 oz/1 cup self-raising (self-rising) flour, sifted
10 ml/2 tsp grated lemon rind
225 g/8 oz ginger nut biscuits (gingersnaps)
pineapple wedges and leaves, to decorate

FOR THE FILLING AND COATING
750 ml/1¼ pints/3 cups double (heavy) cream
30 ml/2 tbsp kirsch
225 g/8 oz fresh pineapple, finely chopped
115 g/4 oz/1⅓ cups desiccated (dry unsweetened shredded) coconut, toasted

1 Preheat the oven to 200°C/400°F/ Gas 6. Grease and line a 28 x 18 cm/ 11 x 7 in Swiss roll tin (jelly roll pan). and a 20 cm/8 in round springform cake tin (pan). Put 50 g/2 oz/4 tbsp of the butter, the sugar, eggs, flour and lemon rind in a bowl and beat until light and fluffy. Spread the mixture in the Swiss roll tin and bake for 10–12 minutes, until firm and golden.

2 Meanwhile, melt the remaining butter in a pan, crush the biscuits and stir in. Press the crumb mixture over the base of the round cake tin.

3 When the cake is cooked, turn it out on to a sheet of non-stick baking parchment sprinkled with caster sugar. Remove the lining paper.

4 Make the filling and coating. Whip the cream and combine half of it with the kirsch and the chopped pineapple. Spread the mixture over the cake and then cut the cake into four long strips.

5 Roll up the first strip of cake and filling and stand it on one end in the tin on the biscuit base. Wrap the remaining strips around to form a 20 cm/8 in cake. Chill for 15 minutes.

6 Carefully remove the cake from the tin and place it on a serving plate. Spoon some of the remaining cream into a piping (pastry) bag and spread the rest over top and side of the cake. Cover with toasted coconut. Pipe swirls of cream on top of the cake and decorate with pineapple wedges and leaves.

COOK'S TIP: Give a marbled effect to the cake by colouring half the sponge mixture with a few drops of food colouring. Put alternate spoonfuls of plain and tinted into the tin and swirl with a skewer before baking.

Caramel Meringue Gâteau with Sloe Gin

Two crisp rounds of orange meringue are filled with a refreshing blend of cream, mango, grapes and sloe gin.

Serves 8

INGREDIENTS
4 egg whites
225 g/8 oz/1 cup soft light
    brown sugar
3 drops of white wine vinegar
3 drops of vanilla extract
10 ml/2 tsp grated orange rind
whipped cream, to decorate

FOR THE FILLING AND
    CARAMEL TOPPING
300 ml/½ pint/1¼ cups double
    (heavy) cream
45 ml/3 tbsp sloe gin
1 mango, chopped
225 g/8 oz mixed green and black
    seedless grapes, halved
75 g/3 oz/6 tbsp granulated sugar

1 Preheat the oven to 160°C/325°F/ Gas 3. Base-line two 20 cm/8 in sandwich tins (pans). Whisk the egg whites until stiff. Add half the sugar and continue to whisk until the meringue softens again.

2 Fold in the remaining sugar, the white wine vinegar, vanilla extract and grated orange rind. Divide the mixture between the tins, spread evenly and bake for 40 minutes. Leave to cool.

3 Make the filling. Whip the double cream in a large bowl until it is fairly thick, then carefully fold in the sloe gin, chopped mango and halved green and black grapes using a wooden spoon.

4 Gently spread one meringue layer with the whipped cream and fruit mixture, then place the second meringue layer on top of the filling and press it down firmly but carefully, so that the delicate meringue does not break. Transfer the gâteau to a serving plate.

5 Line a baking sheet with baking parchment. Put the sugar for the caramel topping into a heavy pan. Heat gently until it melts. Increase the heat and cook, without stirring, until it becomes golden and a spoonful hardens when dropped into cold water.

6 Drizzle some of the caramel on to the baking parchment to make decorative shapes and allow these to cool and harden. Drizzle the remaining caramel over the gâteau. Decorate the top with the whipped cream and stand the cooled caramel shapes upright in the cream.

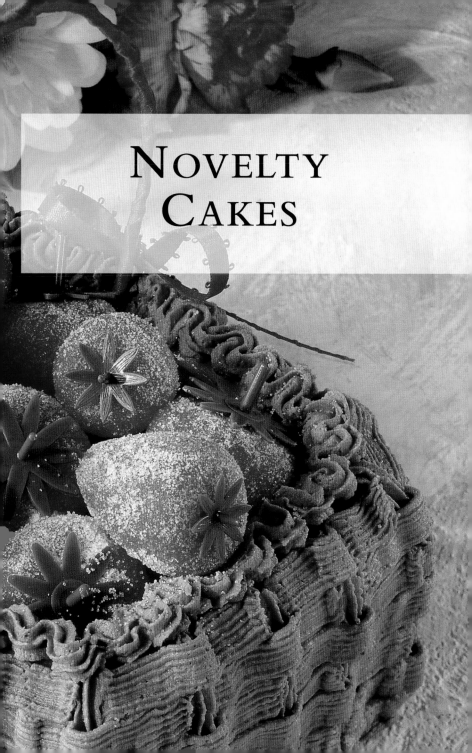

NOVELTY
CAKES

The Beautiful Present Cake

For a best friend, mother, grandmother, aunt or sister, this beautiful cake can mark any special occasion.

Serves 15–20

INGREDIENTS
2 x quantity quick-mix sponge cake, baked in a 23 cm/9 in square cake tin (pan)
1 quantity butter icing
60 ml/4 tbsp apricot glaze
1¼ x quantity marzipan
1⅔ x quantity sugarpaste (fondant) icing
purple and pink food colouring and pen

1 Cut the cake in half horizontally. Sandwich together with butter icing, place on a cake board and brush with apricot glaze. On a surface dusted with icing (confectioners') sugar roll out the marzipan to about 5 mm/¼ in thick and use to cover the cake.

2 Colour about five-eights of the sugarpaste purple. Roll out on a lightly dusted surface and use to cover the cake. With a heart-shaped cookie cutter, stamp out hearts, remove them with a knife, knead the trimmings and reserve wrapped in clear film (plastic wrap).

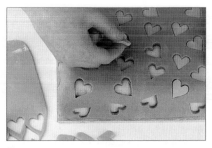

3 Colour the remaining icing pink and roll out to a 5 mm/¼ in thickness. Cut out hearts to fill the spaces. Wrap the trimmings and reserve.

4 Roll out the pink icing and cut into three strips 2 cm/¾ in wide and 30 cm/12 in long. Lay two at right angles across the centre of cake, brushing with a little water to secure. Reserve the trimmings. Divide the remaining strip into quarters and arrange in the centre of the cake to make a bow. Secure with a little water and reserve the trimmings.

5 Roll out all the remaining icing and cut two rounds of each colour with a small fluted cutter. Roll the edges with a cocktail stick (toothpick) to make frilled petals. Make two small purple balls for flower centres. Assemble the flowers and secure to the cake with a little water. Make a name tag from the trimmings. Write a name with a food-colouring pen and secure to the cake.

Terracotta Flowerpot

Ideal for celebrating a gardener's birthday or Mother's Day, this flowerpot cake is filled with a colourful arrangement of icing flowers and foliage.

Serves 15

INGREDIENTS
1 x quantity Madeira cake, baked in a
    1.2 litre/2 pint/5 cup pudding bowl
175 g/6 oz/generous ½ cup jam
½ x quantity butter icing
30 ml/2 tbsp apricot glaze
2 x quantity sugarpaste (fondant) icing
orange-red, red, silver, green, purple and
    yellow food colouring
2 chocolate flakes, crushed
2 x quantity royal icing

1 Slice the cake into three layers and stick together with jam and butter icing. Cut out a shallow circle from the cake top, leaving a 1 cm/½ in rim.

2 Brush the outside of the cake and rim with apricot glaze. Tint 400 g/ 14 oz/2½ cups of the sugarpaste dark orange-red and cover the cake and rim. Reserve the trimmings. Leave to dry.

3 Use the trimmings to make decorations and handles for the flowerpot. Leave to dry on baking parchment before attaching using a little water. Sprinkle the chocolate flakes into the pot for soil.

4 Tint a small piece of sugarpaste very pale orange-red. Use to make a seed bag. When dry, paint on a pattern in food colouring. Tint two small pieces of icing red and silver. Make a trowel and leave to dry over a wooden spoon handle.

5 Tint the remaining icing green, purple and a small piece yellow. Use to make the flowers and leaves, attaching together with royal icing. Score leaf veins with the back of a knife. Make grass and seeds from trimmings. Leave to dry on baking parchment.

6 Place the leaves and flowers in the flowerpot with the seed bag, trowel, seeds and grass arranged around it.

Sun Cake

Whatever the star sign of the month, this cheerful sun cake would be a bright way to celebrate anyone's birthday.

Serves 10–12

INGREDIENTS

2 x quantity quick-mix sponge cake,
    baked in 2 x 15 cm/6 in round tins (pans)
25 g/1 oz/2 tbsp unsalted (sweet) butter
450 g/1 lb/4 cups sifted icing
    (confectiones') sugar
120 ml/4 fl oz/½ cup apricot glaze
2 large egg whites
1–2 drops glycerine
juice of 1 lemon
30 ml/2 tbsp water
yellow and orange
    food colouring

2 Brush the warm apricot glaze over the cake.

1 For the sunbeams cut one of the cakes into eight equal wedges. Cut away a rounded piece from the base of each so that they fit neatly up against the sides of the whole cake. Make butter icing with the butter and 25 g/1 oz/2 tbsp of the icing sugar. Place the whole cake on a 40 cm/ 16 in board and attach the sunbeams with the butter icing.

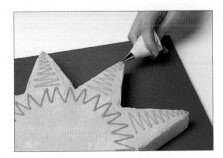

3 For the icing, beat the egg whites until stiff. Gradually add the icing sugar, glycerine and lemon juice, and beat for 1 minute. Reserve a small amount of icing for decoration, then tint the remainder yellow and spread over the cake. Tint the reserved icing bright yellow and orange. Pipe the details on to the cake.

COOK'S TIP: If necessary, thin the icing with water or add icing (confectioners') sugar to thicken.

A Basket of Strawberries

Quick and easy to make, a perfect surprise for a birthday. Don't be put off by the icing technique, it's much easier than it looks!

Serves 6–8

INGREDIENTS

1 x quantity quick-mix sponge cake,
    baked in a 450 g/1 lb loaf tin (pan)
45 ml/3 tbsp apricot glaze
1½ x quantity marzipan
1 x quantity chocolate-flavour
    butter icing
red food colouring
50 g/2 oz/¼ cup caster (superfine) sugar
10 plastic strawberry stalks
30 cm/12 in thin red ribbon

1 Level the top of the cake and make it perfectly flat. Score a 5 mm/¼ in border around the edge and scoop out the inside to make a shallow hollow. Brush the sides and border edges of the cake with apricot glaze.

2 Roll out 275 g/10 oz/scant 2 cups of the marzipan, cut into rectangles and use to cover the sides of the cake, overlapping the borders. Press the edges together to seal.

3 Using a basketweave nozzle, pipe vertical lines of chocolate–flavour butter icing 2.5 cm/1 in apart all around the sides of the cake. Pipe short horizontal lines alternately crossing over and then stopping at the vertical lines to give a basketweave effect. Using a star nozzle, pipe a decorative line of icing around the top edge of the basket to finish.

4 Tint the remaining marzipan red and mould it into ten strawberry shapes. Roll the shapes in the caster sugar and press a plastic stalk into each top. Carefully arrange the strawberries in the "basket".

5 For the basket handle, fold 30 x 7.5 cm/12 x 3 in strip of foil into a thin strip and wind the ribbon around it to cover. Bend up the ends and then bend into a curve. Push the ends into the sides of the cake. Decorate with bows made from ribbon.

The Beehive

The perfect cake for an outdoors spring or summer party. Take the bees along separately on their wires and insert them into the cake at the picnic.

Serves 8–10

INGREDIENTS

2 x quantity marzipan
icing (confectioners') sugar, for dusting
1 x quantity quick-mix sponge cake, baked
   in a 900 ml/1½ pint/3¾ cup pudding bowl
75 ml/5 tbsp apricot glaze
black food colouring
20 cm/8 in square of rice paper
25 g/1 oz sugarpaste (fondant) icing
florist's wire covered in florist's tape

1 Cut off about 175 g/6 oz of marzipan and set aside, wrapped in clear film (plastic wrap). Knead the remainder on a surface lightly dusted with icing sugar, then roll into a long, thin sausage shape. If it breaks, make more than one sausage. Place the cake, dome side up, on a cake board and brush with apricot glaze.

2 Starting at the back of the base, coil the marzipan sausage around the cake. Place any joins at the back.

3 With a small, sharp knife, cut an arched doorway at the front. Remove the cut-out section and cut away some of the cake to make a hollow.

4 To make six bees, halve the reserved marzipan and colour one half black. Set aside a cherry-sized ball of black marzipan, wrapped in clear film.

5 Divide the remaining marzipan into 12 small balls in each colour. To make a bee, pinch together two balls of each colour, alternately placed. Secure with a little water, if necessary. Cut the rice paper into six pairs of wings and stick to the bees with water.

452

6 Use the reserved black marzipan and the sugarpaste icing to make the faces. Then cut the florist's wire into various lengths and pierce the bees from underneath. Once secure, press the other end of the wire into the cake. The wire must be removed before serving.

Mobile Phone Cake

For the upwardly mobile, this novel cake just has to be the business!

Serves 8–10

INGREDIENTS

1 x quantity quick-mix sponge cake, baked
   in a 23 x 13 cm/9 x 5 in loaf tin (pan)
30 ml/2 tbsp apricot glaze
1 x quantity sugarpaste (fondant) icing
black food colouring
10 small square sweets
30–45 ml/2–3 tbsp icing
   (confectioners') sugar
2.5–5 ml/½–1 tsp water

1 Turn the cake upside down. Make
a 2.5 cm/1 in diagonal cut 2.5 cm/
1 in from one end. Cut down
vertically to remove the wedge.
Remove the middle of the cake to the
wedge depth up to 4 cm/1½ in from
the other end.

2 Place the cake on a board and
brush with apricot glaze. Tint 275 g/
10 oz/1¾ cups of the sugarpaste icing
black. Use to cover the cake,
smoothing it over the carved shape.
Reserve the trimmings.

3 Tint the remaining sugarpaste icing
grey. Cut a piece to fit the hollowed
centre, leaving a 1 cm/½ in border, and
another piece 2.5 cm/1 in square.
Stamp out the centre of the square
with a diamond-shape cutter. Secure
all the pieces on the cake with water.

4 Position the sweets and a small
piece of foil for the display panel. For
the glacé icing, mix the icing sugar
with the water and tint black. With a
small round nozzle, pipe border lines
around the edges of the phone,
including the grey pieces of sugarpaste.
Pipe the numbers on the keys.

5 Roll a sausage shape from the
reserved black sugarpaste for the aerial.
Indent one side of the top with a knife
and secure the aerial with water.

VARIATION: If preferred, use a
little extra sugarpaste for the dial
pad instead of the sweets.

Artist's Box & Palette

Making cakes is an art in itself, and this cake proves it. It is the perfect celebration cake for artists of all ages.

Serves 30

INGREDIENTS
1¼ x quantity rich fruit cake, baked in a
    20 cm/8 in square tin (pan)
45 ml/3 tbsp apricot glaze
1 x quantity marzipan
2⅓ x quantity sugarpaste (fondant) icing
chestnut, yellow, blue, black, silver,
    paprika, green and mulberry
    food colouring
90 g/3½ oz/⅔ cup royal icing

1 Brush the cake with the apricot glaze. Cover in marzipan and leave to dry overnight.

2 Make a template of a painter's palette that will fit the cake top. Tint 175 g/6 oz/generous 1 cup of the sugarpaste very pale chestnut. Cut out the palette shape from the tinted sugarpaste, place on baking parchment and leave to dry overnight.

3 Tint 450 g/1 lb/3 cups of the sugarpaste icing dark chestnut. Use to cover the cake. Secure the cake on a board with royal icing. Leave to dry.

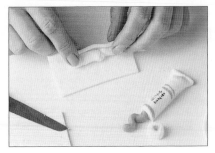

4 Divide half the remaining sugarpaste icing into seven equal parts and tint yellow, blue, black, silver, paprika, green and mulberry. Make all the decorative pieces for the box and palette, using the remaining white sugarpaste for the paint tubes. Leave to dry on baking parchment.

5 Paint black markings on the paint tubes and chestnut wood markings on the box.

6 Position all the sugarpaste pieces on the cake and board using royal icing. Leave to dry.

COOK'S TIP: Start modelling the cake decorations the day before assembling.

457

Glittering Star Cake

With a quick flick of a paintbrush you can give a sparkling effect to this glittering cake.

Serves 20–25

INGREDIENTS
1 x quantity rich fruit cake, baked in a
    20 cm/8 in round tin (pan)
40 ml/2½ tbsp apricot glaze
1½ x quantity marzipan
450 g/1 lb/3 cups sugarpaste (fondant) icing
silver, gold, lilac shimmer, red sparkle, glitter
    green and primrose sparkle food colouring
    and powder tints
90 g/3½ oz/⅔ cup royal icing

1 Brush the cake with the apricot glaze. Use two-thirds of the marzipan to cover the cake. Leave to dry overnight.

2 Cover the cake with the sugarpaste icing. Leave to dry.

3 Place the cake on a large sheet of baking parchment. Dilute a little powdered silver food colouring and, using a loaded paintbrush, flick it all over the cake to give a spattered effect. Allow to dry.

4 Make templates of two different-size moon shapes and three irregular star shapes. Divide the remaining marzipan into six pieces and tint silver, gold, lilac shimmer, red sparkle, glitter green and primrose. Using the templates, cut into stars and moons, cutting some of the stars in half.

5 Place the cut-outs on baking parchment, brush each with its own colour powder tint. Allow to dry.

6 Secure the cake on a board with royal icing. Arrange the stars and moons at different angles all over the cake, attaching with royal icing, and position the halved stars upright as though coming out of the cake. Allow to set.

COOK'S TIP: Stored in an airtight container, the cake will keep for up to 3 weeks.

Lucky Horseshoe Cake

This horseshoe-shaped cake, made to wish "good luck", is made from a round cake cut to shape. Use a crimping tool for the edge.

Serves 30–35

INGREDIENTS

1½ x quantity rich fruit cake, baked in a
  25 cm/10 in round tin (pan)
60 ml/4 tbsp apricot glaze
2 x quantity marzipan
3 x quantity sugarpaste (fondant) icing
peach and blue food colouring
3 mm/⅛ in wide blue ribbon
edible silver balls
90 g/3½ oz/⅔ cup royal icing

1 Make a horseshoe template and use to shape the cake. Brush the cake with apricot glaze. Cover the cake with marzipan using the template and 350 g/12 oz/2¼ cups of marzipan for the top, and measuring the inside and outside of the cake to cover with the remaining marzipan. Place on a board and leave overnight.

2 Tint 800 g/1¾ lb/5¼ cups of the sugarpaste icing peach. Cover the cake in the same way. Crimp the top edge.

3 Draw and measure the ribbon insertion on the template. Cut 13 pieces of ribbon fractionally longer than each slit. Make the slits in the icing through the template with a scalpel. Insert the ribbon with a pointed tool. Leave to dry overnight.

4 Tint half the remaining sugarpaste icing pale blue. Cut out nine blue small horseshoe shapes. Mark each horseshoe with a sharp knife. Cut out 12 large and 15 small blossoms with blossom cutters. Press a silver ball into the centres of the larger blossoms. Dry. Repeat with the white icing. Decorate the cake, securing with royal icing.

Bluebird Bon Voyage Cake

This cake with its marble-effect sky is sure to see someone off on an exciting journey in a very special way.

Serves 12–15

INGREDIENTS
1 x quantity royal icing
blue food colouring
2½ x quantity sugarpaste (fondant) icing
1 x quantity Madeira cake, baked in a
 20 cm/8 in round tin (pan)
1 x quantity butter icing
45 ml/3 tbsp apricot glaze
edible silver balls
thin pale blue ribbon

1 Make two-thirds of the royal icing softer, to use for filling in. Make the rest stiffer for the outlines and further piping. Tint the softer icing bright blue. Cover and leave overnight.

2 Make two different-size bird templates, and use to draw four large and five small birds on to baking parchment. Turn the paper over. Using a No 1. writing nozzle and white icing, pipe the outlines, then fill in with blue icing. Leave to dry for at least 2 days.

3 Tint two-thirds of the sugarpaste icing blue. Form all the icing into small rolls and place them alternately together on a work surface. Form into a round and lightly knead to marble.

4 Cut the cake horizontally into three and sandwich together with the butter icing. Brush with apricot glaze. Roll out the marbled icing and use to cover the cake and a board. Place the cake on the board, flush with the edge.

5 Using the No. 1 writing nozzle and the stiffer royal icing, pipe a wavy line around the edge of the board. Position the balls evenly in the icing. Secure the birds to the cake with royal icing. Pipe beads of white icing for eyes and stick on a ball. Drape the ribbon between the beaks, securing with icing.

COOK'S TIP: The finished cake can be kept for up to 1 week in an airtight container.

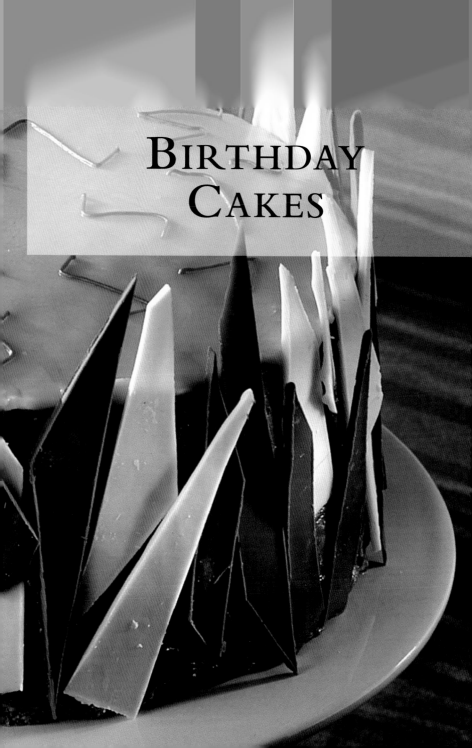

BIRTHDAY CAKES

Flickering Candle Cake

Stripy icing candles are flickering and ready to blow out on this birthday celebration cake for all ages.

Serves 15–20

INGREDIENTS
1⅓ x quantity Madeira cake mix
1 x quantity butter icing
45 ml/3 tbsp apricot glaze
2½ x quantity sugarpaste (fondant) icing
pink, yellow, purple and jade
    food colouring
edible silver balls
edible-ink pens

1 Preheat the oven to 160°C/325°F/ Gas 3. Grease and line a 20 cm/8 in square cake tin (pan). Spoon in the mixture, tap the tin lightly to level and bake for 1¼–1½ hours, until a metal skewer inserted into the centre comes out clean. Place the tin on a wire rack for 10 minutes, then turn the cake out on to the rack to cool.

2 Cut the cake horizontally into three layers. Sandwich the layers together with the butter icing and brush the cake with the apricot glaze.

3 Roll out 500 g/1¼ lb/3¾ cups of the sugarpaste icing on a surface lightly dusted with icing (confectioners') sugar. Use the sugarpaste icing to cover the cake completely and trim the edges neatly. Place the cake on a 23 cm/9 in square cake board.

4 Divide the remaining icing into quarters and colour them pink, yellow, purple and jade. Roll out the jade icing and cut into six 1 cm/½ in strips of unequal length, but each long enough to go up the side and on to the top of the cake. Make a diagonal cut at one end of each. Roll out the yellow icing and stamp out six flames with a leaf-shaped cutter. Place a silver ball in each flame.

5 Stick the candles on the cake with a little water. Mould small strips, fractionally longer than the candles' width, from the yellow and purple icing. Stick alternate colour strips on the candles at a slight angle. Stick the flames at the top.

6 Roll out the pink icing and the remaining purple icing and cut out wavy pieces. Stick on the cake above the candles. Gather the pink trimmings into a ball.

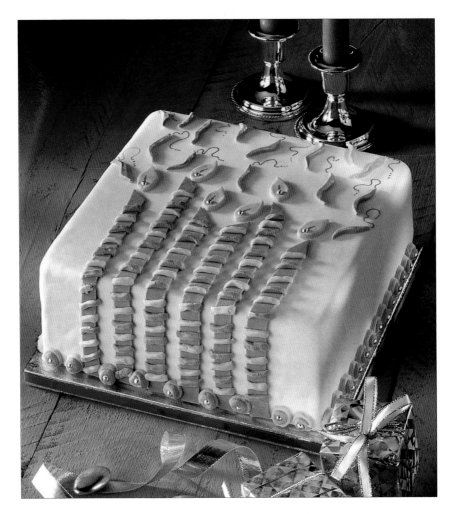

7 Roll out the remaining yellow icing and stamp out circles with a small round cutter or the end of a piping nozzle. Make small balls from the remaining pink icing and stick them to the yellow circles. Press a silver ball into the centre of each decoration. Stick the decorations around the bottom of the cake.

8 Draw wavy lines and dots coming from the purple and pink wavy icing with food colouring pens. Decorate the sides of the cake board with jade ribbon, securing it with a little softened sugar paste.

Birthday Parcel

Here is a birthday cake that is all wrapped up and ready to eat. Change the pattern by using different shaped cutters.

Serves 10

INGREDIENTS
⅔ x quantity Madeira cake mix
¾ x quantity orange-flavour butter icing
45 ml/3 tbsp apricot jam, warmed
   and strained
1⅓ x quantity sugarpaste (fondant) icing
blue, orange and green food colouring

1 Preheat the oven to 160°C/325°F/ Gas 3. Grease and line a 15 cm/6 in square cake tin (pan). Spoon in the mixture, tap to level it and bake for 1 hour 10 minutes, or until a metal skewer inserted into the centre comes out clean. Place the tin on a wire rack for 10 minutes, then turn the cake out on to the rack to cool completely.

2 Cut the cake in half horizontally and sandwich together with the butter icing. Brush the cake with the jam. Colour three-quarters of the sugarpaste icing blue. Divide the remaining icing in half and colour one half orange and the other green.

3 Roll out the blue icing on a surface lightly dusted with icing (confectioners') sugar and use it to cover the cake. Place on the cake board. Stamp out circles and triangles from the icing with cocktail cutters, lifting out to expose the cake.

4 Roll out the orange and green icing and stamp out circles and triangles. Fill the holes in the blue icing with the orange and green shapes. Gather the trimmings to use for the ribbons.

5 Roll out the orange trimmings and cut three strips about 2 cm/¾ in wide and long enough to go over each corner of the cake. Roll out the green trimmings and cut three very thin strips the same length as the orange ones. Place the orange and green strips next to each other to give three striped ribbons and stick together with a little water.

6 Stick one striped ribbon over one corner of the cake. Stick a second strip over the opposite corner. Cut the remaining ribbon in half. Bend each half to make loops and stick both to the ribbon over one corner of the cake to form a loose bow.

Eighteenth Birthday Cake

A really striking and sophisticated cake for a lucky someone celebrating their eighteenth birthday.

Serves 80

INGREDIENTS
1⅓ x quantity rich fruit cake mix
45 ml/3 tbsp apricot glaze
2½ x quantity marzipan
4⅔ x quantity sugarpaste (fondant) icing
black food colouring
30 ml/2 tbsp royal icing

1 Preheat the oven to 150°C/300°F/Gas 2. Grease and line a 33.5 x 20 cm/13½ x 8 in diamond-shaped deep cake tin (pan). Spoon in the mixture, smooth the top, make a slight dip in the centre and bake for 3¼–3¾ hours, until a metal skewer put into the centre comes out clean. Cool in the tin, then turn out.

2 Brush the cake with glaze and place it on a cake board. Roll out the marzipan on a surface lightly dusted with icing (confectioners') sugar. Use to cover the cake and trim the edges.

3 Roll out 1.1 kg/2½ lb/3⅓ cups of the sugarpaste icing on a surface lightly dusted with icing sugar and use to cover the cake, trimming the edges. Knead the trimmings into the remaining sugarpaste and colour it black. Roll out two-thirds and cut into four strips the width and length of each section of the cake board.

4 Brush the board with glaze, place each strip in position and trim. Roll out one-quarter of the remaining sugarpaste and stamp out the number 18 with a special cutter or using a template. Leave on a piece of foam sponge to dry. Roll out some more sugarpaste and use a cocktail cutter to stamp out 40 triangles for the bow ties and 20 for the glasses.

5 Roll out some more sugarpaste and stamp out 20 circles for the music notes and 10 bases for the glasses with a tiny round cutter. Cut the bases in half. Cut out thin strips for the tails of the notes and the stems of the glasses.

6 Colour the royal icing black and spoon into a piping (icing) bag fitted with a No. 1 plain writing nozzle. With tiny beads of icing, join the bow ties together, attach the music notes to their tails and the glasses to their stems and bases. Leave to dry.

7 Arrange the numbers, notes, glasses and bow ties over the top of the cake, then stick them down with a bead of icing. Finish the decoration with black and white ribbons.

Twenty-first Birthday Cake

This cake looks good in any pale colour or simply white. Add the colour with the ribbons and write your own message.

Serves 80

INGREDIENTS

1⅔ x quantity rich fruit
    cake mix
45 ml/3 tbsp apricot glaze
2½ x quantity marzipan
2 x quantity royal icing
blue food colouring
500 g/1¼ lb ready-made
    petal paste
cornflour (cornstarch), for dusting

1 Preheat the oven to 150°C/300°F/ Gas 2. Grease and line a 25 cm/10 in round deep cake tin (pan). Spoon in the mixture, smooth the top, make a depression in the centre and bake for 3¾ hours, until a metal skewer inserted into the centre comes out clean. Cool in the tin, then turn out.

2 Brush the cake with glaze and place on a 30 cm/12 in round cake board. Roll out the marzipan on a surface dusted with icing (confectioners') sugar. Use to cover the cake and trim the edges.

3 Colour the royal icing pale blue. Flat-ice the top and side of the cake with three layers of smooth royal icing, leaving each to dry before adding the next, then ice the cake board.

4 Colour the petal paste pale blue. Roll out one-third on a surface lightly dusted with cornflour. Stamp out two squares with a 7.5 cm/3 in fluted cutter. Stamp out an oval from one square with a 5 cm/2 in plain cutter. Make two tiny holes with a No. 2 plain writing nozzle on the left hand edge on both squares to match. Continue to make a cut-out pattern all around the front of the card. Leave on a piece of foam sponge to dry.

5 Roll out some more petal paste. Stamp out 25 shapes with a club-shaped cocktail cutter, allowing for breakage. Use a tiny petal cutter to cut out three shapes on each piece. Leave to dry thoroughly. Roll out the remaining paste and stamp out two end shapes for the keys with the club cutter. Cut out the remaining parts of the key shapes with a sharp knife. Pattern the keys with tiny cutters. Leave to dry.

6 Tie plain pale and royal blue ribbons around the board, securing with a pin. Fit looped royal blue ribbon around the side of the cake and secure with a bead of icing.

7 Spoon blue icing into a piping bag fitted with a No. 3 plain writing nozzle. Arrange 18 cut-out sugar pieces around the top edge of the cake and secure with a bead of icing. Leave to dry. Pipe a shell edging around the base and between the cut-outs on top.

8 Write your message on the plain card with a food colouring pen and decorate the keys. Thread narrow royal blue ribbon around the card and through the matching holes to join it. Tie in a bow with long ends.

9 Thread matching ribbon through the cut-out sugar pieces, joining the ends with a bead of icing. Tie a bow and stick it to the side of the cake with a bead of icing. Attach the card and the keys with icing and leave to dry.

473

Flower Birthday Cake

Pretty piped sugar flowers and coral and white ribbons decorate this charming birthday cake.

Serves 40

INGREDIENTS
¾ x quantity rich fruit cake mix
30 ml/2 tbsp apricot glaze
1½ x quantity marzipan
3¾ x quantity royal icing
yellow and orange food colouring

1 Preheat the oven to 150°C/300°F/ Gas 2. Grease and line a 18 cm/7 in round deep cake tin (pan). Spoon in the mixture, smooth the top, make a slight depression in the centre and bake for 2½–2¾ hours, until a metal skewer inserted into the centre comes out clean. Leave to cool in the tin, then turn out.

2 Brush the cake with the apricot glaze. Roll out the marzipan on a surface lightly dusted with icing (confectioners') sugar and use to cover the cake. Transfer to a 23 cm/9 in round cake board. Flat-ice the top and side of the cake with three layers of royal icing, leaving each to dry, then ice the cake board.

3 Snip an inverted V shape off the point of a baking parchment piping (icing) bag. Fit another bag with a petal nozzle, a third with a No. 1 plain writing nozzle and a fourth with a medium star nozzle.

4 Colour one-third of the remaining icing yellow and then colour 15 ml/ 1 tbsp of the icing orange. Pipe the narcissi using the petal nozzle for the petals and the writing nozzle for the centres. Make four white narcissi with yellow centres and nine yellow narcissi with orange centres.

5 Pipe nine simple white flowers with the snipped bag and add yellow centres with the plain nozzle. Leave to dry on baking parchment.

6 Arrange the flowers on the top of the cake, securing them with a little icing. With white icing and a star nozzle, pipe shell edging all around the top and base of the cake.

7 With white icing and a No. 2 plain writing nozzle, pipe "Happy Birthday" on either side of the flowers.

8 Place white ribbon around the board and secure with a pin. Place coral ribbon around the board and side of the cake, securing with a bead of icing. Over-pipe the writing with orange icing and a No. 1 plain writing nozzle. Tie a bow and stick to the cake with a bead of icing. Leave to dry.

Birthday Bowl of Strawberries

With its hand-painted picture and moulded fruit, this is the ideal cake to celebrate a summer birthday.

Serves 20

INGREDIENTS
1 x quantity Madeira cake mix
1 x quantity butter icing
45 ml/3 tbsp apricot glaze
2 x quantity sugarpaste (fondant) icing
pink, red, yellow, green and claret
   food colouring
cornflour (cornstarch), for dusting
yellow powdered food colouring

1 Preheat the oven to 160°C/325°F/ Gas 3. Grease and line a 20 cm/8 in petal-shaped cake tin (pan). Spoon in the mixture, tap lightly to level and bake for 1¼ hours, until a metal skewer inserted into the centre comes out clean. Place the tin on a wire rack for 10 minutes, then turn the cake out on to the rack to cool.

2 Colour the butter icing pink. Cut the cake horizontally into three and sandwich together with the butter icing. Brush with the glaze. Roll out 500g/1¼ lb/3¾ cups of the sugarpaste icing on a surface that has been lightly dusted with icing (confectioners') sugar. Use to cover the cake and trim. Place the cake on a 25 cm/10 in petal-shaped cake board and leave to dry for 12 hours.

3 Colour three-quarters of the remaining sugarpaste red. Divide the rest in half and colour one half yellow and the other green. Dust your hands with cornflour and mould the red icing into strawberries.

4 Make tiny oval shapes from the yellow icing and press on to the strawberries. Shape the green icing into flat circles and snip round the edges with scissors. Curl the edges slightly and stick to the top of the strawberries with a little water. Leave to dry on baking parchment.

5 Put red, green, yellow and claret food colouring on a palette and dilute slightly with a little water. Paint the outline of the bowl with the claret food colouring, then fill in the pattern. Add highlights with a little of the yellow powdered food colouring.

6 Finish painting the pattern, filling in the strawberries in the bowl and around the edge of the cake.

7 Decorate the cake with red and green ribbons. Stick two moulded strawberries to the top and arrange the others around the bottom.

Frosted Flower Cake

If pansies are not in season, use other edible flowers – just coordinate the colour of the icing and decoration.

Serves 20–25

INGREDIENTS
1 x quantity rich fruit cake mix
45 ml/3 tbsp apricot glaze
1½ x quantity marzipan
1⅔ x quantity royal icing
orange food colouring
about 7 orange and
    purple pansies
1 egg white, lightly beaten
caster (superfine) sugar, for frosting

1 Preheat the oven to 150°C/300°F/ Gas 2. Grease and line a 20 cm/8 in round deep cake tin (pan). Spoon in the mixture, smooth the top, make a slight depression in the centre and bake for 2¾–3¼ hours, until a metal skewer inserted into the centre comes out clean. Cool in the tin, then turn out on to a wire rack.

2 Brush the cake with the glaze. Roll out the marzipan on a surface lightly dusted with icing (confectioners') sugar and use to cover the cake.

3 Secure the cake to a 25 cm/10 in round cake board with a little icing. Colour one-quarter of the icing pale orange. Flat-ice the cake with three or four layers of icing, using orange for the top and white for the sides. Leave each layer to dry.

4 Wash the pansies and dry on kitchen paper. Leave a short piece of stem attached. Brush both sides of the petals with egg white. Holding the flowers by the stems, sprinkle them evenly with sugar, then shake off the excess. Leave to dry on a wire rack covered with baking parchment.

5 Spoon some white icing into a piping (icing) bag fitted with a No. 19 star nozzle. Pipe a row of scrolls around the top of the cake. Pipe a second row of scrolls in the opposite direction, directly underneath. Pipe another row of scrolls around the bottom of the cake.

6 Spoon some orange icing into a piping bag fitted with a No. 1 writing nozzle. Pipe around the outline of the top of each scroll. Pipe a row of orange dots under the reverse scrolls and a double row of dots above the bottom row of scrolls. Arrange the pansies on top of the cake. Decorate with a wide and a narrow purple ribbon.

479

Cloth of Roses Cake

It is almost too pretty to eat, so make this for a very special birthday.

Serves 20–25

INGREDIENTS
1 x quantity rich fruit cake mix
45 ml/3 tbsp apricot glaze
1½ x quantity marzipan
2⅔ x quantity sugarpaste (fondant) icing
yellow, orange and green food colouring
cornflour (cornstarch), for dusting
⅛ x quantity royal icing

1 Preheat the oven to 150°C/300°F/Gas 2. Grease and line a 20 cm/8 in round deep cake tin (pan). Spoon in the mixture, smooth the top, make a slight depression in the centre and bake for 2¾–3¼ hours, until a metal skewer inserted into the centre comes out clean. Cool in the tin, then turn out on to a wire rack.

2 Brush the cake with the glaze. Roll out the marzipan on a surface lightly dusted with icing (confectioners') sugar and use to cover the cake. Cut a template from baking parchment: draw a 25 cm/10 in circle. Use a 7 cm/2¾ in plain cutter as a guide to draw half circles 2.5 cm/1 in wide around the outside of the large circle. Cut out.

3 Colour 350 g/12 oz/2¼ cups of the sugarpaste pale yellow and roll out on a work surface lightly dusted with icing sugar. Use to cover the cake. Place the cake on a 25 cm/10 in cake board.

4 Colour 350 g/12 oz/2¼ cups of the remaining sugarpaste pale orange and roll out to a 30 cm/12 in circle. Place the template on the icing and cut out. Brush the cake with water and cover with the orange icing so that the scallops fall just over the edge. Curl them slightly and leave to dry.

5 Reserve about one-quarter of the remaining sugarpaste for the leaves and divide the rest into quarters. Colour them pale yellow, deep yellow, orange and marbled yellow and orange.

6 Dust your hands with cornflour. To make the roses, take a small ball of sugarpaste and form into a cone. Form a piece into a petal slightly thicker at the base. Press around the cone, so it sits above the top. Curl the end.

7 Repeat with several more petals, making them slightly larger each time and attaching them so they just overlap. Cut off the base. Make about 18 roses and dry on baking parchment.

8 Colour the remaining sugarpaste green. Roll out thinly and stamp out about 24 leaves with a petal cutter. Leave to dry on baking parchment.

9 Arrange the leaves and roses on the cake, securing them with a bead of royal icing. Decorate the cake with a thin yellow ribbon.

481

Celebration Rose and Fruit Cake

Covered with delicately flavoured rose water icing, this luscious cake is decorated with frosted roses.

Serves 20–25

INGREDIENTS
1 x quantity rich fruit cake mix
900 g/2 lb/5½ cups icing
   (confectioners') sugar
3 egg whites
5 ml/1 tsp distilled rose water
2.5 ml/½ tsp lemon juice
120 ml/4 fl oz/½ cup liquid glucose
45 ml/3 tbsp rose jelly
8–9 roses
caster (superfine) sugar, for frosting

1 Preheat the oven to 150°C/300°F/ Gas 2. Grease and line a 20 cm/8 in round deep cake tin (pan). Spoon in the mixture, smooth the top, make a slight depression in the centre and bake for 2¾–3¼ hours, until a metal skewer inserted into the centre comes out clean. Cool in the tin, then turn out on to a wire rack.

2 Sift the icing sugar into a bowl and beat in two of the egg whites, the rose water, lemon juice and liquid glucose with a wooden spoon. Knead until the mixture forms a smooth, pliable icing.

3 Transfer the cake to a 25 cm/10 in round cake board. Brush the top and side with the rose jelly, warming it first, if necessary. Roll out the icing on a surface lightly dusted with icing sugar. Position the icing on the cake, smoothing the top and the sides. Frill out at the base of the cake and trim off any excess.

4 Wash the roses and dry on kitchen paper. Leave a little of the stem still attached. Lightly beat the remaining egg white. Brush both sides of the rose petals with the egg white. Holding the flowers by the stems, sprinkle them evenly with sugar, then shake off the excess. Leave to dry on a wire rack covered with baking parchment.

5 If necessary, trim the stems of the roses. Arrange three roses on top of the cake and the remainder around the frill at the base.

Jazzy Chocolate Gâteau

With its modern and sophisticated appearance, this would make a good birthday cake for a teenager.

Serves 12–15

INGREDIENTS
2 x quantity chocolate-flavoured quick-mix
    sponge mix
75 g/3 oz plain (semisweet) chocolate
75 g/3 oz white chocolate
½ x quantity fudge frosting
120 ml/8 tbsp chocolate
    hazelnut spread

FOR THE COFFEE GLACE ICING
115 g/4 oz/1 cup icing (confectioners') sugar
5 ml/1 tsp weak coffee
30 ml/2 tbsp warm water

1 Preheat the oven to 160°C/325°F/ Gas 3. Grease and line two 20 cm/8 in round cake tins (pans). Divide the cake mixture equally between the tins, smooth the surfaces and bake for 20–30 minutes, until a metal skewer inserted into the centres comes out clean. Turn out on to a wire rack.

2 Meanwhile, cover a large baking sheet with baking parchment. Melt the plain and white chocolate in separate bowls over pans of simmering water, stirring until smooth, then pour on to the baking sheet.

3 Spread out evenly with a palette knife or metal spatula and leave to cool until firm enough to cut. When the chocolate no longer feels sticky, cut out random shapes and set aside.

4 Sandwich the two cooled cakes together with the fudge frosting and transfer to a serving plate.

5 To make the icing, sift the sugar into a bowl, stir in the coffee and gradually stir in sufficient water to give the consistency of thick cream. Beat until smooth. Spread the icing on top of the cake almost to the edges.

6 Spread the side of the cake with enough chocolate hazelnut spread to cover. Arrange the chocolate pieces around the side of the cake, pressing them into the spread. Spoon about 45 ml/3 tbsp of the spread into a piping bag fitted with a No. 1 plain nozzle and pipe "jazzy" lines over the icing.

Divine Chocolate Cake

This very rich cake would be the best possible way to say "Happy Birthday" to a chocoholic.

Serves 18–20

INGREDIENTS
225 g/8 oz fine quality dark (bittersweet)
  chocolate, chopped
115 g/4 oz/½ cup unsalted (sweet) butter,
  cut into pieces
170 ml/5½ fl oz/⅔ cup water
250 g/9 oz/1¼ cups granulated sugar
10 ml/2 tsp vanilla extract
2 eggs, separated
170 ml/5½ fl oz/⅔ cup buttermilk or
  sour cream
365 g/12½ oz/2 cups plain (all-purpose) flour
10 ml/2 tsp baking powder
5 ml/1 tsp bicarbonate of soda
  (baking soda)
pinch of cream of tartar
chocolate curls, raspberries and icing
  (confectioners') sugar, to decorate

FOR THE CHOCOLATE FUDGE FILLING
450 g/1 lb fine quality couverture
  chocolate or dark (bittersweet)
  chocolate, chopped
225 g/8 oz/1 cup unsalted (sweet) butter
75 ml/3 fl oz/⅓ cup brandy or rum
215 g/7½ oz/¾ cup seedless
  raspberry preserve

FOR THE CHOCOLATE GANACHE GLAZE
250 ml/8 fl oz/1 cup double (heavy) cream
225 g/8 oz couverture chocolate or dark
  (bittersweet) chocolate, chopped
30 ml/2 tbsp brandy or rum

1 Preheat the oven to 180°C/350°F/ Gas 4. Grease and line a 25 cm/10 in springform tin (pan).

2 Heat the chocolate, butter and water in a small pan, stirring frequently, until smooth. Remove from the heat, transfer to a bowl, beat in the sugar and cool. Lightly beat the egg yolks, then beat into the chocolate mixture with the vanilla extract.

3 Fold in the buttermilk or sour cream. Sift the flour, baking powder and bicarbonate of soda into a bowl, then fold into the chocolate mixture. Beat the egg whites and cream of tartar with an electric mixer until stiff peaks form, then fold into the chocolate mixture.

4 Pour the mixture into the tin and bake for 45–50 minutes, until the cake begins to shrink from the side of the tin. Place the tin on a wire rack for 10 minutes, then turn the cake out on to the rack to cool.

5 To make the filling, heat the chocolate, butter and 60 ml/4 tbsp of the brandy or rum in a pan, stirring frequently, until smooth. Remove from the heat and ser aside to cool and thicken.

6 Cut the cake horizontally into three layers. Heat the raspberry preserve and remaining brandy or rum, stirring frequently until smooth. Spread thinly over each layer and leave to set.

7 Place the bottom layer in the cleaned tin. Spread with half the filling, top with the second layer and spread with the remaining filling. Top with the final layer, coated side down.

8 Gently press together, cover and chill for 4–6 hours or overnight. Remove the cake from the tin and set on a wire rack over a tray.

9 To make the glaze, bring the cream to the boil in a pan. Remove from the heat, add all the chocolate and stir until smooth. Stir in the brandy or rum, strain and set aside for 4–5 minutes to thicken. Whisk until smooth and shiny.

10 Pour the glaze over the cake, smoothing with a metal spatula. Leave to set, then transfer to a serving plate and decorate with chocolate curls and raspberries. Dust with icing sugar.

Chocolate Box with Caramel Mousse & Berries

For chocolate lovers this luscious chocolate box makes the ideal birthday cake. Choose berries and fruit that are in season

Serves 8–10

INGREDIENTS
275 g/10 oz plain (semisweet) chocolate,
  broken into pieces

FOR THE CARAMEL MOUSSE
4 x 50 g/2 oz chocolate-coated caramel bars,
  coarsely chopped
20 ml/4 tsp milk or water
350 ml/12 fl oz/1½ cups double
  (heavy) cream
1 egg white

FOR THE CARAMEL SHARDS
120 ml/8 tbsp granulated sugar
50 ml/2 fl oz/¼ cup water

FOR THE TOPPING
115 g/4 oz white chocolate, chopped
350 ml/12 fl oz/1½ cups double
  (heavy) cream
450 g/1 lb mixed berries or cut-up fruits, such
  as raspberries, strawberries and blackberries
  or nectarine and orange segments

1 To make the box, line a 23 cm/9 in baking tin (pan) with foil. Melt the plain chocolate in a bowl over a pan of simmering water, stirring constantly until smooth. Pour into the tin and keep tilting to coat the base and sides evenly. Chill for 45 minutes, until firm.

2 To make the mousse, put the caramel bars and milk or water in a bowl set over a pan of simmering water and stir until melted. Remove from the heat and cool for 10 minutes, stirring occasionally. Whip the cream with an electric mixer until soft peaks form. Stir a spoonful of the cream into the caramel mixture, then fold in the rest. In a separate bowl, beat the egg white until just stiff, then fold it into the mousse. Pour into the chocolate box and chill for 6–8 hours or overnight.

3 To make the caramel shards, lightly oil a baking sheet. Dissolve the sugar in the water over low heat, stirring gently, then boil for 4–5 minutes, until the mixture turns pale gold. Immediately pour on to the oiled sheet, tilting to spread evenly. Do not touch the hot caramel. Cool, then lift off the sheet and break into pieces with a metal spatula. Set aside.

4 For the topping, heat the white chocolate with 120 ml/4 fl oz/½ cup cream over a low heat, stirring frequently, until smooth. Strain and leave to cool, stirring occasionally. Beat the remaining cream with an electric mixer until firm peaks form. Stir a spoonful of cream into the chocolate mixture, then fold in the remainder.

5 Remove the mousse-filled box from the foil by peeling it carefully from the sides and the base. Slide on to a serving plate. Spoon the chocolate-cream mixture into a piping (icing) bag fitted with a medium star nozzle and pipe rosettes or shells over the surface of the mousse. Decorate with fruits and caramel shards.

White Chocolate Cake

Make this superb cake for an extra special birthday, such as a fiftieth.

Serves 40–50

INGREDIENTS
FOR THE TWO CAKES
2 x 600 g/1 lb 5 oz/4 cups plain
 (all-purpose) flour
2 x 10 ml/2 tsp bicarbonate of soda
 (baking soda)
2 x pinch of salt
2 x 225 g/8 oz white chocolate, chopped
2 x 250 ml/8 fl oz/1 cup whipping cream
2 x 225 g/8 oz/1 cup unsalted (sweet) butter
2 x 400 g/14 oz/2 cups caster (superfine) sugar
2 x 6 eggs
2 x 10 ml/2 tsp lemon extract
2 x grated rind of 1 lemon
2 x 325 ml/11 fl oz/1⅓ cups buttermilk
whipped cream, chocolate leaves and fresh
 flowers, to decorate

FOR THE LEMON SYRUP
90 g/3½ oz/½ cup granulated sugar
120 ml/4 fl oz/½ cup water
30 ml/2 tbsp fresh lemon juice

FOR THE BUTTERCREAM (2 BATCHES)
2 x 350 g/12 oz white chocolate, chopped
2 x 500 g/1¼ lb/2½ cups cream cheese
2 x 275 g/10 oz unsalted (sweet) butter
2 x 30 ml/2 tbsp fresh lemon juice
2 x 2.5 ml/½ tsp lemon extract

FOR ASSEMBLING
175 g/6 oz/⅔ cup lemon curd
50–115 g/2–4 oz/4–8 tbsp unsalted (sweet)
 butter, softened

1 Start by making one cake. Preheat
the oven to 180°C/350°F/Gas 4.
Grease and line a 30 cm/12 in cake
tin (pan).

2 Sift the flour, bicarbonate of soda
and salt into a bowl. Heat the chocolate
and cream over a medium heat,
stirring, until smooth. Set aside to
cool. Beat the butter with an electric
mixer until creamy, add the sugar and
beat for 2–3 minutes. Beat in the eggs.
Slowly beat in the chocolate mixture,
lemon extract and rind. On low speed,
alternately beat in the flour in four
batches and the buttermilk in three
batches until smooth.

3 Pour into the tin and bake for
1 hour, until a metal skewer inserted
into the centre comes out clean. Place
the tin on a wire rack for 10 minutes,
then turn out on to the rack to cool.
Make a second cake. For the syrup,
dissolve the sugar in the water over a
medium heat, stirring. Off the heat, stir
in the lemon juice and let cool.

4 To make the buttercream, put the
chocolate in a bowl set over a pan of
simmering water and stir until melted.
Remove from the heat and cool slightly.
Beat the cream cheese until smooth
with an electric mixer. Gradually beat
in the chocolate, then the butter, lemon
juice and extract. Make a second batch.

5 To assemble, cut each cake in half horizontally. Spoon the syrup over each layer, allowing it to soak in, then repeat. Sandwich the layers of each cake together with lemon curd.

6 Gently beat the buttercream, then spread one-quarter on top of one cake. Place the other cake on top. Spread a little softened butter over the top and side. Chill for 15 minutes. Place the cake on a serving plate and spread the remaining buttercream on the top and side.

7 Spoon the whipped cream into a piping (icing) bag fitted with a small star nozzle and pipe shells carefully around the edges. Decorate with the leaves and flowers.

491

Chocolate Fruit Birthday Cake

A moist Madeira chocolate cake is decorated with eye-catching fruit moulded from coloured marzipan.

Serves 30

INGREDIENTS

1 x quantity chocolate-flavoured
   Madeira cake mix (see Cook's Tip)
45 ml/3 tbsp apricot glaze
1 x quantity marzipan
1⅓ x quantity chocolate fudge frosting
red, yellow, orange, green and purple
   food colouring
cloves
angelica strips

1 Preheat the oven to 160°C/325°F/ Gas 3. Grease and line an 18 cm/7 in square cake tin (pan). Spoon in the mixture, tap lightly to level the surface and bake for 1¼ hours, until a metal skewer inserted into the centre comes out clean. Place the tin on a wire rack for 10 minutes, then turn the cake out on to the rack to cool.

2 Cut a slice off the top of the cake to level, if necessary, then invert on to a 20 cm/8 in square cake board. Brush with the glaze. Roll out two-thirds of the marzipan on a surface lightly dusted with icing (confectioners') sugar to a 25 cm/10 in square. Use to cover and trim the cake. Reserve the trimmings.

3 Place the cake on a wire rack over a tray and pour over the warm fudge frosting, spreading quickly with a metal spatula. Leave for 10 minutes, then return to the cake board.

4 Spoon the frosting from the tray into a piping (icing) bag fitted with a medium gâteau nozzle. Pipe a row of stars around the top edge and base of the cake. Leave to set.

5 Using the reserved marzipan, food colouring, cloves and angelica strips, model a selection of fruits.

6 Fit a strip of looped yellow ribbon around the cake and secure with a pin. Decorate the top of the cake with the colourful marzipan fruits.

COOK'S TIP: To flavour the cake mix, omit the lemon rind and vanilla extract and stir in 15 ml/1 tbsp unsweetened cocoa powder blended with 15 ml/1 tbsp boiling water just before adding the eggs.

493

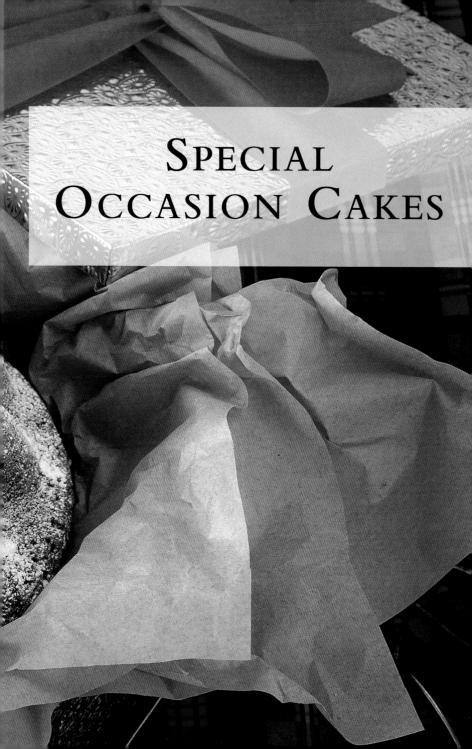

SPECIAL
OCCASION CAKES

Christening Sampler

Instead of embroidering a sampler to welcome a newborn baby, why not make a sampler cake to celebrate?

Serves 30

INGREDIENTS
1¼ x quantity rich fruit cake, baked in a
   20 cm/8 in square tin (pan)
45 ml/3 tbsp apricot glaze
1 x quantity marzipan
2 x quantity sugarpaste (fondant) icing
brown, yellow, orange, purple, cream, blue,
   green and pink food colouring

1 Brush the cake with apricot glaze. Roll out the marzipan, cover the cake and leave to dry overnight. Roll out 150 g/5 oz/1 cup of the sugarpaste icing to fit the cake top. Brush the top with water and cover with the icing.

2 Colour 300 g/11 oz/2 cups of the icing brown and roll out four pieces to the length and about 1 cm/½ in wider than the cake sides. Brush the sides with water and cover with icing, folding over the extra width at the top and cutting the corners at an angle to make a frame. Place on a cake board.

3 With a fine paintbrush, paint fine lines over the sides with watered–down brown food colouring to represent wood grain.

4 Take the remaining icing and colour small amounts yellow, orange, brown, purple and cream and two shades of blue, green and pink. Leave a little white.

5 Use these colours to shape the ducks, teddy bear, bulrushes, water, branch and leaves. Cut out a pink heart with a cookie cutter and make the baby's initial from white icing. Mix the white and pink icings together for the apple blossom flowers.

6 Make the shapes for the border. Attach the decorations to the cake with a little water. Use the leftover colours to make "threads". Arrange in loops around the base of the cake on the cake board.

Double Heart Engagement Cake

For a celebratory party, these sumptuous cakes make the perfect centrepiece.

Serves 20

INGREDIENTS
350 g/12 oz plain (semisweet) chocolate
2 x quantity chocolate-flavour
   quick-mix sponge cakes,
   baked in 20 cm/8 in
   heart-shaped tins (pans)
2 x quantity coffee-flavour
   butter icing
icing (confectioners') sugar, for dusting
fresh raspberries, to decorate

1 Melt the chocolate in a heatproof bowl over a pan of hot water (you may find it easier to work with half the chocolate at a time). Pour the chocolate on to a smooth, non-porous surface and spread it out with a metal spatula. Leave to cool slightly until just set, but not hard.

2 To make the chocolate curls, hold a large sharp knife at a 45° angle to the chocolate and push it along the chocolate in short sawing movements. Leave to set on baking parchment.

COOK'S TIP: The finished cakes can be kept for up to 3 days in an airtight container in the refrigerator.

3 Cut each cake in half horizontally. Use one-third of the butter icing to sandwich the cakes together. Use the remaining icing to coat the tops and sides of the cakes.

4 Place the cakes on heart–shaped cake boards. Generously cover the tops and sides of the cakes with the chocolate curls, pressing them gently into the butter icing.

5 Sift a little icing sugar over the top of each cake and decorate with raspberries. Chill until ready to serve.

Valentine's Box of Chocolates

This special cake would also make a wonderful gift for Mother's Day. Choose her favourite chocolates to go inside.

Serves 10–12

INGREDIENTS
1½ x quantity chocolate-flavour quick-mix sponge cake, baked in a 20 cm/8 in heart-shaped tin (pan)
⅔ x quantity marzipan
120 ml/4 fl oz/½ cup apricot glaze
3 x quantity sugarpaste (fondant) icing
red food colouring
length of ribbon tied in a bow, and a pin
225 g/8 oz/about 16–20 hand-made chocolates
small paper sweet (candy) cases

2 Roll the marzipan into a long sausage to the measured length of the string. Place on the cake around the outside edge. Brush both sections of the cake with apricot glaze. Tint the sugarpaste icing red and cut off one-third. Cut another 50 g/2 oz/⅓ cup portion from the larger piece. Set aside. Use the large piece to cover the base section of cake.

3 Stand the lid on a raised surface. Use the reserved one-third of sugarpaste icing to cover the lid. Roll out the remaining piece of icing and stamp out small hearts with a cookie cutter. Stick them around the edge of the lid with water. Secure the ribbon bow on top of the lid with the pin.

1 Place the cake on a 23 cm/9 in square piece of stiff card, draw around it, and cut the heart shape out to make a template. It will be used to support the box lid. Using a sharp knife, cut through the cake horizontally, just below the dome. Place the top section on the card and the base on a board. Use a piece of string to measure around the outside of the base.

4 Place the chocolates in the paper cases and arrange in the cake base. Position the lid slightly off-centre, to reveal the chocolates. **Do not forget to remove the ribbon and pin before serving the cake.**

Mother's Day Basket

Every mother would love to receive a cake like this on Mother's Day.
Choose fresh flowers to decorate the top.

Serves 12

INGREDIENTS

1½ x quantity orange-flavour quick-mix
  sponge cake, baked in a fluted dish
  or brioche mould
3 x quantity orange-flavour
  butter icing
1 m/1 yd x 1 cm/½ in wide
  mauve ribbon
50 cm/20 in x 3 mm/⅛ in wide spotted
  mauve ribbon
fresh flowers

1 Spread the side of the cake with
one-third of the butter icing and place
upside down on a board.

2 Half fill a piping (icing) bag fitted
with a basket-weave nozzle with
butter icing. Pipe a vertical line down
the side of the cake, then pipe four
horizontal lines across the vertical line,
starting at the top of the cake and
equally spacing the lines apart.

3 Pipe another vertical line of icing
on the edge of the horizontal lines,
then pipe four horizontal lines across
this between the spaces formed by the
previous horizontal lines, to form a
basket-weave. Continue until the sides
are completely covered.

4 Invert the cake on to the cake
board and spread the top with butter
icing. Pipe a shell edging, using the
basket-weave nozzle, to neaten the top
edge. Continue to pipe the basket-
weave icing across the top of the cake,
starting at the edge. Leave the cake to
set in a cool place.

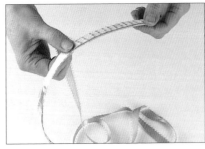

5 Fold a piece of foil in half, then half
again and continue to fold until you
have a strip several layers thick. Using
the 1 cm/½ in wide mauve ribbon,
bind the strip to cover the foil; bend
up the end to secure the ribbon. Bend
the foil to make a handle, and press
into the icing.

6 Choose some flowers and make a neat arrangement tied with the spotted ribbon on top of the cake just before serving. Tie a bow and pin it to the sides of the cake.

COOK'S TIP: Wrap the flower stalks in silver paper, if liked.

Simnel Cake

This is a traditional Easter cake, but is delicious at any time of year.

Serves 10–12

INGREDIENTS

225 g/8 oz/1 cup butter, softened
225 g/8 oz/generous 1 cup caster
  (superfine) sugar
4 eggs, beaten
500 g/1¼ lb/3⅓ cups mixed dried fruit
115 g/4 oz/½ cup glacé (candied) cherries
45 ml/3 tbsp sherry (optional)
275 g/10 oz/2½ cups plain (all-purpose) flour
15 ml/1 tbsp mixed (apple pie) spice
5 ml/1 tsp baking powder
675 g/1½ lb/4½ cups yellow marzipan
1 egg yolk, beaten
ribbons, sugared eggs and sugarpaste
  animals, to decorate

1 Preheat the oven to 160°C/325°F/
Gas 3. Grease and line a deep
20 cm/8 in round cake tin (pan).

2 Beat the butter and sugar until
fluffy. Gradually beat in the eggs. Stir
in the fruit, cherries and sherry, if
using. Sift over the flour, mixed spice
and baking powder, then fold in.

3 Roll out half the marzipan to a
20 cm/8 in round. Spoon half the cake
mixture into the cake tin and place the
round of marzipan on top. Add the
other half of the cake mixture and
smooth the surface.

4 Bake for 2½ hours, or until golden
and springy to the touch. Leave in the
tin for 15 minutes, then turn out on to
a wire rack, peel off the lining paper
and leave to cool.

5 Roll out the reserved marzipan
to fit the cake. Brush the cake
top with egg yolk and place the
marzipan circle on top. Flute the
edges and make a lattice pattern on
top with a fork.

6 Brush the top of the marzipan with
more egg yolk. Put the cake on
a baking sheet and grill (broil) for
5 minutes to brown the top lightly.
Cool before decorating with ribbons,
sugared eggs and sugarpaste animals.

Hallowe'en Pumpkin

This is the time for spooky cakes, and witches may even burst out of them. Make the cake and butter icing your favourite flavour.

Serves 15

INGREDIENTS

1 x quantity Madeira cake, baked in two
  1.2 litre/2 pint/5 cup pudding bowls
1 x quantity orange-flavour butter icing
1½ x quantity sugarpaste (fondant) icing
orange, black and yellow food colouring
90 g/3½ oz/⅔ cup royal icing

1 Trim the widest ends of the cakes so that they will fit together. Split each cake in half horizontally, then sandwich the layers together with butter icing. Trim one end narrower for a better shape and to form the base. Cover the cake with the remaining butter icing.

2 Colour 350 g/12 oz/2¼ cups of the sugarpaste icing orange. Roll out and cover the cake, trimming to fit. Reserve the trimmings. Mark segments on the icing with a skewer. Paint the markings of pumpkin flesh with watered–down orange food colouring.

3 Cut and tear the sugarpaste trimmings into jagged pieces, to make the place where the witch bursts out. Attach to the cake with a little water.

4 Colour three-quarters of the remaining sugarpaste icing black. Colour a little of the remainder yellow and leave the rest white. Use black and white icing to make the witch's head, arms and body, joining them with royal icing.

5 Make the cape and hat from black icing. Shape the cauldron, broomstick and cat's head from black and yellow icing, securing the cauldron handle with royal icing when dry. Leave to dry.

6 Use a sharp knife to make the pumpkin features from the remaining black icing. Attach to the pumpkin with a little water. Secure the witch on the top of the cake with royal icing and arrange her accoutrements around the base.

Spiced Christmas Cake

This light cake mixture is flavoured with spices and fruit. It can be served with a dusting of icing sugar and decorated with holly leaves.

Serves 6–8

INGREDIENTS
225 g/8 oz/1 cup butter, plus 15 ml/1 tbsp
15 ml/1 tbsp fresh white breadcrumbs
225 g/8 oz/1 cup caster (superfine) sugar
50 ml/2 fl oz/¼ cup water
3 eggs, separated
225 g/8 oz/2 cups self-raising (self-rising) flour
7.5 ml/1½ tsp mixed (apple pie) spice
25 g/1 oz/2 tbsp chopped angelica
25 g/1 oz/2 tbsp mixed (candied) peel
50 g/2 oz/¼ cup glacé (candied) cherries
50 g/2 oz/½ cup walnuts, chopped
icing (confectioners') sugar, to dust

1 Preheat the oven to 180°C/350°F/ Gas 4. Brush a 20 cm/8 in, 1.5 litre/2½ pint/6¼ cup fluted ring mould with 15 ml/1 tbsp melted butter. Coat the greased ring mould with fresh white breadcrumbs, shaking to remove any excess crumbs.

2 Place the butter, sugar and water in a pan. Heat gently, stirring occasionally, until melted. Boil for 3 minutes, until syrupy, then set aside to cool.

3 Whisk the egg whites until stiff. Sift the flour and spice into a bowl, add the angelica, mixed peel, cherries and walnuts and stir well to mix. Add the egg yolks.

4 Pour the cooled syrup into the bowl and beat together with a wooden spoon to form a soft batter. Gradually fold in the egg whites, using a plastic spatula, until the mixture is evenly blended.

5 Pour into the mould and bake for 50–60 minutes, or until the cake springs back when pressed. Turn out and cool on a wire rack. Dust the cake thickly with icing sugar and decorate with a sprig of holly.

Christmas Stocking Cake

This charming fruit cake is easy to decorate in festive style.

Makes 1 x 20 cm/8 in square cake

INGREDIENTS

1 x 20 cm/8 in square rich fruit cake
45 ml/3 tbsp apricot glaze
2 x quantity marzipan
4 x quantity sugarpaste (fondant) icing
15 ml/1 tbsp royal icing
red and green ribbons
red and green food colouring

1 Brush the cake with the apricot glaze and place on a 25 cm/10 in square cake board. Cover the cake with marzipan.

2 Set aside 225 g/8 oz/1½ cups of the sugarpaste icing. Cover the cake with the remainder and leave to dry. Secure the red ribbon around the board and the green ribbon around the cake with royal icing.

3 Divide the reserved sugarpaste icing in half and roll out one half. Using a template cut out two sugarpaste stockings, one 5 mm/¼ in larger all around. Put the smaller one on top of the larger one. Reserve the remaining white icing.

4 Divide the other half of the sugarpaste into two and tint one half red and the other green.

5 Roll out and cut seven 1 cm/½ in strips from each colour. Alternate the strips on top of the stocking. Roll lightly to fuse and press the edges together. Leave to dry.

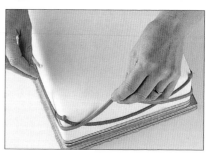

6 Shape the remaining white sugarpaste into four parcels. Trim with red and green sugarpaste ribbons. Use the remaining red and green sugarpaste to make thin strips to decorate the cake sides. Secure in place with royal icing. Stick small sugarpaste balls over the joins. Arrange the stocking and parcels on the cake top.

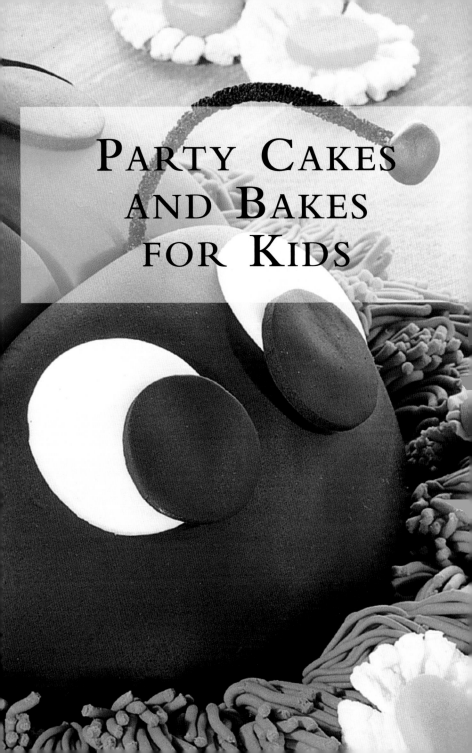

PARTY CAKES
AND BAKES
FOR KIDS

Monster Meringues

Children will be clamouring for more of these crisp, mouth-watering meringues, whipped cream and tangy summer fruits.

Serves 4

INGREDIENTS
3 egg whites
175 g/6 oz/¾ cup caster (superfine) sugar
15 ml/1 tbsp cornflour (cornstarch)
5 ml/1 tsp white wine vinegar
few drops of vanilla extract
225 g/8 oz/1½ cups assorted red
    summer fruits
300 ml/½ pint/1¼ cups double
    (heavy) cream
1 passion fruit

1 Preheat the oven to 140°C/275°F/ Gas 1. Using a pencil, draw eight 10 cm/4 in circles on two sheets of non-stick baking parchment which will fit on two baking sheets. Place the paper face-down on the baking sheets.

2 Whisk the egg whites until they are stiff, then gradually add the caster sugar, whisking well after each separate addition until the mixture has become very stiff.

3 Using a metal spoon, gently stir in the cornflour, vinegar and vanilla extract. Put the meringue mixture into a large piping (pastry) bag fitted with a large star nozzle.

4 Pipe a solid layer of meringue in four of the drawn circles and then pipe a lattice pattern in the other four. Cook in the oven for 1¼–1½ hours, swapping the shelf positions after 30 minutes, until lightly browned. The paper will peel off the back easily when the meringues are cooked. Allow to cool.

5 Roughly chop most of the summer fruits, reserving a few for decoration. Whip the cream and spread it over the solid meringue shapes. Scatter the chopped fruit on top. Halve the passion fruit, scoop out the seeds with a teaspoon and scatter them over. Top with a lattice lid and serve with the reserved whole fruits.

Kooky Cookies

Cut out these easy cookies in lots of different shapes and let your imagination run wild with the decorating, using lots of bright colours.

Makes 20

INGREDIENTS
115 g/4 oz/1 cup self-raising
   (self-rising) flour
5 ml/1 tsp ground ginger
5 ml/1 tsp bicarbonate of soda (baking soda)
50 g/2 oz/¼ cup sugar
50 g/2 oz/¼ cup butter, softened
30 ml/2 tbsp golden (light corn) syrup

FOR THE ICING
115 g/4 oz/½ cup butter, softened
225 g/8 oz/2 cups icing (confectioners') sugar
5 ml/1 tsp lemon juice
few drops of food colouring
coloured writing icing
coloured sweets

1 Sift the self-raising flour, ground ginger and bicarbonate of soda into a large mixing bowl. Add the sugar, then carefully rub in the softened butter with your fingertips, lifting the mixture above the bowl, until it resembles fine breadcrumbs.

2 Add the golden syrup and mix to a dough. Preheat the oven to 190°C/375°F/Gas 5. Grease a baking sheet.

3 Roll out to 3 mm/⅛ in thick on a lightly floured surface. Stamp out shapes with cookie cutters and transfer to the prepared baking sheet. Bake for 5–10 minutes before transferring to a wire rack to cool.

4 To make the icing, beat the butter in a bowl until light and fluffy. Add the icing sugar a little at a time and continue beating. Add the lemon juice and food colouring. Spread over some of the cooled cookies and leave to set.

5 To make each cookie individual, decorate some with coloured sweets just before the icing has set completely. Leave the other cookies until the icing has set and then decorate them with a variety of coloured writing icing.

Mint-surprise Chocolate Cupcakes

Exclamations of delight will be heard as children discover the creamy, mint filling that is hidden within these little cupcakes, which are also topped with minty chocolate icing.

Makes 12

INGREDIENTS
225 g/8 oz/2 cups plain (all-purpose) flour
5 ml/1 tsp bicarbonate of soda (baking soda)
pinch of salt
50 g/2 oz/½ cup unsweetened
   cocoa powder
150 g/5 oz/10 tbsp unsalted (sweet)
   butter, softened
300 g/11 oz/1½ cups caster
   (superfine) sugar
3 eggs
5 ml/1 tsp peppermint extract
250 ml/8 fl oz/1 cup milk

FOR THE MINT CREAM FILLING
300 ml/½ pint/1¼ cups double (heavy) or
   whipping cream
5 ml/1 tsp peppermint extract

FOR THE CHOCOLATE MINT GLAZE
175 g/6 oz plain (semisweet) chocolate
115 g/4 oz/½ cup unsalted (sweet) butter
5 ml/1 tsp peppermint extract

1 Preheat the oven to 180°C/350°F/ Gas 4. Line a 12-hole bun tray with individual paper cases. Into a mixing bowl, sift together the flour, bicarbonate of soda, pinch of salt and cocoa powder.

2 Using a hand-held electric mixer, beat the butter and sugar in a large mixing bowl until light and creamy.

3 Add the eggs to the butter and sugar one at a time, beating well after each addition, then beat in the peppermint extract. On low speed, beat in the flour mixture alternately with the milk until just blended. Spoon into the prepared paper cases.

4 Bake for 12–15 minutes until a thin skewer inserted in the centre of a bun comes out clean: do not over-bake.

5 Immediately remove the cupcakes from the tin to a wire rack to cool completely. When they are cool, remove the paper cases.

6 To make the filling, whip the cream and peppermint extract in a small bowl until stiff peaks form. Spoon into a small icing bag fitted with a small, plain tip. Push the tip into the bottom of a cupcake and squeeze gently, releasing about 15 ml/1 tbsp of cream into the centre. Repeat with the remaining cupcakes.

7 To make the glaze, melt the chocolate and butter in a pan over low heat, stirring until smooth. Remove from the heat and stir in the peppermint extract. Cool, then spread on top of each cake.

Chunky Choc Bars

An easy cake that needs no cooking and is a smash-hit with kids.

Makes 12

INGREDIENTS
350 g/12 oz plain (semisweet) chocolate
115 g/4 oz/½ cup butter
400 g/14 oz can evaporated (unsweetened condensed) milk
225 g/8 oz digestive biscuits (graham crackers), broken
50 g/2 oz/⅓ cup raisins
115 g/4 oz/⅔ cup dried peaches, chopped
50 g/2 oz/½ cup hazelnuts or pecans, chopped

2 Beat the evaporated milk into the chocolate and butter mixture. Add the biscuits, raisins, peaches and nuts and mix well until all the ingredients are coated in chocolate.

3 Turn the mixture into the prepared tin, making sure it is pressed well into the corners. Leave the top craggy. Put in the refrigerator and leave to set.

1 Line an 18 x 28 cm/7 x 11 in cake tin (pan) with clear film (plastic wrap). Put the chocolate and butter in a large bowl over a pan of hot but not boiling water and leave to melt. Stir until well mixed.

4 Lift the cake out of the tin using the clear film and then carefully peel it off. Cut the cake into 12 bars and keep chilled until ready to serve.

VARIATION: Experiment with different fruits and nuts. Try replacing the peaches with chopped dried apples and the chopped hazelnuts or pecans with toasted blanched almonds.

Drum

This is a colourful cake for very young children, who will find it so realistic that they may want to play it!

Makes a 15 cm/6 in round cake

INGREDIENTS

15 cm/6 in round quick-mix sponge cake
50 g/2 oz/¼ cup butter icing
apricot glaze
350 g/12 oz/2¼ cups marzipan
1¼ x quantity sugarpaste (fondant) icing
red, blue and yellow
   food colourings

1 Split the cake and fill with the butter icing. Place on a 20 cm/8 in round cake board and brush with the hot apricot glaze.

2 Cover the cake with a layer of marzipan and leave it to dry overnight.

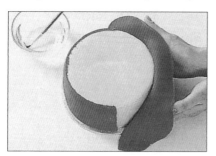

3 Colour half the sugarpaste icing red. Reserve a small amount for the drumsticks, then roll out to 25 x 30 cm/10 x 12 in and cut in half. Stick to the sides of the cake with water, smoothing the joins neatly.

4 Reserve a little white icing for the drumsticks, then roll out a circle to fit the top of the cake.

5 Divide the rest of the sugarpaste icing in half. Colour one half blue and the other yellow. Divide the blue into four equal pieces and roll each piece into a sausage long enough to go half way round the cake. Stick around the base and top of the cake with water.

6 Using a sharp knife, mark the blue edging of the cake into six around the top and bottom using a circle of baking parchment that has been folded to show six wedges.

7 Roll the yellow fondant icing into strands long enough to cross diagonally from top to bottom to form the drum strings. Roll the rest of the yellow fondant icing into 12 small balls and stick where the strings join the drum.

8 Using the remaining red and white fondant icing, knead together until streaky and roll two balls and sticks 15 cm/6 in long. Dry overnight. Stick together with a little royal icing to make the drumsticks.

Banjo Cake

The perfect cake for a musical child. It can be set on a large tray or you could cut out a card template to support it.

Serves 15–20

INGREDIENTS

2 x quantity quick-mix sponge cake,
  baked in one 20 cm/8 in round tin (pan)
  and one 18 cm/7 in square tin
115 g/4 oz/6 tbsp seedless raspberry
  jam, warmed
2⅔ x quantity sugarpaste (fondant) icing
lime green food colouring
2 coloured sticks of liquorice
4 round lollipops
60 ml/4 tbsp coloured vermicelli
pieces of flat green liquorice
2 long red liquorice bootlaces
4 long green liquorice bootlaces
ribbon and 2 pins, for the strap
sugarpaste stars (optional)

1 Cut the dome off the round cake and place bottom side up. Cut the dome off the square cake, then cut in half down the middle. Place together in a banjo shape. Draw round them on stiff card and cut out to make a reinforcing template.

2 Stamp out a shallow hole in the round cake with a 5 cm/2 in cutter. Place the cakes on the base and brush with the jam.

3 Colour the sugarpaste icing lime green and roll out to a 62 x 25 cm/ 25 x 10 in rectangle. Cover the banjo, easing the icing into the hollow and down the sides. Make finger indentations along the length of the neck on each side.

4 Cut off four 1 cm/½ in pieces from 1 liquorice stick and press into the top end of the banjo neck. Place the remaining piece and the other liquorice stick next to the hollow. Dip the lollipops in water and then in the coloured vermicelli. Press them into the sides of the neck end to line up with the liquorice.

5 Place the flat liquorice pieces side by side at the base, securing with a little water. Cut the red bootlace into 5 cm/2 in lengths. Position them along the neck to make frets, securing with water if necessary.

COOK'S TIP: The finished cake can be made up to 2 days in advance and kept in a cool, dry place.

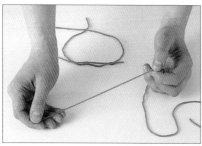

6 Dip the green bootlaces in hot water and stretch until straight. Wrap one end of the bootlace strings around the liquorice sticks and attach the other ends to the flat liquorice pieces. Secure the ribbon strap with pins and decorate the banjo with sugarpaste stars, if wished. **Do not forget to remove the pins before serving.**

Teddy's Birthday

Young children will adore this jolly-faced teddy bear with his own cake.

Makes a 20 cm/8 in round cake

INGREDIENTS
20 cm/8 in round quick-mix sponge cake
115 g/4 oz/1¼ cups butter icing
apricot glaze
350 g/12 oz/2½ cups marzipan
1¼ x quantity sugarpaste (fondant) icing
brown, pink, red, blue and black
   food colourings
115 g/4 oz/¾ cup royal icing
silver balls
1.5 m/1½ yds ribbon, 2.5 cm/1 in wide, and
   candles, to decorate

1 Split the cake and fill with the butter icing. Place on a 25 cm/10 in round cake board and brush with hot apricot glaze. Cover with a layer of marzipan, then sugarpaste icing. Using a template, mark the design on top of the cake.

2 Colour one-third of the remaining sugarpaste icing pale brown. Colour a piece pink, a piece red, some blue and a tiny piece black. Using a template, cut out the pieces to make the teddy.

3 Place the pieces in position. Stick down by lifting the edges and brushing the undersides with water. Roll ovals for the eyes and stick in place with the nose and eyebrows. Cut out a mouth and press flat.

4 Tie the ribbon around the cake. Colour the royal icing blue and pipe a border around the base of the cake using a no. 7 shell tube.

5 Pipe tiny stars around the small cake using a no. 7 star tube and inserting silver balls. Place the candles on the small cake.

COOK'S TIP: For a 20 cm/8 in round cake, follow the instructions for the 15 cm/6 in cake, but use three eggs, 175 g/6 oz/¾ cup caster (superfine) sugar, 175 g/6 oz/¾ cup butter or margarine, 175 g/6 oz/1½ cups self-raising (self-rising) flour, 4 ml/¾ tsp baking powder and 30 ml/2 tbsp water. Bake for 45–55 minutes.

Ballerina

This cake requires patience and plenty of time for the decoration.

Makes a 20 cm/8 in round cake

INGREDIENTS
20 cm/8 in round quick-mix sponge cake
115 g/4 oz/1¼ cups butter icing
apricot glaze
450 g/1 lb/3 cups marzipan
1¼ x quantity sugarpaste (fondant) icing
pink, green, yellow, brown and blue
    food colourings
115 g/4 oz/¾ cup royal icing
1.5 m/1½ yds ribbon, 2.5 cm/1 in wide

1 Split the cake and fill with the butter icing. Place on a 25 cm/10 in round cake board and brush with hot apricot glaze. Cover with a layer of marzipan then a layer of sugarpaste icing. Leave to dry overnight.

2 Divide the remaining sugarpaste icing into three; colour one flesh tones and the other two contrasting pinks. Roll out each colour and use 5 mm/¼ in and 9 mm/⅜ in flower cutters with ejectors to cut out 12 flowers and three tiny flowers from the paler pink fondant. Set aside to dry.

3 Using a template, carefully mark the position of the ballerina. Cut out the body from flesh-coloured icing and stick in position with water. Round off the edges gently with a finger. Cut out a bodice from the darker pink sugarpaste and stick in place.

4 To make the tutu, work swiftly as the thin sugarpaste dries quickly and will crack. Roll out the darker pink sugarpaste to 3 mm/⅛ in thick and cut out a fluted circle with a small plain inner circle. Cut into quarters and, with a cocktail stick (toothpick), roll along the fluted edge to stretch it.

5 Attach the frills to the waist with a little water. Repeat with two more layers, using a cocktail stick to shape the frills and cotton wool to hold them in place until dry. For the final layer of frills, use the paler pink sugarpaste and cover with a short dark frill, as the bodice extension. Leave to dry overnight.

6 Attach flowers as the hoop. Colour a little royal icing green and pipe tiny leaves. Paint on the face and hair. Stick tiny flowers around the head. Cut pale pink shoes and stick on, and paint ribbons. Pipe the flower centres from dark pink royal icing. Pipe royal icing around the base with a no. 7 shell tube. Tie with pink ribbon, to decorate.

COOK'S TIP: For this size cake, follow the steps for the 15 cm/6 in cake, but use three eggs, 175 g/6 oz/ ¾ cup sugar, 175 g/6 oz/¾ cup butter or margarine, 175 g/6 oz/ 1½ cups flour, 4 ml/¾ tsp baking powder and 30 ml/2 tbsp water. Bake for 45–55 minutes.

Child's Fairy Cake

Allow yourself plenty of time for decorating this enchanting novelty cake.

Serves 6–8

INGREDIENTS
1 x quantity quick-mix sponge cake mix
⅓ x quantity butter icing
30 ml/2 tbsp apricot glaze
1 x quantity marzipan
⅛ x quantity royal icing
pink sparkle lustre powder
silver balls

FOR THE SUGARPASTE ICING
450 g/1 lb/4 cups icing
   (confectioners') sugar
1 egg white
27½ ml/5½ tsp liquid glucose
blue, pink, yellow and gold food colouring

1 Preheat the oven to 160°C/325°F/Gas 3. Grease and line a 20 cm/8 in round cake tin (pan). Spoon in the mixture, smooth the surface and bake for 30-40 minutes, until a skewer inserted in the centre comes out clean. Turn out and cool on a wire rack.

2 To make the sugarpaste icing, put the icing sugar, egg white and glucose in a food processor or mixer and process until the mixture resembles fine breadcrumbs. Knead well until smooth and pliable, adding a drop of water if it is too dry. Set aside 50 g/2 oz/¼ cup in a plastic bag in the refrigerator and colour the remainder pale blue, kneading well.

3 Cut the cake in half horizontally and sandwich together with the butter icing. Place on a 25 cm/10 in round cake board and brush with the glaze. Roll out the marzipan and use to cover the cake. Roll out the blue sugarpaste icing and use to cover the cake. Leave to dry overnight.

4 Using a template, mark the position of the fairy. Spoon the royal icing into a piping (icing) bag with a No. 1 nozzle and pipe the outline of each wing. Pipe a second line inside the first. With a damp paint brush, brush long strokes in from the edges, leaving more icing at the edges and fading away to a thin film near the base. Leave to dry for 1 hour. Brush with dry lustre powder.

5 Colour a little of the white sugarpaste icing flesh colour. Roll out and cut out the body. Stick on the cake with a little water. Round sharp edges with your finger. Cut out the bodice and shoes and stick in place. Cut out a wand and star and leave to dry.

6 Make the tutu frills one at a time. Roll out a small piece of sugarpaste to 3 mm/⅛ in thick and stamp out a circle with a small fluted cutter. Cut it into quarters and roll a cocktail stick (toothpick) along the fluted edge to stretch it and give fullness.

7 Stick one frill to the waist. Repeat with the other layers, tucking the sides in neatly. Use a cocktail stick to arrange the frills and support the folds with small pieces of cotton wool until dry.

8 Brush a little lustre powder over the edge of the tutu. Paint on the hair and face, stick on the wand and star and paint the star gold. Pipe a border of royal icing around the board using a No. 7 star nozzle and place a silver ball on alternate points. Leave to dry.

9 Colour a little royal icing yellow and pipe over the hair. Paint with a touch of gold colouring.

Mermaid Cake

Pretty, elegant and flavoured with delicious chocolate, this cake must be every little girl's dream. The cake can be filled with butter icing.

Serves 6–8

INGREDIENTS

1 x quantity chocolate-flavour quick-mix
   sponge cake, baked in a
   900 g/2 lb loaf tin (pan)
450 g/1 lb plain (semisweet) chocolate
25 g/1 oz/3 cups
   unflavoured popcorn
1½ x quantity sugarpaste (fondant) icing
lilac and pink
   food colouring
1 Barbie- or Sindy-type doll
45 ml/3 tbsp apricot glaze,
   plus a little extra
1 egg white, lightly beaten
demerara (raw) sugar
sea shells (optional)

1 Place the cake on a cake board. Melt the chocolate over a pan of simmering water. Stir in the popcorn until evenly coated, then spoon around the sides of the cake and on the board. Spread any remaining melted chocolate over the top of the cake.

2 Colour about three-quarters of the sugarpaste icing lilac and the remainder pink. Reserve the pink icing and one-third of the lilac icing wrapped in clear film (plastic wrap). Roll out the remaining lilac icing to a rectangle wide enough to wrap around the doll's legs and about 5 cm/2 in longer.

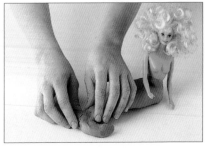

3 Brush the doll from the waist down with the apricot glaze, then wrap her in the sugarpaste, lightly squeezing and pinching to make it stick. Pinch the end of the tail to form a fin shape, curling the ends slightly. Position the mermaid on the cake.

4 Roll out the remaining lilac and the pink sugarpaste icing and stamp out scales with a small crescent-shaped cutter. Cover with clear film to prevent them from drying out. Starting at the fin, brush the crescents with a tiny amount of egg white and stick them to the tail, overlapping them, until it is completely covered.

5 Cut a shell-shaped bra top from the trimmings. Make indentations with the back of a knife and secure in place with a little apricot glaze.

6 Scatter demerara sugar around the base of the cake for sand and add a few real shells, if you like. Remove the doll before serving.

Racing Track

A cake to thrill all eight-year-old racing-car enthusiasts. It is relatively simple to make and can be decorated with as many cars as you like.

Makes 1 cake

INGREDIENTS
2 x 15 cm/6 in round quick-mix sponge
    cakes
½ x quantity butter icing
1½ x quantity sugarpaste (fondant) icing
blue and red food colourings
apricot glaze
1 quantity marzipan
⅛ x quantity royal icing
candles and 2 small racing cars,
    to decorate

1 Split the cakes and fill with the butter icing. Cut off a 1 cm/½ in piece from one side of each cake and then place both the cakes on a 25 x 35 cm/ 10 x 14 in cake board with the flat edges together.

2 Colour about 450 g/1 lb/4½ cups of the sugarpaste icing pale blue. Brush the cakes with hot apricot glaze. Cover with a layer of marzipan, then with the pale blue sugarpaste icing.

3 Mark a 5 cm/2 in circle in the centre of each cake. Roll out the remaining white sugarpaste icing, cut out two fluted circles and stick in the marked spaces.

4 Colour the royal icing red. Pipe a shell border around the base of the cake using a no. 8 star tube.

5 Pipe a track for the cars on the cake using a no. 2 plain tube. Place the candles on the two white circles and arrange the cars on the track.

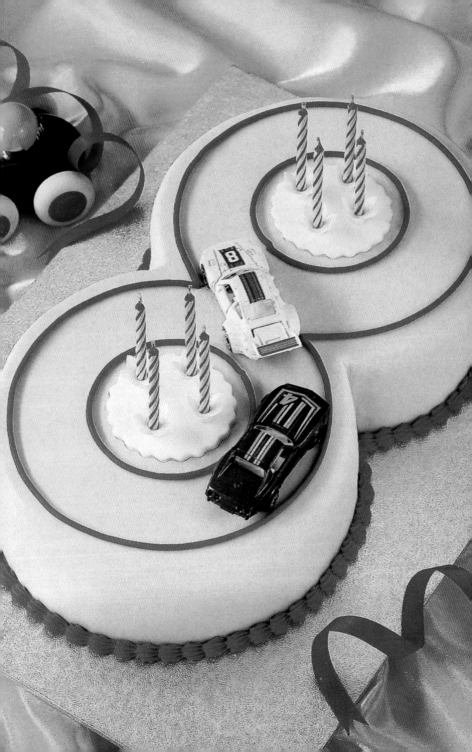

Computer Game

The perfect cake to bake for a computer game fanatic.

Makes 1 cake

INGREDIENTS
15 cm/6 in square quick-mix sponge cake
115 g/4 oz/1¼ cups butter icing
apricot glaze
1 x quantity sugarpaste
   (fondant) icing
black, blue, red and yellow
   food colourings
225 g/8 oz/1½ cups marzipan
¼ x quantity royal icing

1 Split the cake and fill with the butter icing. With a sharp, serrated knife, cut 2.5 cm/1 in off one side of the cake and 1 cm/½ in off the other. Round the corners slightly. Place on a 20 cm/8 in square cake board and brush with hot apricot glaze.

2 Colour 225 g/8 oz/1½ cups of the sugarpaste icing black. Cover the cake with a layer of marzipan, then with most of the black sugarpaste icing.

3 With a wooden cocktail stick (toothpick), mark the speaker holes and position of the screen and knobs.

4 Colour half the remaining white sugarpaste icing pale blue, roll out and cut out a 6 cm/2½ in square for the screen. Stick in the centre of the game with a little water.

5 Colour a small piece of sugarpaste icing red and the rest yellow. Cut out the start switch 2.5 cm/1 in long from the red and the controls from the yellow. Stick into position with water.

6 Roll the remaining black sugarpaste into a long, thin sausage and use it to edge the screen and around the base of the cake.

7 With a fine paintbrush, draw the game on to the screen with a little blue colour. Pipe letters on to the buttons with a little royal icing.

Smiley Kite

The face on this happy kite is a great favourite with children of all ages.

Makes 1 cake

INGREDIENTS
25 cm/10 in square quick-mix sponge cake
225 g/8 oz/2⅓ cups butter icing
apricot glaze
2 x quantity sugarpaste (fondant) icing
yellow, red, green, blue and black
   food colourings
450 g/1 lb/3 cups marzipan
115 g/4 oz/¾ cup royal icing

1 Split the cake and fill with the butter icing. Mark 15 cm/6 in from one corner down two sides and, guided by a ruler, cut down to the opposite corner on both sides. Place diagonally on a 30 cm/12 in square cake board and brush with hot apricot glaze.

2 Colour 450 g/1 lb/3 cups of the sugarpaste icing pale yellow. Divide the remainder into five portions leaving one white and colour the other four red, green, blue and black. Wrap each piece in clear film (plastic wrap).

3 Cover the cake with a layer of marzipan, then a layer of the yellow fondant, leaving some for the tail.

4 Using a template, mark the happy face on the kite. Pipe a shell border around the base of the cake. Cut out the face, bow tie and buttons from the different colours of fondant icing and stick in place with a little water.

5 To make the kite's tail, roll out each colour separately and cut two 4 x 1 cm/ 1½ x ½ in lengths from the blue, red and green fondants. Pinch them to shape into bows.

COOK'S TIP: For the cake, follow the steps for the 15 cm/6 in round cake, but use 8 eggs, 450 g/1 lb/2¼ cups caster (superfine) sugar, 450 g/ 1 lb/2 cups butter or margarine, 450 g/1 lb/4 cups self-raising (self-rising) flour, 10 ml/2 tsp baking powder and 105 ml/ 7 tbsp water. Bake for 1½–1¾ hours.

6 Roll most of the remaining yellow into a long rope and lay it on the board in a wavy line from the narrow end of the kite, then stick the bows in place with water. Roll balls of yellow fondant, stick on the board with a little royal icing and press in candles.

Dumper Truck

Any large round biscuits will work well for the wheels and all sorts of coloured sweets can go into the truck.

Serves 8–10

INGREDIENTS
1½ x quantity quick-mix sponge cake mix
90 ml/6 tbsp apricot glaze
2⅔ x quantity sugarpaste (fondant) icing
yellow, red and blue food colouring
about 12 sandwich wafer biscuits
4 coconut swirl cookies
115 g/4 oz coloured sweets (candies)
5 cm/2 in piece blue liquorice stick
demerara (raw) sugar, for the sand

1 Preheat the oven to 180°C/350°F/ Gas 4. Grease and line a 900 g/2 lb/ 5 cup loaf tin (pan). Spoon the cake mixture into the tin, smooth the surface and bake for 40–45 minutes, until a metal skewer inserted into the centre comes out clean. Transfer to a wire rack to cool.

2 Cut off the top of the cake. Cut off one-third of the cake for the cabin. Holding the larger piece cut side up, cut a hollow in the centre, leaving a 1 cm/½ in border. Brush with glaze.

3 Colour 350 g/12 oz/2¼ cups of the icing yellow. Set aside a piece the size of a walnut. Roll out the remainder on a surface lightly dusted with icing (confectioners') sugar to 5 mm/¼ in thick. Use to cover the larger piece of cake. Trim the bottom edges.

4 Colour 350 g/12 oz/2¼ cups of the remaining icing red. Set aside one-third and roll out the remainder to 5 mm/¼ in thick. Brush the remaining piece of cake with glaze, cover with the icing and trim the edges.

5 Break off and set aside a piece of the reserved red icing the size of a walnut and roll out the remainder. Brush an 18 x 7.5 cm/7 x 3 in piece of cake card with glaze and cover with the icing.

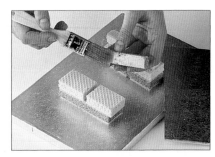

6 Brush the wafers with glaze and stick together in two equal piles. Place them on a 30 x 18 cm/12 x 7 in cake board about 7.5 cm/3 in apart. Place the covered cake card on top.

7 Place a little of the remaining white icing about halfway along the card. Place the dumper, slightly tilted, on top and the red cabin in front. Stand the coconut cookies in position for wheels.

8 Roll out the reserved yellow icing to a 5 x 2.5 cm/2 x 1 in rectangle. Colour the remaining icing blue and roll out thinly. Stamp out eyes with a crescent cutter. Roll out the reserved red icing and stamp out a mouth. Stick the yellow panel to the front of the cabin with water and stick on the features. Fill the dumper with sweets and push a piece of liquorice into the top of the cabin. Scatter the sugar around the truck to make sand.

Train Cake

This quick-and-easy train cake is made from a shaped tin, so all you need to do is decorate it!

Serves 8–10

INGREDIENTS

1½ x quantity quick-mix sponge cake, baked
   in a train-shaped tin (pan),
   about 35 cm/14 in long
2 x quantity butter icing
yellow food colouring
red liquorice bootlaces
90–120 ml/6–8 tbsp
   coloured vermicelli
4 liquorice wheels
pink and white cotton wool balls

1 Slice off the top surface of the cake to make it flat. Place diagonally on a cake board.

2 Tint the butter icing yellow. Use half of it to cover the cake.

COOK'S TIP: If you can't find a train-shaped tin (pan), cook the cake mix in a 23 cm/9 in square tin and cut out the shape.

3 Using a round nozzle and a quarter of the remaining butter icing, pipe a straight border around the top edge of the cake.

4 Place the red liquorice bootlaces on the piped border. Shape the bootlaces around the curves of the train to make a border. Pipe another butter–icing border inside the first border.

5 Using a small star nozzle and the remaining butter icing, pipe small stars over the top of the cake. Add extra liquorice and pipe other details, if you like. Use a metal spatula to press on the coloured vermicelli all around the sides of the cake.

6 Press the liquorice wheels in place for the wheels of the train. Pull a couple of balls of cotton wool apart for the steam and stick on to the cake board with butter icing.

Lion Cake

This spectacular cake is surprisingly easy to make and would be perfect for an animal lover or a Leo.

Serves 10–15

INGREDIENTS
1½ x quantity quick-mix sponge cake mix
1 x quantity orange-flavoured butter icing
orange and red food colouring
1½ x quantity yellow marzipan
⅙ x quantity sugarpaste (fondant) icing
red or orange liquorice bootlaces
long and round marshmallows

1 Preheat the oven to 180°C/350°F/ Gas 4. Grease and line a 25 x 30 cm/ 10 x 12 in tin (pan). Spoon in the cake mixture, smooth the top and bake for 45–50 minutes, until a metal skewer inserted into the centre comes out clean. Leave in the tin for 5 minutes, then turn out on to a wire rack to cool.

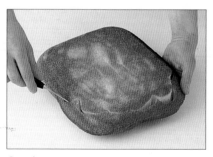

2 Place the cake base side up and cut an uneven scallop design around the edge. Turn the cake over and trim the top so that it sits squarely. Place it on a 30 cm/12 in square cake board.

3 Colour the butter icing orange and spread it evenly over the surface and down the sides of the cake.

4 Roll out 115 g/4 oz/¾ cup of the marzipan on a surface lightly dusted with icing (confectioners') sugar to a 15 cm/6 in square. Place in the centre of the cake, pressing down to secure.

5 Grate the remaining marzipan on to baking parchment. With a metal spatula, gently press it on to the cake to cover the sides and the top up to the edges of the face panel.

6 Colour the sugarpaste icing red and roll out on a surface lightly dusted with icing sugar. Stamp out a nose using a heart-shaped cutter and stick on the cake with a little water. With your fingers, roll two thin short strands for the mouth and stick on the cake.

7 Cut the liquorice bootlaces into lengths for the whiskers and place on the cake. Flatten two round marshmallows for eyes and stick on the cake with a little water. Cut the long marshmallows into 5 cm/2 in lengths and snip along one side to make the eyebrows. Stick on the cake with a little water.

Merry-go-round Cake

Choose your own figures to sit on the merry-go-round, from chocolate animals to jelly bears.

Serves 16–20

INGREDIENTS
1⅓ x quantity lemon-flavoured quick-mix
   sponge cake mix
60 ml/4 tbsp apricot glaze
1⅔ x quantity sugarpaste (fondant) icing
orange and yellow food colouring
8 x 18 cm/7 in long candy sticks
sweet (candy) figures

1 Preheat the oven to 180°C/350°F/ Gas 4. Grease and line two 20 cm/8 in round sandwich tins (pans). Spoon two-thirds of the cake mixture into one tin and the rest into the other, smooth the top and bake for 30–60 minutes, until a metal skewer inserted into the centres comes out clean. Leave in the tins for 5 minutes, then turn on to a wire rack.

2 Place the larger cake upside down on a 23 cm/9 in round fluted cake board. Place the smaller cake right side up on an 18 cm/7 in round piece of stiff card. Brush both with the glaze.

3 Roll out two-thirds of the icing on a surface dusted with icing (confectioners') sugar. Add a few spots of orange food colouring with a cocktail stick (toothpick). Roll the icing into a sausage shape, fold in half and roll out again. Repeat until it is streaked.

4 Roll out two-thirds of the orange icing and cover the larger cake. Roll out the remaining orange icing and cover the smaller cake. Trim and reserve the trimmings.

5 Using a candy stick, make eight holes evenly around the edge of the larger cake, leaving a 2 cm/¾ in border. Press the stick right through the cake to the board.

6 Knead the reserved orange icing until evenly coloured, then roll out thinly. Stamp out nine stars with a small star-shaped cutter and reserve.

7 Colour the remaining icing yellow. Roll it out and stamp out nine stars with a larger star-shaped cutter. Place the smaller cake on an upturned bowl and stick eight large and eight small stars around the edge with a little water. Stick the remaining stars on top.

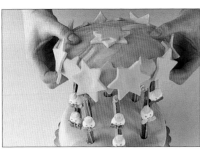

8 Secure the sweet figures to the candy sticks with reserved icing trimmings. Leave them to set for 30 minutes. Place the candy sticks in the holes in the larger cake. Assemble the cake just before serving. Lift the smaller cake, with its card base, on to the candy sticks, making sure it balances before letting go.

Indian Elephant

You can also make this delightful pachyderm for someone who loves to travel. Be as colourful as you like with the decoration.

Serves 30

INGREDIENTS

1¾ x quantity Madeira cake mix
2 x quantity butter icing
½ x quantity marzipan
black, green, yellow and pink
   food colouring
chocolate coins
silver balls
brown and white
   chocolate buttons
2 flat, round-shaped sweets (candies)
115 g/4 oz/2 cups desiccated (dry
   unsweetened shredded) coconut
30 ml/2 tbsp apricot glaze

1 Preheat the oven to 160°C/325°F/ Gas 3. Grease and line a 30 cm/12 in square cake tin (pan). Spoon in the mixture, tap lightly to level the surface and bake for 1½ hours, until a metal skewer inserted into the centre comes out clean. Place the tin on a wire rack for 10 minutes, then turn the cake out on to the rack to cool.

2 Make a template from stiff paper in the shape of an elephant and place on top of the cake. Cut out the shape with a sharp knife and transfer to a 35 cm/14 in cake board.

3 Colour the icing pale grey and cover the top and sides of the cake. Swirl with a metal spatula. Swirl black food colouring highlights into the icing with a cocktail stick (toothpick).

4 Roll out half the marzipan on a surface lightly dusted with icing (confectioners') sugar. Cut out shapes for the tusk, headpiece and blanket. Colour the remaining marzipan green, yellow and pink. Roll and cut out patterns for the blanket, headpiece, trunk and tail. Roll small balls of yellow and pink marzipan for the anklets.

5 Place the patterns and decorations in position. Cut the white chocolate buttons in half for toenails and make an eye from the sweets.

6 Colour the desiccated coconut green. Brush the cake board with the apricot glaze and sprinkle with the coconut.

Mouse in Bed

This cake is suitable for almost any age. Make the mouse well ahead to allow it time to dry.

Serves 8–10

INGREDIENTS

1 x quantity quick-mix sponge cake, baked in a 20 cm/8 in square tin (pan)
⅓ x quantity butter icing
45 ml/3 tbsp apricot glaze
1 x quantity marzipan
2 x quantity sugarpaste (fondant) icing
blue and pink food colouring and pens

1 Cut 5 cm/2 in off one side of the cake. Split and fill the main cake with butter icing. Place on a cake board. With the cake off-cut, shape a hollowed pillow, the torso and the legs of the mouse. Brush the cake with apricot glaze and cover with marzipan. Cover the pillow and mouse's torso and legs in the same way. Leave to dry overnight.

2 Cover the cake and pillow with white sugarpaste icing. Lightly frill the edge of the pillow with a fork.

3 To make the valance, roll out 350 g/12 oz/2¼ cups of sugarpaste icing and cut into four 7.5 cm/3 in wide strips. Attach to the bed with water. Arrange the pillow and mouse's body on the cake.

4 For the quilt, tint 75 g/3 oz/½ cup of sugarpaste icing blue and roll out to an 18 cm/7 in square. Mark with a diamond pattern and with a flower cutter. Cover the mouse with the quilt.

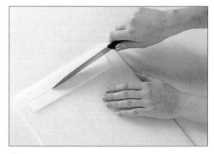

5 Cut a 2.5 x 18 cm/1 x 7 in white sugarpaste icing strip for the sheet, mark the edge and place over the quilt, tucking it under at the top edge.

6 Tint 25 g/1 oz/2 tbsp of marzipan pink and make the head and paws of the mouse. Put the head on the pillow, tucked under the sheet, and the paws over the edge of the sheet. Use food colouring pens to draw on the face of the mouse.

Number 7 Cake

Any combination of colours will work well for this marbled cake.

Serves 8–10

INGREDIENTS
1½ x quantity quick-mix sponge cake, baked
 in a 23 x 30 cm/9 x 12 in tin (pan)
1 x quantity orange-flavour butter icing
60 ml/4 tbsp apricot glaze
2 x quantity sugarpaste (fondant) icing
blue and green food colouring
rice paper sweets (candies)

1 Place the cake flat side up and cut out the number seven. Slice the cake horizontally, sandwich together with the butter icing and place on a board.

2 Brush the cake evenly with apricot glaze. Divide the sugarpaste icing into three and tint one of the pieces blue and another green. Set aside 50 g/ 2 oz/⅓ cup from each of the coloured icings.

3 Knead together the large pieces of blue and green icing with the third piece of white icing to marble. Use to cover the cake.

4 Immediately after covering, use a small "7" cutter to remove sugarpaste shapes in a random pattern from the covered cake.

5 Roll out the reserved blue and green sugarpaste icing and stamp out shapes with the same cutter. Use these to fill the stamped-out shapes from the cake. Decorate the board with some rice paper sweets.

COOK'S TIP: If you are unsure about shaping the number seven cake freehand, you can purchase or hire shaped cake tins from specialist cake decorating shops.

Ladybird Cake

Children will love this colourful and appealing ladybird (ladybug), and it is very simple to make.

Serves 10–12

INGREDIENTS

1½ x quantity quick-mix sponge cake,
    baked in a 1.2 litre/2 pint/5 cup
    pudding bowl
½ x quantity butter icing
60 ml/4 tbsp lemon curd, warmed
3 x quantity sugarpaste
    (fondant) icing
red, black and green food colouring
5 marshmallows
50 g/2 oz/4 tbsp marzipan
2 pipe cleaners

2 Colour 350 g/12 oz/2¼ cups of the icing black, roll out three-quarters and use to cover the smaller piece of cake for the head. Place both cakes on a cake board and press together.

3 Roll out 50 g/2 oz/⅓ cup of icing and cut out two 5 cm/2 in rounds for the eyes, then stick to the head with water. Roll out the remaining black icing and cut out eight 4 cm/1½ in rounds. Use two of these for the eyes and stick the others on to the body.

1 Cut the cake in half horizontally and sandwich together with the butter icing. Cut vertically through the cake, about a third of the way in. Brush both pieces with the lemon curd. Colour 450 g/1 lb/3 cups of the sugarpaste icing red. Roll out to 5 mm/¼ in thick and cover the larger piece of cake to make the body. Using a skewer, make an indentation down the centre for the wings.

4 Place the ladybird on a cake board. Colour some icing green and squeeze through a garlic crusher to make grass. Flatten the marshmallows, snip and stick a marzipan round in the centre of each. Colour pipe cleaners black and press a ball of black icing on to the end of each. Arrange the grass and flowers around the ladybird. If you have sufficient trimmings, make baby ladybirds as well, if you like.

ICE CREAMS

Fresh Strawberry Ice Cream

You can make this ice cream by hand if you freeze it over a period of several hours, whisking it every hour or so.

Serves 6

INGREDIENTS
300 ml/½ pint/1¼ cups creamy milk
1 vanilla pod (bean)
3 large (US extra large) egg yolks
225 g/8 oz/2 cups strawberries
juice of ½ lemon
75 g/3 oz/¾ cup icing (confectioners') sugar
300 ml/½ pint/1¼ cups double (heavy) cream
strawberries, to serve

1 Put the milk and the vanilla pod into a pan and bring to the boil over a low heat. Remove from the heat. Leave for 20 minutes, then remove the vanilla pod. Strain the milk into a bowl containing the egg yolks and whisk well.

2 Return the mixture to the clean pan and heat, stirring, until the custard just coats the back of the spoon. Pour the custard into a bowl, cover the surface with clear film (plastic wrap) and set aside to cool.

3 Reserve a few strawberries for serving, and purée the rest with the lemon juice in a food processor or blender. Press the strawberry purée through a sieve (strainer) into a bowl, stir in the icing sugar and set aside.

4 Whip the cream to soft peaks, then gently but thoroughly fold it into the custard with the strawberry purée. Pour the mixture into an ice cream maker. Churn for 20–30 minutes, or until the mixture holds its shape.

5 Transfer the ice cream to a freezer container, cover and freeze until firm. Soften for about 10 minutes before serving. Serve with whole or sliced strawberries.

COOK'S TIP: Use free-range (farm-fresh) eggs if possible.

Exotic Fruits with Mango and Ginger Ice Cream

Exotic fruits are now widely available: choose your fruits with care, taking colour, shape and taste into account, then use them to create your own still life with this marvellous mango ice cream.

Serves 6–8

INGREDIENTS
2 large ripe mangoes, peeled, stoned (pitted)
  and roughly chopped
2 pieces preserved stem ginger
  plus 30 ml/2 tbsp ginger syrup
250 ml/8 fl oz/1 cup double (heavy) cream

FOR THE DECORATION
1 star fruit (carambola), thickly sliced
1 mango, peeled and cut into wedges
1 cantaloupe melon, cut into wedges
6 strawberries, cut in half
1 small bunch frosted grapes

1 Purée the mangoes in a food processor with the preserved ginger and ginger syrup, until smooth.

2 Whip the cream in a large bowl until it forms fairly firm peaks. Fold in the mango purée.

3 Transfer to a freezer container. Freeze for 2 hours, then beat with an electric mixer until smooth. Return the ice cream to the freezer and freeze for at least 8 hours. Alternatively, use an ice cream maker, following the manufacturer's instructions.

4 About 30 minutes before serving, transfer the ice cream to the refrigerator to soften slightly. Arrange the prepared fruit on individual plates and add two scoops of ice cream to each one.

Avocado & Lime Ice Cream

In some parts of the world, avocados are frequently eaten as desserts. In fact, their rich texture makes them perfect for a smooth, creamy and delicious ice cream.

Serves 4–6

INGREDIENTS
4 egg yolks
300 ml/½ pint/1¼ cups whipping cream
115 g/4 oz/generous ½ cup granulated sugar
2 ripe avocados, peeled and stoned (pitted)
grated rind of 2 limes
juice of 1 lime
2 egg whites
avocado slices and fresh mint, to decorate

1 Beat the egg yolks in a bowl. In a pan, heat the whipping cream with the sugar, stirring it well until it dissolves.

2 As the cream rises to the top of the pan at the point of boiling, remove it from the heat.

3 Gently pour the beaten egg yolks into the scalded cream, adding them in small amounts from a height above the pan and stirring well. Allow the mixture to cool, stirring it occasionally, then chill.

4 Mash the avocados until they are smooth, then beat them into the custard with the lime rind and juice. Taste for sweetness; ice cream should be quite sweet before freezing as it loses flavour when ice-cold.

5 Pour the ice cream mixture into a shallow freezer container and freeze it until it is slushy. Remove from the freezer and beat it well to stop large ice crystals from forming. Return the mixture to the freezer for 3 hours and repeat the beating process once more.

6 Whisk the egg whites until softly stiff and fold into the ice cream. Return the mixture to the freezer and freeze until firm. Soften in the refrigerator for about 30 minutes before serving, decorated with avocado slices and sprigs of fresh mint.

COOK'S TIP: You can use an ice cream maker for this recipe but omit the egg whites as the paddle will beat in air.

Apricot Ice Cream under a Caramel Cage

Caramel is a favourite with confectioners because of its decorative possibilities. It is used here to create a cage to cover a tea-scented apricot ice cream.

Serves 6–8

INGREDIENTS
450 g/1 lb/2 cups dried apricots
900 ml/1½ pints/3¾ cups cold
   Earl Grey tea
115 g/4 oz/½ cup soft light brown sugar
30 ml/2 tbsp brandy or gin
   (optional)
300 ml/½ pint/1¼ cups whipping cream

FOR THE DECORATION
500 g/1¼ lb/2½ cups caster
   (superfine) sugar
175 ml/6 fl oz/¾ cup water
120 ml/4 fl oz/½ cup liquid glucose
oil, for greasing

1 Place the apricots in a large bowl. Pour the cold Earl Grey tea over, cover and soak the apricots for 4 hours or overnight.

2 Pour the apricots and the tea into a pan. Add the brown sugar. Bring to the boil, stirring to dissolve the sugar. Simmer gently for 15–20 minutes, until the apricots are tender. Allow to cool.

3 Process the apricots with the cooking liquid in a food processor to a rough purée; the apricots should be chopped but still identifiable. Stir in the brandy or gin, if using.

4 Whip the cream in a large bowl until soft peaks form. Fold in the apricot purée and mix well. Transfer to a freezer container and freeze for 2 hours. Beat with an electric mixer until smooth, then return to the freezer for at least 8 hours. Alternatively, place in an ice cream maker and freeze according to the manufacturer's instructions.

5 Meanwhile, make the decoration. Place the sugar and water in a small pan. Heat gently, stirring until the sugar dissolves. Bring to the boil and add the liquid glucose. Cook until the mixture is a pale caramel. Cool slightly. Lightly oil the back of a ladle.

6 Using a teaspoon, trail caramel over the upturned ladle in horizontal and vertical lines, until a "cage" is built. Leave to harden, then gently ease off. Repeat to make six to eight "cages". To serve, place a "cage" over scoops of ice cream.

Stem Ginger Ice Cream

This rich and flavourful ice cream goes beautifully with sliced fresh pears and bananas or with gooseberry and apple purée.

Serves 4

INGREDIENTS
15 ml/1 tbsp clear honey
4 egg yolks
600 ml/1 pint/2½ cups double (heavy) cream,
   lightly whipped
4 pieces preserved stem ginger, chopped into
   tiny dice

1 Place the honey and 150 ml/
¼ pint/⅔ cup water in a small pan
and heat gently until the honey is
completely dissolved. Remove from
the heat and allow to cool.

2 Place the egg yolks in a large bowl
and whisk gently until pale and frothy.
Slowly add the honey syrup and fold
in the whipped cream.

3 Pour the mixture into a plastic
freezer container and freeze for about
45 minutes, or until the ice cream is
freezing at the edges.

4 Transfer to a bowl and whisk again.
Mix in the stem ginger, reserving a
few pieces for decoration. Freeze again
for 2–4 hours. Serve in scoops,
decorated with stem ginger.

Mint Ice Cream

Fresh mint from the garden gives this ice cream a wonderful flavour.

Serves 4–6

INGREDIENTS
8 egg yolks
75 g/3 oz/6 tbsp caster (superfine) sugar
600 ml/1 pint/2½ cups single
   (light) cream
1 vanilla pod (bean)
60 ml/4 tbsp chopped fresh mint
fresh mint sprigs, to decorate

1 Using an electric beater or balloon whisk, beat the egg yolks and sugar until pale and light. Transfer to a small pan. In a separate pan, bring the cream and vanilla pod to the boil.

2 Remove the pod and pour the hot cream on to the egg mixture, whisking. Continue whisking to ensure that the eggs are mixed into the cream. Gently heat until the custard thickens enough to coat the back of a wooden spoon. Remove from the heat and allow to cool.

3 Stir in the chopped mint, transfer to a freezer container and freeze until mushy. Whisk to break down the ice crystals. Freeze for 3 hours, then whisk again. Freeze for at least 6 hours, until hard. Serve, decorated with mint sprigs.

Old-fashioned Chocolate Ice Cream

A classic and a great favourite with young and old alike.

Serves 8

INGREDIENTS

750 ml/1¼ pints/3 cups whipping cream
250 ml/8 fl oz/1 cup milk
1 vanilla pod (bean), split in half
150 g/5 oz/¾ cup plus
  2.5 ml/½ tsp caster (superfine) sugar
115 g/4 oz plain (semisweet)
  chocolate, grated
4 egg yolks

1 Put 250 ml/8 fl oz/1 cup of the cream in a heavy pan with the milk and the vanilla pod. Heat until bubbles appear round the edge of the pan.

2 Add 150 g/5 oz/¾ cup of the sugar and the chocolate. Heat almost to boiling point, stirring until the chocolate is melted and smooth.

3 In a heatproof bowl, lightly beat the egg yolks. Add the hot mixture, stirring constantly.

4 Set the bowl over a pan of simmering water. Stir until the custard thickens enough to coat the spoon. Strain into a bowl. Stir in the remaining cream and sugar. Cool and then transfer to an ice cream maker and freeze. Serve in scoops.

Rippled Chocolate Ice Cream

A heavenly ice cream marbled with rich chocolate.

Serves 4

INGREDIENTS

60 ml/4 tbsp chocolate and
   hazelnut spread
450 ml/¾ pint/scant 2 cups double
   (heavy) cream
15 ml/1 tbsp icing (confectioners')
   sugar, sifted
50 g/2 oz plain (semisweet)
   chocolate, chopped
plain (semisweet) chocolate curls,
   to decorate

1 Mix the spread and 75 ml/5 tbsp of the cream in a bowl.

2 Place the remaining cream and the icing sugar in a second bowl and beat until softly whipped.

3 Lightly fold in the chocolate mixture with the chopped chocolate until the mixture is rippled. Transfer to a freezer container and freeze for about 3–4 hours, until firm.

4 Remove the ice cream from the freezer about 30 minutes before serving to allow it to soften slightly. Spoon or scoop into dessert dishes or glasses and top each serving with a few plain chocolate curls.

White Chocolate Raspberry Ripple Ice Cream

Freeze ice cream in a soufflé dish or other attractive bowl so that it can be served directly at the table.

Serves 8

INGREDIENTS
250 ml/8 fl oz/1 cup milk
450 ml/¾ pint/scant 2 cups
　　whipping cream
7 egg yolks
25 g/1 oz/2 tbsp granulated sugar
225 g/8 oz fine-quality white
　　chocolate, chopped
5 ml/1 tsp vanilla extract
fresh mint sprigs, to decorate

FOR THE RASPBERRY RIPPLE SAUCE
275 g/10 oz packet frozen
　　raspberries in light syrup, thawed,
　　or 275 g/10 oz jar reduced-sugar
　　raspberry preserve
10 ml/2 tsp corn syrup
15 ml/1 tbsp lemon juice
15 ml/1 tbsp cornflour (cornstarch) mixed
　　with 15 ml/1 tbsp water

1 To make the sauce, press the raspberries and their syrup through a sieve into a pan. Add the corn syrup, lemon juice and cornflour mixture. (If using raspberry preserve, omit the cornflour, but add the water.) Bring to the boil, stirring frequently, and simmer for 1–2 minutes, until syrupy. Pour into a bowl and cool, then chill.

2 In a pan, bring the milk and 250 ml/8 fl oz/1 cup of the cream to the boil. Beat the egg yolks and sugar for 2–3 minutes with a hand-held mixer, until thick and creamy.

3 Pour the hot milk over the yolks and return to the pan. Cook gently until the custard coats the back of a wooden spoon, stirring constantly. Do not allow to boil or the custard will curdle.

4 Remove the pan from the heat and stir in the white chocolate until smooth. Pour the remaining cream into a medium bowl. Strain the hot custard into the bowl and add the vanilla. Blend and cool to room temperature, then chill until cold. Transfer the custard to an ice cream maker and freeze according to the manufacturer's instructions.

5 When the mixture is frozen, but still soft, transfer one-third of the ice cream to a serving bowl. Spoon over some raspberry sauce. Cover with another third of the ice cream and more sauce. Cover with the remaining ice cream and more sauce.

6 With a knife or spoon, lightly marble the sauce into the ice cream. Cover and freeze until hard. Allow the ice cream to soften for about 30 minutes in the refrigerator before serving with the remaining raspberry sauce, decorated with mint.

Pistachio Halva Ice Cream

Halva is made from sesame seeds and is available in several flavours. This ice cream, studded with chunks of pistachio-flavoured halva, is as unusual as it is irresistible.

Serves 6

INGREDIENTS
3 egg yolks
115 g/4 oz/generous ½ cup caster (superfine) sugar
300 ml/½ pint/1¼ cups single (light) cream
300 ml/½ pint/1¼ cups double (heavy) cream
115 g/4 oz pistachio halva
unsalted pistachio nuts, chopped, to decorate

1 Whisk the yolks with the sugar in a bowl until thick. Pour the single cream into a pan and bring to the boil, stir into the egg-yolk mixture.

2 Transfer the mixture to a double boiler or a heatproof bowl placed over a pan of gently simmering water. Cook, stirring continuously, until the custard is thick enough to coat the back of a spoon. Strain into a bowl and leave to cool.

3 Whisk the double cream lightly, then whisk in the cooled custard. Crumble the halva into the mixture and stir in gently with a metal spoon.

4 Pour the halva mixture into a freezer container. Cover and freeze for 3 hours or until half-set. Stir well, breaking up any ice crystals, then return to the freezer until frozen solid. Alternatively, freeze in an ice cream maker, following the manufacturer's instructions.

5 Remove the ice cream from the freezer about 30 minutes before serving so that it softens enough for scooping, and to allow the full flavour to develop. Serve decorated with chopped pistachio nuts.

Brown Bread & Hazelnut Ice Cream

Toasted breadcrumbs add to the sweet nuttiness of this ice cream, which is served with a tangy blackcurrant sauce.

Serves 6

INGREDIENTS
50 g/2 oz/½ cup roasted and chopped
    hazelnuts, ground
75 g/3 oz/1½ cups wholemeal
    (whole-wheat) breadcrumbs
50 g/2 oz/4 tbsp demerara (raw) sugar
3 egg whites
115 g/4 oz/generous ½ cup caster
    (superfine) sugar
300 ml/½ pint/1¼ cups double (heavy) cream
few drops of vanilla extract
fresh mint sprigs, to decorate

FOR THE SAUCE
225 g/8 oz/2 cups blackcurrants
75 g/3 oz/6 tbsp caster (superfine) sugar
15 ml/1 tbsp crème de cassis

1 Combine the hazelnuts and breadcrumbs and demerara sugar on a baking sheet. Place under a medium grill (broiler) and cook, stirring frequently, until the mixture is crisp and evenly browned. Set aside.

2 Whisk the egg whites in a bowl until stiff, then gradually whisk in the caster sugar until thick and glossy. Whip the cream to soft peaks and fold into the meringue with the bread-crumb mixture and vanilla extract.

3 Spoon the mixture into a 1.2 litre/ 2 pint/5 cup loaf tin (pan). Smooth the top level, then cover and freeze for several hours, or until firm.

4 Meanwhile, make the sauce. Strip the blackcurrants from their stalks using a fork and put the blackcurrants in a small bowl with the remaining caster sugar. Toss gently to mix and leave for 30 minutes.

5 Purée the blackcurrants in a blender or food processor, then press through a nylon sieve (strainer) until smooth. Add the crème de cassis and chill well.

6 To serve, turn out the ice cream on to a plate and cut into slices. Arrange each slice on a serving plate, spoon over a little sauce and decorate with fresh mint sprigs.

Hazelnut Ice Cream

This popular flavour is an especially good partner to chocolate ice cream.

Serves 4–6

INGREDIENTS
75 g/3 oz/¾ cup hazelnuts
115 g/4 oz/⅔ cup granulated sugar
475 ml/16 fl oz/2 cups milk
10 cm/4 in piece vanilla pod (bean)
4 egg yolks

1 Spread the hazelnuts out on a baking sheet and place under a medium grill (broiler) for 5 minutes, shaking to turn the nuts over. Remove from the heat and allow to cool slightly. Place the nuts on a dishtowel and rub them with the cloth to remove their dark outer skin. Chop very finely, or grind in a food processor with 25 g/1 oz/2 tbsp of the sugar.

2 Make the custard. Heat the milk with the vanilla pod in a small pan. Remove from the heat as soon as small bubbles start to form on the surface. Do not let it boil.

3 Beat the egg yolks with a wire whisk or electric beater. Gradually incorporate the remaining sugar and continue beating for about 5 minutes, until the mixture is pale yellow. Add the milk very gradually, pouring it in through a sieve and discarding the vanilla pod. Stir constantly until all the milk has been added.

4 Pour the mixture into the top of a double boiler, or into a heatproof bowl placed over a pan of simmering water. Add the chopped nuts. Stir over a medium heat until the water in the pan is boiling and the custard thickens enough to lightly coat the back of a spoon. Remove from the heat and allow to cool.

5 Freeze in an ice cream maker following the manufacturer's instructions, or pour the mixture into a freezer container and freeze for about 3 hours until set. Remove from the container and chop roughly into 7.5 cm/3 in pieces. Place in the bowl of a food processor and process.

6 Return to the freezer container and freeze until firm. Repeat the freezing-chopping process two or three times, until a smooth consistency is achieved. Serve in scoops.

Pistachio & Almond Ice Cream

This unusual ice cream, based on an old Indian recipe, uses canned evaporated milk and is packed with nuts and dried and candied fruit.

Serves 4–6

INGREDIENTS
3 x 400 ml/14 fl oz cans evaporated (unsweetened condensed) milk
3 egg whites, whisked until peaks form
350 g/12 oz/3 cups icing (confectioners') sugar, sifted
175 g/6 oz/1½ cups pistachio nuts, chopped
75 g/3 oz/scant ½ cup sultanas (golden raisins)
75 g/3 oz/¾ cup flaked (sliced) almonds
25 g/1 oz glacé (candied) cherries, halved

2 Open the cans and empty the milk into a large, chilled bowl. Whisk until it doubles in quantity, then fold in the egg whites and icing sugar.

1 Remove the labels from the cans of evaporated milk and lay the cans down in a pan with a tight-fitting cover. Fill the pan with water to reach three-quarters of the way up the cans. Bring to the boil, cover and simmer for 20 minutes. Leave to cool completely, then chill the cans in the refrigerator for 24 hours.

3 Gently fold in the remaining ingredients, seal the bowl with clear film (plastic wrap) and leave in the freezer for 1 hour.

4 Remove from the freezer and mix using a fork. Transfer to a serving bowl and freeze again. Remove from the freezer 10 minutes before serving.

French–style Coupe Glacé with Chocolate Ice Cream

Extra-rich chocolate ice cream creates this luxurious dessert.

Serves 6

INGREDIENTS
225 g/8 oz dark (bittersweet) chocolate, chopped
250 ml/8 fl oz/1 cup milk mixed with 250 ml/8 fl oz/1 cup single (light) cream
3 egg yolks
50 g/2 oz/generous ¼ cup granulated sugar
350 ml/12 fl oz/1½ cups double (heavy) cream
15 ml/1 tbsp vanilla extract
chocolate triangles, to decorate

FOR THE ESPRESSO CREAM
45ml/3 tbsp instant espresso powder, dissolved in 45 ml/3 tbsp boiling water, cooled
350 ml/12 fl oz/1½ cups double (heavy) cream
30 ml/2 tbsp coffee-flavour liqueur

FOR THE CHOCOLATE ESPRESSO SAUCE
300 ml/½ pint/1¼ cups double (heavy) cream
30 ml/2 tbsp instant espresso powder, dissolved in 45 ml/3 tbsp boiling water
300 g/11 oz dark (bittersweet) chocolate, chopped
30 ml/2 tbsp coffee-flavour liqueur

1 Prepare the ice cream. In a pan over a low heat, melt the chocolate with 120 ml/4 fl oz/½ cup of the milk mixture, stirring frequently. Remove from the heat. In another pan, over medium heat, bring the remaining milk mixture gently to the boil.

2 In a bowl beat the egg yolks and sugar for 2–3 minutes with a hand-held mixer, until thick. Pour the hot milk mixture over the yolks, whisking constantly. Return to the pan and cook over medium heat until the custard thickens. (Do not boil or the custard will curdle.) Stir in the melted chocolate.

3 Pour the double cream into a bowl and strain the custard into the bowl. Add the vanilla. Cool, then chill until cold. Transfer to an ice cream maker and freeze.

4 To make the espresso cream, stir the dissolved espresso powder into the cream and beat until it holds soft peaks. Add the liqueur and beat for 30 seconds. Spoon into a piping (pastry) bag with a medium star nozzle and chill.

5 Prepare the sauce. In a pan over medium heat, bring the cream and dissolved espresso powder to the boil. Remove from the heat and add the chocolate. Stir until it is melted. Add the liqueur and strain into a bowl. Keep warm.

6 To serve, soften the ice cream for 15 minutes at room temperature. Pipe a layer of espresso cream into the bottom of six wine goblets. Add scoops of ice cream. Spoon over the chocolate sauce and top with cream. Serve the remaining sauce separately.

Chocolate Mint Ice Cream Pie

Much simpler to make than you would expect from its luxurious appearance, this makes an excellent dessert for entertaining.

Serves 8

INGREDIENTS
75 g/3 oz/½ cup plain (semisweet) chocolate chips
40 g/1½ oz/3 tbsp butter or margarine
50 g/2 oz crisped rice cereal
1 litre/1¾ pints/4 cups mint-chocolate-chip ice cream
75 g/3 oz plain (semisweet) chocolate

1 Line a 23 cm/9 in flan tin (pie pan) with foil. Place a round of baking parchment over the foil.

2 In a heatproof bowl set over a pan of barely simmering water, or in a double boiler, melt the chocolate chips and butter or margarine. Remove the bowl from the heat and gently stir in the cereal, a little at a time. Leave to cool for 5 minutes.

3 Press the chocolate–cereal mixture evenly over the bottom and up the sides of the prepared tin, forming a 1 cm/½ in rim. Chill until hard.

4 Carefully remove the cereal base from the tin and peel off the foil and baking parchment. Return the base to the flan tin.

5 Remove the ice cream from the freezer and allow to soften for 10 minutes. Spread evenly in the crust. Freeze for about 1 hour, until firm.

6 For the decoration, have the chocolate at room temperature and draw the blade of a swivel-headed vegetable peeler along the smooth surface of the chocolate to shave off short, wide curls. Chill the chocolate curls until needed and sprinkle them over the ice cream just before serving.

Coffee Ice Cream Sandwiches

A great combination of contrasting textures united by flavour: sweet, crunchy biscuits sandwiched together with cool, smooth ice cream.

Makes 8

INGREDIENTS
115 g/4 oz/½ cup butter or margarine, softened
50 g/2 oz/generous ¼ cup caster (superfine) sugar
115 g/4 oz/1 cup plain (all-purpose) flour
30 ml/2 tbsp instant coffee powder
icing (confectioners') sugar, for dusting
450 ml/¾ pint/scant 2 cups coffee ice cream
30 ml/2 tbsp unsweetened cocoa powder

1 Lightly grease two or three large baking sheets.

2 With an electric mixer or wooden spoon, beat the butter or margarine until soft. Beat in the caster sugar. Add the flour and coffee and mix by hand to form an evenly blended dough. Wrap in a plastic bag and chill for at least 1 hour.

3 Lightly dust a work surface with icing sugar. Knead the dough on the sugared surface for a few minutes to soften it slightly. Using a rolling pin dusted with icing sugar, roll out the dough to 3 mm/⅛ in thickness. With a 6 cm/2½ in fluted cutter, cut out 16 rounds. Transfer the rounds to the prepared baking trays. Chill for at least 30 minutes.

4 Preheat the oven to 150°C/300°F/ Gas 2. Bake the biscuits (cookies) for about 30 minutes, until they are lightly golden. Leave the biscuits to cool and firm up before transferring them from the baking sheets to a wire rack to cool completely.

5 Remove the ice cream from the freezer and allow to soften for 10 minutes at room temperature. Spread the ice cream evenly over the flat side of eight of the biscuits and top with the remaining biscuits.

6 Arrange the ice cream sandwiches on a baking sheet. Cover and freeze for at least 1 hour, or longer if a firmer sandwich is desired. Sift the cocoa powder over the top before serving.

VARIATION: Other flavours of ice cream could be used for the filling. Try strawberry, vanilla, chocolate or one containing chopped hazelnuts or almonds.

Amaretto Ice Cream in Brandy Snap Baskets

Almond-flavoured liqueur gives this ice cream a wonderful depth of flavour.

Serves 4–6

INGREDIENTS
750 ml/1¼ pints/3 cups vanilla ice
　cream, softened
30 ml/2 tbsp amaretto liqueur
15 ml/1 tbsp orange juice
1.5 ml/¼ tsp vanilla extract
thinly pared orange rind, to decorate

FOR THE BRANDY SNAP BASKETS
50 g/2 oz/ 4 tbsp butter
50 g/2 oz/generous ¼ cup caster
　(superfine) sugar
75 g/3 oz/¼ cup golden (light
　corn) syrup
5 ml/1 tsp ground ginger
grated rind and juice of
　1 lemon
50 g/2 oz/½ cup plain (all-purpose) flour

1 Preheat the oven to 180°C/350°F/ Gas 4. Lightly grease and line three baking sheets with baking parchment.

2 Beat the vanilla ice cream until soft and creamy, then beat in the liqueur, orange juice and vanilla extract. Return to the tub, or a similar container, for freezing. Set the freezer at its coldest temperature and freeze the ice cream until firm.

3 To make the brandy snap baskets, put the butter, sugar, golden syrup and ground ginger into a pan. Heat gently, stirring constantly, until the butter has melted, then remove from the heat and stir in the lemon rind and juice, followed by the flour.

4 The mixture hardens quickly, so bake only two brandy snaps at a time. Put spoonfuls of mixture on the baking sheets. Bake for 10–12 minutes, until golden. Cool for a few seconds.

5 Lift each brandy snap in turn with a metal spatula and drape over a small orange or the outside of an upturned cup. Leave to cool and harden, then invert on to plates. Add scoops of amaretto ice cream, decorate with thin strips of orange rind and serve.

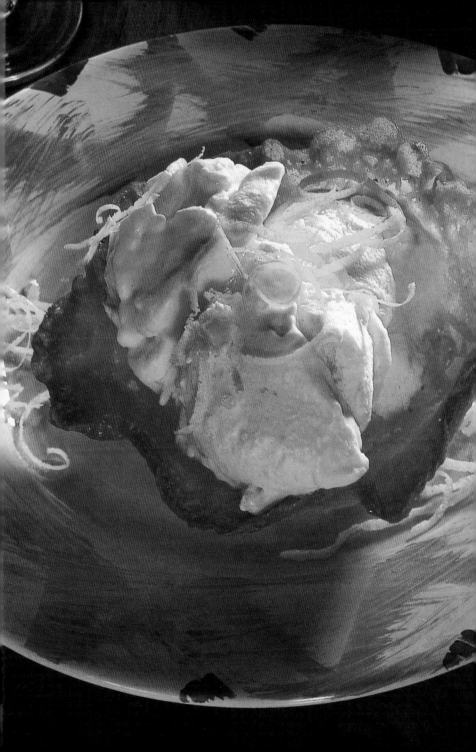

Coffee & Chocolate Bombe

The delicious combination of Marsala and chocolate transforms bought ice cream in this fancy dessert.

Serves 6–8

INGREDIENTS
15–18 savoiardi (Italian sponge fingers)
about 175 ml/6 fl oz/¾ cup sweet Marsala
75 g/3 oz amaretti
about 475 ml/16 fl oz/2 cups coffee ice cream, softened
about 475 ml/16 fl oz/2 cups vanilla ice cream, softened
50 g/2 oz dark (bittersweet) or plain (semisweet) chocolate, grated
chocolate curls and sifted cocoa powder or icing (confectioners') sugar, to decorate

1 Line a 1 litre/1¾ pint/4 cup bowl with a piece of damp muslin (cheesecloth), letting it hang over the edge. Trim the sponge fingers to fit the bowl.

2 Pour the Marsala into a dish. Dip a sponge finger in the Marsala, turning it quickly so that it becomes saturated but does not disintegrate. Stand it in the bowl, sugared side out. Repeat with the remaining sponge fingers to line the bowl fully.

3 Fill in the base and any gaps around the side with any trimmings and sponge fingers cut to fit. Chill for about 30 minutes.

4 Put the amaretti in a large bowl and crush them with the end of a rolling pin. Add the coffee ice cream and any remaining Marsala and beat until mixed. Spoon into the sponge-finger-lined bowl.

5 Press the ice cream against the sponge to form an even layer with a hollow in the centre. Freeze for 2 hours until firm.

6 Put the vanilla ice cream and grated chocolate in a bowl and beat together until evenly mixed. Spoon into the hollow in the centre of the bowl. Smooth the top, then cover with the overhanging muslin. Place in the freezer overnight.

7 To serve, run a palette knife or metal spatula between the muslin and the bowl, then unfold the top of the muslin. Invert a chilled serving plate on top, then invert the bowl so that the bombe is upside-down on the plate. Carefully peel off the muslin. Decorate the dessert with the chocolate curls, then sift cocoa powder or icing sugar over. Serve immediately.

Cranberry Bombe

This attractive dessert features smooth buttermilk vanilla ice cream enclosing a colourful cranberry and orange sorbet.

Serves 6

INGREDIENTS
FOR THE SORBET CENTRE
175 g/6 oz/1½ cups fresh or
    frozen cranberries
150 ml/¼ pint/⅔ cup orange juice
finely grated rind of ½ orange
2.5 ml/½ tsp mixed (apple pie) spice
50 g/2 oz/generous ¼ cup golden caster
    (superfine) sugar

FOR THE OUTER LAYER
1 quantity Buttermilk Vanilla Ice Cream
30 ml/2 tbsp chopped angelica
30 ml/2 tbsp mixed chopped (candied) peel
15 ml/1 tbsp flaked (sliced) almonds,
    toasted

1 For the sorbet, put the cranberries, orange juice, rind and spice in a pan and cook gently until the fruit is soft. Add the sugar, then purée until almost smooth. Leave to cool.

2 Allow the vanilla ice to soften slightly, then stir in the chopped angelica, mixed peel and almonds.

3 Pack into a 1.2 litre/2 pint/5 cup bowl and hollow out the centre. Freeze until firm.

4 Fill the hollowed-out centre of the bombe with the cranberry mixture, smooth over and freeze until firm. To serve, turn out and cut into slices.

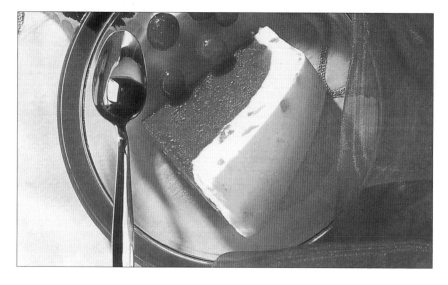

Rocky Road Ice Cream

This classic sweet ice cream is packed with contrasting textures and flavours.

Serves 6

INGREDIENTS

115 g/4 oz plain (semisweet) chocolate,
  broken into squares
150 ml/¼ pint/⅔ cup milk
300 ml/½ pint/1¼ cups double
  (heavy) cream
115 g/4 oz/1½ cups chopped marshmallows
50 g/2 oz/½ cup glacé (candied)
  cherries, chopped
50 g/2 oz/½ cup crumbled shortbread
30 ml/2 tbsp chopped walnuts
chocolate sauce, to serve

1 Melt the chocolate in the milk in a pan over a low heat, stirring from frequently. Remove the pan from the heat and leave to cool completely.

2 Whip the cream in a bowl until it just holds its shape. Beat in the chocolate mixture.

3 Pour the mixture into an ice cream maker and churn until it is thick and almost frozen. Alternatively, pour into a container suitable for use in the freezer, freeze until ice crystals form around the edges, then whisk vigorously until smooth.

4 Stir the marshmallows, cherries, crumbled shortbread and nuts into the iced mixture, then return to the freezer container and freeze until firm. Allow the ice cream to soften at room temperature for 15-20 minutes before serving with chocolate sauce.

Blackberry Ice Cream

The sharpness of blackberries gives a delicious vibrancy to this superb and elegant ice cream. A delightful autumn dessert.

Serves 4–6

INGREDIENTS
500 g/1¼ lb/5 cups blackberries, hulled,
 plus extra, to decorate
75 g/3 oz/6 tbsp caster (superfine) sugar
30 ml/2 tbsp water
300 ml/½ pint/1¼ cups
 whipping cream
crisp dessert biscuits (cookies),
 to serve

1 Put the blackberries, sugar and water into a pan. Bring to the boil, cover and simmer for 5 minutes, until the berries are just soft.

2 Press the fruit through a sieve (strainer) placed over a bowl, to make a purée. Leave to cool, then chill.

3 If you are using an ice cream maker, churn the purée for 10–15 minutes, until it is thick, then gradually pour in the cream. Continue to churn until it is firm enough to scoop.

4 If you are making the ice cream by hand, whip the cream until it is just thick but still soft enough to fall from a spoon, then mix it with the chilled purée. Pour into a freezerproof container and freeze for 2 hours.

5 Mash the mixture with a fork, or beat with an electric mixer to break up the ice crystals. Return it to the freezer for 4 hours more, beating the mixture again after 2 hours. Scoop into dishes and decorate with blackberries. Serve with biscuits.

Buttermilk Vanilla Ice Cream

Enriched with just a little double cream, this unusual ice cream tastes far
more luxurious than it really is. Serve it with fresh fruit or fruit purée.

Serves 4

INGREDIENTS
250 ml/8 fl oz/1 cup buttermilk
60 ml/4 tbsp double (heavy) cream
1 vanilla pod (bean) or 2.5 ml/½ tsp
    vanilla extract
2 eggs
30 ml/2 tbsp clear honey

1 Place the buttermilk and cream in a
pan with the vanilla pod, if using, and
heat gently until almost boiling.
Remove the vanilla pod.

2 Place the eggs in a heatproof bowl
over a pan of hot water and whisk
until they are pale and thick.

3 Pour in the heated buttermilk in
a thin stream, whisking hard. Continue
whisking over the hot water until the
mixture thickens slightly and coats the
back of a spoon.

4 Whisk in the clear honey and
vanilla extract, if using. Spoon the
mixture into a freezer container and
freeze until firm.

5 When the mixture is firm enough
to hold its shape, spoon it on to a
sheet of baking parchment. Form it
into a long smooth sausage shape and
roll it up in the paper. Freeze again
until it is firm. Serve the ice cream
in slices.

Summer Fruit Salad Ice Cream

What could be more cooling on a hot summer day than fresh summer fruits, lightly frozen in this irresistible ice?

Serves 6

INGREDIENTS

900 g/2 lb/6–7 cups mixed soft summer fruits, such as raspberries, strawberries, blackcurrants and redcurrants
2 eggs
225 g/8 oz/1 cup low fat Greek (US strained plain) yogurt
175 ml/6 fl oz/¾ cup red grape juice
15 ml/1 tbsp powdered gelatine

1 Reserve half the fruit and purée the remainder in a food processor, or rub it through a sieve.

2 Separate the eggs and whisk the yolks and the yogurt into the mixed fruit purée.

3 Heat the grape juice in a pan until it is almost boiling, then remove it from the heat. Sprinkle the gelatine over the grape juice and stir to dissolve the gelatine completely.

4 Whisk the dissolved gelatine mixture into the fruit purée and then pour the mixture into a freezer container. Freeze until half-frozen and slushy in consistency.

5 Whisk the egg whites with an electric hand-held mixer until they are stiff. Quickly fold them into the half-frozen mixture.

6 Return to the freezer and freeze until almost firm. Scoop into individual serving dishes or glasses and add the reserved soft fruits.

COOK'S TIP: Red grape juice has a good flavour and improves the colour of the ice, but if it is not available, use cranberry, apple or orange juice instead.

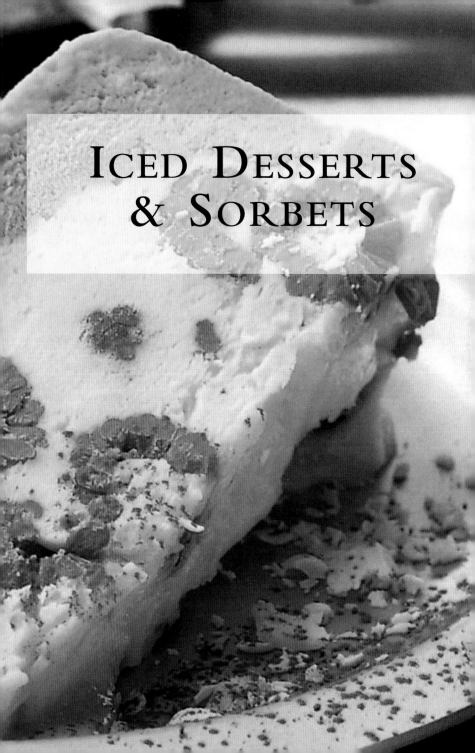

ICED DESSERTS & SORBETS

Chocolate Ice with Red Fruits

The chill that thrills – that's chocolate ice. For a really fine texture, it helps to have an ice-cream maker, which churns the mixture as it freezes, but you can make it by hand quite easily.

Serves 6

INGREDIENTS
475 ml/16 fl oz/2 cups water
45 ml/3 tbsp clear honey
115 g/4 oz/generous ½ cup caster
  (superfine) sugar
75 g/3 oz/¾ cup unsweetened cocoa powder
50 g/2 oz dark (bittersweet) chocolate,
  broken into squares
400 g/14 oz soft red fruits, such as
  raspberries, redcurrants or strawberries

1 Place the water, honey, sugar and cocoa in a pan. Heat gently, stirring occasionally, until the sugar has completely dissolved.

2 Remove from the heat, add the chocolate and stir until melted. Leave until cool.

3 Pour into an ice cream maker and churn until frozen. Alternatively, pour into a freezer container, freeze until slushy, whisk until smooth, then freeze again. Whisk for a second time before the mixture hardens completely.

4 Remove from the freezer 10–15 minutes before serving so that the ice softens slightly. Serve in scoops, with the soft fruits.

COOK'S TIP: This chocolate ice looks attractive if served in small, oval scoops shaped with two spoons – simply scoop out the sorbet with one tablespoon, then use another to smooth it off and transfer it to the serving plate.

Iced Oranges

These little sorbets served in the fruit shell were originally sold in the beach cafés in the south of France. They are pretty and easy to eat – a good picnic treat to pack in the cool-box.

Serves 8

INGREDIENTS
150 g/5 oz/¾ cup granulated sugar
juice of 1 lemon
14 medium oranges
icing (confectioners') sugar, to taste
8 fresh bay leaves, to decorate

1 Put the granulated sugar in a heavy pan. Add half the lemon juice and 120 ml/4 fl oz/½ cup water. Heat gently, stirring, until the sugar has dissolved. Bring to the boil and boil for 2–3 minutes, until the syrup is clear. Leave to cool.

2 Slice the tops off 8 of the oranges, to make "hats" for the sorbets. Scoop out the flesh of the oranges and reserve. Put the empty orange shells and "hats" on a tray and place in the freezer until needed.

3 Grate the rind of the remaining oranges and add to the syrup. Squeeze the juice from the oranges and from the reserved flesh. There should be 750 ml/1¼ pints/3 cups. Squeeze another orange or add bought orange juice, if necessary.

4 Stir the orange juice, remaining lemon juice and 90 ml/6 tbsp water into the syrup. Taste, adding more lemon juice or icing sugar, as desired. Freeze the mixture in an ice cream maker, following the manufacturer's instructions. Alternatively, pour the mixture into a shallow freezer container and freeze for 3 hours.

5 Turn the mixture into a bowl and whisk to break down the ice crystals. Freeze for 4 hours more, until firm, but not solid.

6 Pack the mixture into the orange shells, mounding it up, and set the "hats" on top. Freeze until ready to serve. Just before serving, pierce the tops of the "hats" with a skewer and push a bay leaf into each hole.

COOK'S TIP: Use crumpled kitchen paper to keep the shells upright while the sorbet freezes.

Mango and Lime Ice

Home-made ice cream is utterly delicious and surprisingly easy to make.
Serve this delicately flavoured dessert at the end of a dinner party.

Serves 4–6

INGREDIENTS
2 x 425 g/15 oz cans sliced
  mango, drained
50 g/2 oz/¼ cup caster (superfine)
  sugar
30 ml/2 tbsp lime juice
15 ml/1 tbsp powdered gelatine
350 ml/12 fl oz/1½ cups double (heavy)
  cream, lightly whipped
fresh mint sprigs, to decorate

1 Reserve four slices of mango for decoration and chop the remainder. Place the mangoes in a bowl with the sugar and lime juice. Stir well.

COOK'S TIP: Although fresh mango can be used instead, the canned variety makes this dish especially easy to prepare and tastes just as good.

2 Put 45 ml/3 tbsp hot water in a small heatproof bowl and sprinkle over the gelatine. Place over a pan of gently simmering water and stir until dissolved. Pour on to the mangoes and mix well.

3 Add the lightly whipped cream and fold into the mango mixture. Pour the mixture into a plastic freezer container and freeze until half frozen.

4 Place in a food processor or blender and process until smooth. Spoon back into the container and re-freeze.

5 Remove the ice cream from the freezer 10 minutes before serving and place in the refrigerator. Serve in scoops, decorated with pieces of the reserved sliced mango and fresh mint.

VARIATION: You might like to try using other canned fruit, such as pineapple, to make equally simple ice cream.

Frosted Raspberry & Coffee Terrine

A white chocolate and raspberry layer and a contrasting smooth coffee layer make this attractive-looking dessert doubly delicious.

Serves 6–8

INGREDIENTS
30 ml/2 tbsp flavoured ground coffee,
　e.g. mocha or orange
250 ml/8 fl oz/1 cup milk
4 eggs, separated
50 g/2 oz/¼ cup caster (superfine) sugar
30 ml/2 tbsp cornflour (cornstarch)
150 ml/¼ pint/⅔ cup double
　(heavy) cream
150 g/5 oz white chocolate,
　roughly chopped
115 g/4 oz/⅔ cup raspberries
shavings of white chocolate and
　unsweetened cocoa powder, to decorate

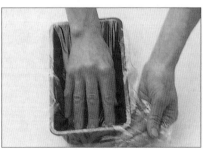

1 Line a 1.5 litre/2½ pint/6¼ cup loaf tin (pan) with clear film (plastic wrap) and put in the freezer to chill. Put the ground coffee in a jug (pitcher). Heat 100 ml/3½ fl oz/scant ½ cup of the milk to near-boiling point and pour over the coffee. Leave to steep.

2 Blend the egg yolks, sugar and cornflour together in a pan and whisk in the remaining milk and the cream. Bring to the boil, stirring constantly, until thickened.

3 Divide the hot mixture between two bowls and add the white chocolate to one, stirring until melted. Strain the coffee through a fine nylon sieve (strainer) into the other bowl and mix well. Leave until cool, stirring occasionally.

4 Whisk two of the egg whites until stiff. Fold into the coffee custard. Spoon into the tin and freeze for 30 minutes. Whisk the remaining whites and fold into the chocolate mixture with the raspberries.

5 Spoon the chocolate mixture into the tin and level before freezing for 4 hours. Turn the terrine out on to a flat serving plate and peel off the clear film. Cover with chocolate shavings and dust with cocoa powder.

COOK'S TIP: After decorating, soften the terrine in the refrigerator for 20 minutes before slicing.

Orange Granita with Strawberries

Granitas are like semi-frozen sorbets, but contain larger particles of ice. Served in Italian cafés, they are very refreshing, particularly in the summer. For this jewel-like dessert use very juicy oranges and really ripe strawberries that do not need any additional sweetening.

Serves 4

INGREDIENTS
6 large juicy oranges
350 g/12 oz ripe strawberries
finely pared strips of orange rind,
  to decorate

1 Squeeze the juice from the oranges and pour into a shallow freezerproof bowl.

COOK'S TIP: Granita will keep for up to 3 weeks in the freezer. Sweet pink grapefruits or deep red blood oranges can be used for a different flavour and colour. Add a little freshly squeezed lemon juice if you prefer a more tart taste.

2 Place the bowl in the freezer set at its coldest temperature. Remove after 30 minutes and beat the semi-frozen juice thoroughly with a wooden spoon until it is smooth.

3 Repeat this beating and freezing process at 30-minute intervals over a 4-hour period. This will break the ice crystals down into small particles to give the correct consistency for an authentic granita.

4 Halve the fresh strawberries and arrange them on a serving plate. Scoop the granita into attractive serving glasses, decorate with strips of orange rind and serve immediately with the strawberries.

Frozen Apple & Blackberry Terrine

Freeze this classic autumn combination to enjoy it at any time of year.

Serves 6

INGREDIENTS
500g/1¼ lb cooking or eating apples
300 ml/½ pint/1¼ cups sweet (hard) cider
15 ml/1 tbsp clear honey
5 ml/1 tsp vanilla extract
200 g/7 oz/1¼ cups fresh or frozen and
    thawed blackberries
15 ml/1 tbsp/1 envelope powdered gelatine
2 egg whites
fresh apple slices and blackberries,
    to decorate

1 Peel, core and chop the apples and place them in a pan with half the cider. Bring to the boil, cover and simmer until tender.

2 Purée the apples in a food processor. Stir in the honey and vanilla and remove half the purée. Add half the blackberries to the processor bowl and pulse until smooth. Press through a strainer to remove the pips (seeds).

3 Heat the remaining cider until it is almost boiling, then sprinkle the gelatine over it and stir until it has completely dissolved. Add half the cider to the apple purée and half to the blackberry and apple purée.

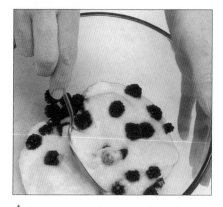

4 Leave the purées to cool until almost completely set. Whisk the egg whites until stiff. Quickly fold into the apple purée. Remove half the apple purée to another bowl. Stir the remaining whole blackberries into half the apple purée and then pour this into a 1.75 litre/3 pint/7½ cup loaf tin (pan), packing down firmly.

5 Top with the blackberry and apple purée, spreading evenly. Add the remaining apple purée and smooth evenly. If necessary, freeze each layer until firm before adding the next.

6 Freeze until firm. To serve, allow to stand at room temperature for about 20 minutes to soften. Serve in slices with fresh apple slices and blackberries.

Iced Pear Terrine with Calvados & Chocolate Sauce

This terrine, based on a classic French dessert, makes a refreshing and impressive end to any meal. For flavour, be sure the pears are fully ripe.

Serves 8

INGREDIENTS
1.5 kg/3–3½ lb ripe Williams pears
juice of 1 lemon
115 g/4 oz/generous ½ cup caster
    (superfine) sugar
10 whole cloves
90 ml/6 tbsp water
julienne strips of unwaxed orange rind,
    to decorate

FOR THE SAUCE
200 g/7 oz plain (semisweet) chocolate
60 ml/4 tbsp hot strong black coffee
200 ml/7 fl oz/scant 1 cup double
    (heavy) cream
30 ml/2 tbsp Calvados or brandy

1 Peel, core and slice the pears. Place them in a pan with the lemon juice, sugar, cloves and water. Cover and simmer for 10 minutes. Remove the cloves. Allow the pears to cool.

2 Process the pears with their juice in a food processor or blender until smooth. Pour the purée into a freezerproof bowl, cover and freeze until firm.

3 Meanwhile, line a 900 g/2 lb loaf tin (pan) with clear film (plastic wrap). Allow the film to overhang the sides. Spoon the frozen pear purée into a food processor or blender. Process until smooth. Pour into the prepared tin, cover and freeze until firm.

4 Make the sauce. Break the chocolate into a large heatproof bowl set over a pan of hot water. When the chocolate has melted, stir in the coffee until smooth. Gradually stir in the cream and then the Calvados or brandy. Remove from the pan and set the sauce aside.

5 About 20 minutes before serving, remove the tin from the freezer. Invert the terrine on to a plate, lift off the clear film and place the terrine in the refrigerator to soften slightly. Warm the sauce over hot water. Place a slice of terrine on each dessert plate and spoon over some of the sauce. Decorate with julienne strips of orange rind and serve immediately.

Strawberry Semi Freddo

Serve this quick strawberry dessert semi-frozen to reap the full flavour.

Serves 4–6

INGREDIENTS
250 g/9 oz/generous 2 cups strawberries
115 g/4 oz/generous ½ cup strawberry jam
250 g/9 oz/generous 1 cup ricotta cheese
200 g/7 oz/scant 1 cup Greek (US strained
    plain) yogurt
5 ml/1 tsp vanilla extract
40 g/1½ oz/3 tbsp caster (superfine) sugar
extra strawberries and mint or lemon balm,
    to decorate

1 Put the strawberries in a bowl and mash them with a fork until broken into small pieces but not completely puréed. Stir in the jam.

2 Drain off any whey from the ricotta. Pour it in a bowl and stir in the yogurt, vanilla extract and sugar.

3 Using a dessertspoon, fold the mashed strawberries into the ricotta mixture until rippled.

4 Spoon into individual freezerproof dishes and freeze until almost solid, about 2 hours. Alternatively, freeze until completely solid, then transfer the ice cream to the refrigerator for about 45 minutes to soften before serving. Serve decorated with extra strawberries and mint or lemon balm.

COOK'S TIPS: Don't mash the strawberries too much or they will liquefy. Freeze in a large freezer container if you don't have suitable small dishes. Thaw slightly in the refrigerator, then scoop into glasses.

Chocolate Fudge Sundaes

This self-indulgent American dish is every chocoholic's dream.

Serves 4

INGREDIENTS
4 scoops each vanilla and coffee ice cream
2 small ripe bananas, sliced
whipped cream
toasted flaked (sliced) almonds

FOR THE SAUCE
50 g/2 oz/⅓ cup soft light brown sugar
120 ml/4 fl oz/½ cup golden
    (light corn) syrup
45 ml/3 tbsp strong black coffee
5 ml/1 tsp ground cinnamon
150 g/5 oz plain (semisweet) chocolate,
    chopped into small pieces
75 ml/3 fl oz/5 tbsp whipping cream
45 ml/3 tbsp coffee-flavoured liqueur
    (optional)

1 Make the sauce. Place the sugar, syrup, coffee and cinnamon in a heavy pan. Bring to the boil, then boil for about 5 minutes, stirring the mixture constantly.

2 Remove from the heat and stir in the chocolate. When the chocolate has melted and the mixture is smooth, stir in the cream and the liqueur, if using. Leave the sauce to cool slightly. If made ahead, reheat the sauce gently until just warm.

3 Fill four glasses with a scoop each of vanilla and coffee ice cream. Top with thin slices of banana, warm fudge sauce, whipped cream and toasted almonds. Serve immediately.

Peach & Cardamom Yogurt Ice

This unusual peach ice cream spiced with cardamom uses yogurt to provide a creamy, velvety texture.

Serves 4

INGREDIENTS
8 cardamom pods
6 peaches, total weight about 500 g/1¼ lb,
    halved and stoned (pitted)
75 g/3 oz/6 tbsp caster (superfine) sugar
30 ml/2 tbsp water
200 ml/7 fl oz/scant 1 cup natural (plain) yogurt

1 Put the cardamom pods on a board and crush them with the base of a ramekin, or use a mortar and pestle.

2 Chop the peaches roughly and put them in a pan. Add the crushed cardamom pods and seeds, the sugar and water. Cover and simmer for 10 minutes or until tender. Cool.

3 Pour the peach mixture into a food processor or blender, process until smooth, then press through a sieve (strainer) placed over a bowl. If you are using an ice cream maker, churn the purée until thick, then scrape it into a freezerproof container. Stir in the yogurt and freeze until firm.

4 If you are making the ice cream by hand, strain the peach purée into a bowl and stir in the yogurt. Pour the mixture into a plastic tub and freeze for 5–6 hours until firm, beating once or twice with a fork, electric mixer or in a food processor to break up the ice crystals. Scoop on to a large platter, or use a melon baller to make miniature scoops in individual dishes. Serve immediately.

Mango & Orange Sorbet

Fresh and tangy, and gloriously vibrant in colour, this sorbet is the perfect finale for a spicy meal.

Serves 2–4

INGREDIENTS
115 g/4 oz/generous ½ cup golden caster
   (superfine) sugar
2 large mangoes
juice of 1 orange
1 egg white (optional)
thinly pared strips of unwaxed orange rind,
   to decorate

1 Gently heat the golden caster sugar and 300 ml/½ pint/1¼ cups water in a pan until the sugar has dissolved. Bring to the boil, then reduce the heat and simmer for 5 minutes. Remove from the heat and leave to cool.

2 Cut away the two sides of the mangoes close to the stone (pit). Peel, then cut the flesh from the stone. Dice the fruit. Process the mango flesh and orange juice in a food processor with the sugar syrup until smooth.

3 Pour the mixture into a freezerproof container and freeze for 2 hours until semi-frozen. Whisk the egg white, if using, until it forms stiff peaks, then stir it into the sorbet. Whisk well to remove any ice crystals and freeze until solid.

4 Transfer the sorbet to the refrigerator 10 minutes before serving. Serve, decorated with orange rind.

Rose-petal Sorbet

This sorbet makes a wonderful end to a summer meal with its fabulous flavour of roses. Remember to use the most scented variety of rose that you can find in the garden.

Serves 4–6

INGREDIENTS

115 g/4 oz/½ cup caster (superfine) sugar
300 ml/½ pint/1¼ cups boiling water
petals of 3 large, scented red or deep-pink
   roses, white ends of petals removed
juice of 2 lemons
300 ml/½ pint/1¼ cups rosé wine
whole crystallized roses or rose petals,
   to decorate

1 Place the sugar in a bowl and add the boiling water. Stir until the sugar has completely dissolved. Add the rose petals and leave to cool completely.

2 Process the mixture in a food processor, then strain. Add the lemon juice and wine and pour into a freezer container. Freeze for several hours, until the mixture has frozen around the edges.

3 Turn the sorbet into a mixing bowl and whisk until smooth. Re-freeze until frozen around the edges. Repeat the whisking and freezing process once or twice more, until the sorbet is pale and smooth. Freeze until firm.

4 Serve the sorbet in individual glass bowls, decorated with crystallized roses or rose petals.

> COOK'S TIP: This sorbet can also be made in an ice cream maker. Churn until firm with a good texture. If the sorbet is too hard, transfer it to the refrigerator for about 30 minutes before serving.

Blackcurrant Sorbet

This luscious sorbet is easily made by hand, but it is important to alternately freeze and blend or process the mixture five or six times.

Serves 6

INGREDIENTS

300 ml/½ pint/1¼ cups plus 30 ml/2 tbsp water
115 g/4 oz/generous ½ cup caster (superfine) sugar
225 g/8 oz/2 cups blackcurrants
30 ml/2 tbsp crème de cassis or other blackcurrant liqueur
5 ml/1 tsp lemon juice
2 egg whites

1 Pour 300 ml/½ pint/1¼ cups of the water into a pan and add the sugar. Place over a low heat until the sugar has dissolved. Bring to the boil and boil rapidly for 10 minutes, then set the syrup aside to cool.

3 Pour the chilled blackcurrant syrup into a freezerproof bowl and freeze until slushy, whisking occasionally. Whisk the egg whites in a grease-free bowl until soft peaks begin to form, then fold into the semi-frozen blackcurrant mixture.

2 Cook the blackcurrants with the remaining 30 ml/2 tbsp water over a low heat for 5–7 minutes. Press the blackcurrants and juice through a sieve (strainer), then stir the purée into the syrup with the liqueur and lemon juice. Cool, then chill for 1 hour.

4 Freeze the mixture again until firm, then spoon into a food processor and process or whisk by hand. Alternately freeze and process or whisk until completely smooth. Serve straight from the freezer.

Raspberry Sorbet with a Soft Fruit Garland

A stunning fresh fruit and herb decoration creates a bold border for the scoops of sorbet.

Serves 6–8

INGREDIENTS
175 g/6 oz/generous ¾ cup caster
   (superfine) sugar
450 g/1 lb/2⅔ cups fresh or thawed
   frozen raspberries
strained juice of 1 orange

FOR THE DECORATION
1 bunch fresh mint
selection of soft fruits, including
   strawberries, raspberries, redcurrants
   and blueberries

2 Mix the syrup with the puréed raspberries and pour into a freezer container. Freeze for 2 hours, or until ice crystals form around the edges of the sorbet. Whisk until smooth, then return to the freezer for 4 hours. Alternatively make the sorbet in an ice cream maker, according to the manufacturer's instructions.

3 About 30 minutes before serving, transfer the sorbet to the refrigerator to soften slightly. Place a large sprig of mint on the rim of a serving plate, then build up a garland, using more mint sprigs.

1 Heat the sugar with 250 ml/ 8 fl oz/1 cup water in a pan until dissolved, stirring occasionally. Bring to the boil, then set aside to cool. Purée the raspberries with the orange juice in a blender or food processor, then use a wooden spoon to press through a sieve (strainer) to remove any seeds.

4 Leaving on the leaves, cut the strawberries in half. Arrange on the mint with the other fruit. Place the fruits at different angles and link the leaves with strings of redcurrants. Place scoops of sorbet in the centre.

Watermelon Sorbet

A slice of this refreshing and colourful sorbet is the perfect way to cool down on a hot, sunny day.

Serves 4–6

INGREDIENTS
½ small watermelon, weighing about
   1 kg/2¼ lb
75 g/3 oz/scant ½ cup caster (superfine) sugar
60 ml/4 tbsp cranberry juice or water
30 ml/2 tbsp lemon juice
fresh mint sprigs, to decorate

1 Cut the watermelon into 4–6 equal-size wedges (depending on the number of servings you require). Scoop out the pink flesh and set aside. Remove the seeds and discard. Reserve the shell.

2 Line a freezerproof bowl, about the same size as the melon, with clear film (plastic wrap). Arrange the melon skins in the bowl to re-form the shell, fitting them together snugly so that there are no gaps. Put in the freezer.

3 Put the caster sugar and cranberry juice or water in a medium-sized heavy pan and stir over a low heat until the sugar dissolves. Bring to the boil and simmer for 5 minutes. Leave the sugar syrup to cool.

4 Put the melon flesh and lemon juice in a blender and process to a smooth purée. Stir in the sugar syrup and pour into a freezer container. Freeze for 3–3½ hours, or until slushy when tested with a fork.

5 Tip the sorbet into a chilled bowl and whisk to break up the ice crystals. Return to the freezer for another 30 minutes, whisk again, then pour into the melon shell and freeze until solid. To serve, cut through the individual slices of watermelon and sorbet and decorate with fresh mint.

Pink Grapefruit Sorbet

This tastebud-tingling citrus sorbet is the perfect way to clear the palate after a rich main course.

Serves 8

INGREDIENTS
175 g/6 oz/generous ¾ cup
   granulated sugar
120 ml/4 fl oz/½ cup water
1 litre/1¾ pints/4 cups strained
   freshly squeezed pink grapefruit juice
15–30 ml/1–2 tbsp lemon juice
icing (confectioners') sugar, to taste
fresh mint sprigs, to decorate

1 In a small, heavy pan, dissolve the granulated sugar in the water over medium heat without stirring. When the sugar has dissolved, boil for 3–4 minutes. Remove from the heat and allow to cool.

2 Pour the cooled sugar syrup into the grapefruit juice. Stir well. Taste the mixture and adjust the flavour by adding some lemon juice or a little icing sugar, if necessary.

3 Pour the mixture into a freezer container and freeze for about 3 hours, until softly set.

4 Remove from the container and chop roughly into 7.5 cm/3 in pieces. Place in a food processor and process until smooth. Return the mixture to the freezer container and freeze again until set.

5 Repeat this freezing and chopping process two or three times, until a smooth consistency is obtained. Alternatively, freeze the sorbet in an ice cream maker, following the manufacturer's instructions. Serve in scoops, decorated with fresh mint.

VARIATION: For orange sorbet, substitute an equal amount of orange juice for the grapefruit juice and increase the lemon juice to 45–60 ml/3–4 tbsp or to taste.

Lime Sorbet

Use ripe, well-flavoured limes for this refreshing sorbet.

Serves 4

INGREDIENTS
250 g/9 oz/generous 1¼ cups
    granulated sugar
600 ml/1 pint/2½ cups water
grated rind of 1 lime
175 ml/6 fl oz/¾ cup lime juice
15–30 ml/1–2 tbsp lemon juice
icing (confectioners') sugar, to taste
curls of lime rind, to decorate

1 In a small, heavy pan, dissolve the granulated sugar in the water, without stirring, over medium heat. When the sugar has dissolved, boil for 5–6 minutes. Remove the syrup from the heat and set aside to cool.

2 Combine the cooled sugar syrup and lime rind and juice in a bowl. Stir well. Taste, and adjust the flavour by adding lemon juice or some icing sugar, if necessary. Do not over-sweeten the mixture.

3 Freeze the lime mixture in an ice cream maker, following the manufacturer's instructions. If you do not have an ice cream maker, pour the mixture into a freezer container and freeze for about 3 hours, until softly set.

4 Remove the mixture from the container and chop roughly into 7.5 cm/3 in pieces. Place in a food processor and process until smooth. Return the mixture to the freezer container and freeze again until set. Repeat this freezing and chopping process two or three times, until a smooth consistency is obtained.

COOK'S TIP: If using an ice cream maker, check the manufacturer's instructions to find out the freezing capacity. If necessary, halve the quantities used in the recipe. If too much mixture is placed in the bowl it will not set.

Mango & Lime Sorbet in Lime Shells

This richly flavoured sorbet looks pretty served in the lime shells, but is also good served in scoops for a more traditional presentation.

Serves 4

INGREDIENTS
4 large limes
1 medium ripe mango
7.5 ml/1½ tsp powdered gelatine
2 egg whites
15 ml/1 tbsp caster (superfine) sugar
finely pared strips of lime rind, to decorate

1 Cut a thick slice from the top of each of the limes, and then cut a thin slice from the bottom end so that they will stand upright. Squeeze the juice from the limes and reserve. Use a small knife to remove all the membrane from the centre.

2 Halve, stone (pit), peel and chop the mango and purée the flesh in a food processor with 30 ml/2 tbsp of the lime juice. Dissolve the gelatine in 45ml/3 tbsp of the lime juice and stir it into the mango mixture.

3 Whisk the egg whites until they hold soft peaks. Whisk in the sugar. Fold the egg white mixture quickly into the mango mixture. Spoon the sorbet into the lime shells. Any that will not fit into the lime shells can be frozen in small ramekins.

4 Overwrap the filled shells with clear film (plastic wrap), and place them in the freezer until the sorbet is firm. Before serving, remove the clear film and allow the shells to stand at room temperature for about 10 minutes; decorate them with strips of lime rind.

COOK'S TIP: If you have lime juice left over from this recipe, it will freeze well for future use. Pour it into a small freezer container, seal it and freeze for up to six months. Or pour 15 ml/1 tbsp into each compartment of an ice-cube tray and freeze the tray.

Lychee & Elderflower Sorbet

The flavour of elderflowers complements lychees wonderfully.

Serves 4

INGREDIENTS
175 g/6 oz/1½ cups caster (superfine) sugar
400 ml/14 fl oz/1⅔ cups water
500 g/1¼ lb fresh lychees, peeled
    and pitted
15 ml/1 tbsp elderflower cordial

1 Place the sugar and water in a pan and heat gently until the sugar has dissolved. Increase the heat and boil for 5 minutes, then add the lychees. Lower the heat and simmer for 7 minutes. Allow to cool.

2 Process the fruit and syrup in a blender or food processor. Press through a sieve (strainer) with a spoon.

3 Stir the elderflower cordial into the strained purée, then pour the mixture into a freezerproof container. Freeze for 2 hours, until ice crystals start to form around the edges.

4 Remove from the freezer and process briefly in a blender or food processor. Repeat twice, then freeze until firm. Transfer the sorbet to the refrigerator for 10 minutes, to soften before serving.

Fresh Orange Granita

A granita is like a water ice with a grainier texture, hence its name.

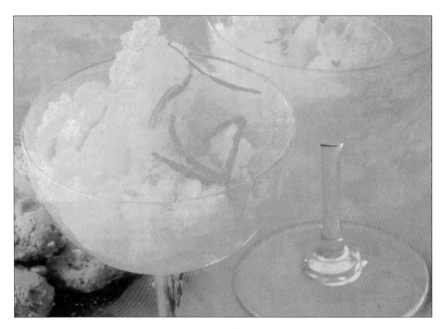

Serves 6

INGREDIENTS
4 large oranges
1 large lemon
150 g/5 oz/²⁄₃ cup sugar
475 ml/16 fl oz/2 cups water
blanched, pared strips of orange and
    lemon rind, to decorate

1 Thinly pare the rind from the
oranges and lemon, taking care to
avoid the white pith, cut into strips
and set aside. Cut the fruit in half and
squeeze the juice into a jug (pitcher).

2 Heat the sugar and water in a
heavy-based pan, stirring over a low
heat until the sugar dissolves.

3 Bring to the boil, add the strips of
rind, then boil to a syrup, without
stirring, for about 10 minutes.

4 Off the heat, add the rind and
shake the pan. Cover until cool. Strain
into a shallow freezerproof dish and
add the reserved juice. Stir well, then
freeze, uncovered, for about 4 hours,
until slushy. Mix with a fork and
freeze again for 4 hours. Soften for
10 minutes before serving.

Chocolate Sorbet

This velvety smooth sorbet is always popular. For a really rich flavour, use the best quality chocolate you can find, with a high percentage of cocoa solids – it makes all the difference.

Serves 6

INGREDIENTS
150 g/5 oz dark (bittersweet) chocolate, chopped
115 g/4 oz plain (semisweet) chocolate, chopped
200 g/7 oz/1 cup caster (superfine) sugar
475 ml/16 fl oz/2 cups water
chocolate curls, to decorate

1 Put all the chocolate in a food processor, fitted with the metal blade, and process for 20–30 seconds until finely chopped.

2 Bring the sugar and water to the boil in a pan over a medium-high heat, stirring until the sugar dissolves. Boil for about 2 minutes, then remove from the heat.

3 With the machine running, pour the hot syrup over the chocolate. Allow the machine to continue running for 1–2 minutes, until the chocolate is completely melted and the mixture is smooth, scraping the mixture from the sides of the bowl once.

4 Strain the chocolate mixture into a large bowl, and leave to cool, then chill, stirring occasionally. Freeze the mixture in an ice cream machine, following the manufacturer's instructions. Allow the sorbet to soften for 5–10 minutes at room temperature and serve in scoops, decorated with chocolate curls.

COOK'S TIP: If you do not have an ice cream machine, freeze the sorbet until firm around the edges. Process it until smooth, then freeze again.

Index

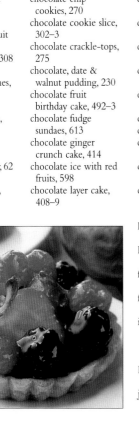